P9-CRA-620

CALHOUN: BASIC DOCUMENTS

C A L H O U N

BASIC DOCUMENTS

edited & introduced by *JOHN M. ANDERSON*

BALD EAGLE PRESS STATE COLLEGE, PA.

Printed in the United States of America

DESIGNED BY ELEANORE RUBIN

FOREWORD

John C. Calhoun was the last major political thinker who was also an active major figure upon the American political scene. He was both a thinker and an active figure during a primary crisis in the history of our nation; yet his basic work on political theory has not been readily available to students since the publication of *A Disquisition on Government* in 1851 and its inclusion in *The Works of John C. Calhoun.*[1] The present reprint of this fundamental analysis in political theory is intended to recover a seminal work and give it the place it deserves upon the contemporary scene.

Calhoun's originality as a political thinker has been obscured by his position in American politics. As a theorist he anticipates much of the latter nineteenth century emphasis upon the close connection of political structure with social classes and regional patterns. In the early nineteenth century he understood and stated the mutual dependence between society and government, something which has since become a widely accepted tenet of political theory. As a representative of the South, however, Calhoun was forced in practice to express his theory in terms of the relation of states to the Federal Government and the place of the plantation society in the nation. His political debates, therefore, are concerned primarily with an aspect of social structure which lost its central character in American society with the end of the Civil War.

The social forces which became formative in later nineteenth century America were economic and industrial rather than legal and cultural. To a great extent Calhoun was aware that this was to be. Thus, even where he most concerns himself with the legal and cultural cause of the South, his speeches on the floor of Congress contain prophetic passages in which the breadth of his theoretical vision moderates his partisan preoccupation. Those of his speeches which are reprinted here delineate the personal position of a man whose developing theoretical insight vividly opened to him a probable future, and whose deep allegiance to a way of life which he knew to be passing was expressed in terms of the social and political ideas of the future.

Calhoun's significance for the present has been noted and stated by a growing number of historians and political philosophers. C. M. Wiltse's definitive three-volume study, *John C. Calhoun*, is an excellent example of this contemporary interest, as is Margaret L. Coit's human picture, *John C. Calhoun: An American Portrait.* Recent interest in Calhoun is found not only in such full length research, but is evidenced in studies of American historical themes in which Calhoun is seen as a significant example. Gamaliel Bradford's *As God Made Them*, R. H. Gabriel's *The Course of American Democratic Thought* and Richard Hofstadter's *The American Political Tradition* see Calhoun from different perspectives but as related to central themes in American history. Finally, recognition of Calhoun's stature as an original political philosopher is evident in Arthur Styron's *The Cast Iron Man: John C. Calhoun and American Democracy*, in the more recent treatment of his thought in A. O. Spain's *The Political Theory of John C. Calhoun* and in the frequency with which his speeches and portions of his longer works are now included in anthologies of American thought. Certainly such testimony of Calhoun's historical importance and contemporary relevance suggests the need for an edition of his work complete enough to give genuine insight into the structure of his thought. It is hoped that the present volume will fill this need.

I wish to express my gratitude to my colleague, Professor Henry A. Finch, for first suggesting the present volume and for continued encouragement and valuable advice in carrying it through to completion; to Gale Anderson for invaluable help in the task of editing and selection, and to J. Mitchell Morse for reading the manuscript and for helpful criticism. I am also indebted to Ralph W. McComb, Director of The Pennsylvania State College Library, and to Mrs. M. K. Spangler, Assistant Librarian, for special permission to use library facilities in preparing the manuscript. Dean Ben Euwema, as is his admirable wont, has encouraged and aided this project in many ways.

JOHN M. ANDERSON

State College, Pennsylvania

CONTENTS

INTRODUCTION

POLITICAL UNITY AND SECTIONALISM

Calhoun's life-long hope for national unity was genuine; his desire for an ideal social and political unity was fundamental to his thought and character. "The community would become a unity," he urges, "by becoming a common centre of attachment of all its parts. And hence, instead of faction, strife, and struggle for party ascendency, there would be patriotism, nationality, harmony and a struggle only for supremacy in promoting the common good of the whole."[1] Such an impartial observer as John Quincy Adams could testify that Calhoun sustained his desires for an ideal unity in politics and society with a rare combination of patriotism and objectivity. He was, Adams says, a ". . . man of fair and candid mind, of honorable principles, of clear and quick understanding, of cool self-possession . . . above all sectional and factious prejudices."[2]

Calhoun's early nationalism was no more intense than that of other major figures of his time. The devices he conceived to perserve the nation, namely, the concurrent voice and nullification, are now mainly of theoretical and historical interest. However, his conception of political order, which he framed in terms of a realistic appraisal of human nature and the social structure of classes and regions, constitutes a claim to contemporary attention which is worthy of evaluation. Calhoun's analysis of American sectionalism and the realities of class struggle not only antedates most social thought of this modern stamp,[3] but is directed by him to showing the mutual dependence of the political and the social order. Calhoun argues that the function of political order is the preservation and establishment of social order. He thus states a relation and a distinction which at once extend the function of government beyond the negative regulation of human behavior to the positive organization of social interests. The same distinction and relation require that government to accept and work with whatever groups or classes exist or may be generated in the social order.

This insight of Calhoun's into political institutions led him to deal with the problem of individual and social conflict in a novel way. His suggestions, although deviating from the American tradition of his time, offer basic ideas toward the solution of the problem of minority relations today. These ideas have a twofold contemporary pertinence. First, they constitute a subtle and profound statement of the major issues pertaining to the political organization of minority groups. Calhoun's experience of the problem of conflict was immediate and he had the analytical mind needed to formulate his experience. Second, these ideas clearly uncover the root issue in minority relations, which is the achievement of a balance between freedom and responsible action. If Calhoun was too willing to sacrifice freedom to security under the pressure of impending conflict, this, of itself, is a lesson for today.

John C. Calhoun was born in 1782, the fourth child in one of the Scotch-Irish families which pushed the American frontier across the Appalachian mountains.[4] His father, Patrick Calhoun, was a personage of some distinction in the up-country of South Carolina, an individualist whom his son remembers as insisting "that the improvements in political science would be found to consist in throwing off many of the restraints then imposed by law and deemed necessary to an organized society."[5] Calhoun's boyhood was but one generation removed from the frontier. His paternal grandmother had been killed by Indians. His father's house was the first framed building in the region. His own preoccupations were, until the age of eighteen, almost completely agricultural. Indeed, he first determined to become a planter, but was dissuaded from this role only when assured by his brother James of the support necessary for "the seven years of study preparatory to entering his profession [of law]."[6] At eighteen Calhoun seems already to have come to his understanding of the place of the individual in society, as shown by his insistence that the conditions for his own social role be met.

The financial contributions of his brother James enabled Calhoun to obtain his first formal education at a local academy, to graduate from Yale and then to attend the law school of Judge Reeve at Litchfield, Connecticut. Success at law was immediate, following the very favorable impression he made at his first appearance before the bar. But Calhoun felt a strong aversion to the practice of law. As he said, "I feel myself now and while I continue in the practice of the law almost as a slave chained down to a particular place and course of life . . . I . . . am determined to forsake it as soon as I can . . ."[7] Election to the South Carolina legislature in 1808, and to Congress in 1810 enabled Calhoun to escape the bondage which society might have exacted of him and to attain to a considerable degree of individual expression.

But individuality came slowly. His initial expressions of opinion in Congress were not original. He accepted the intense nationalism of his time, and to this acceptance he owed his early position of practical influence as a leader among the "war hawks" and his importance in the prosecution of the war which he had urged. Calhoun's ideal of nationalism reflected the hope of his era, and his early expression of this hope differs from the common contemporary expressions only in being phrased in somewhat less florid language. It agrees with the connotation of the ordinary symbols of the nineteenth century, The Eagle of the United States, The Flag, Uncle Sam, Brother Jonathan, the national festival centering around Independence Day, the overt allegiance to national heroes, and the conception of American Destiny. Calhoun, with the American people, conceived of national unity as a support for exalted feelings and as a principle which might give originality and direction to men's attitudes and beliefs. Thus, in the Twelfth Congress, he could say, ". . . He (Mr. Randolph) represents the people of the Western States as willing to plunge the country into war for such base and precarious [i.e., mercenary] motives . . . I see the cause of their ardor, not in such base motives, but in their known patriotism and disinterestedness."[8] Certainly his urging of appropriation of funds for the war of 1812, his plea for internal improvements and for a new national bank are a record testifying to his belief in the national solidarity and power. At this point in his career he could speak of sectionalism as an evil to be avoided:

> In one respect, and in my opinion, in one only, are we materially weak. We occupy a surface prodigiously great . . . We are great, and rapidly—I was about to say fearfully—growing. This is our pride and our danger—our weakness

> and our strength . . . We are under the most imperious obligation to counteract every tendency to disunion . . . Let us then bind the Republic together with a perfect system of roads and canals. Let us conquer space. . . So situated, blessed with a form of Government at once combining liberty and strength, we may reasonably raise our eyes to a most splendid future, if we only act in a manner worthy of our advantages. If, however, neglecting them, we permit a low, sordid, selfish, and sectional spirit to take possession of this House, this happy scene will vanish. We will divide, and in its consequences will follow misery and degradation . . .[9]

If Calhoun, like his compatriots, initially looked to national solidarity for the realization of the meanings of the age, he came in part to change his mind. As Secretary of War in Monroe's cabinet and as Vice-President in 1824 during Adams' presidency, he was first formally nationalist and then silent on the increasingly insistent problems of both economic and cultural sectionalism. By 1828 the Tariff of Abominations and South Carolina's desperate position in the cotton market brought forth an explicit sectional doctrine in his *Exposition and Protest* —Calhoun's authorship, however, remaining secret for some time. Jackson's charge in 1832, that Calhoun changed his mind when he saw that he had lost his chance for the presidency, is thus false in fact, but it shows a true insight into the shift of Calhoun's thought. As Calhoun's thought developed and came more and more accurately to reflect the social and economic realities of his time, the line of political action which he directed began to deviate from the mainstream of American politics. His mature thought, in actual fact, challenged the central tenets of the developing American political tradition, in particular its concept of a monolithic nationalism and of freedom.

Had Calhoun's alliance with Jackson eventually brought him the presidency or had his later efforts to obtain it been successful, the effect of his mature thought on the political tradition of America would have been tremendous. Yet, by 1832 the body of the accepted tradition was so strong as to exclude from ultimate political importance those men like Calhoun who diverged from it and to depose those who, although initially of the common stamp, came to change their minds about such fundamental beliefs.

THE DEVELOPMENT OF SOCIAL STRUCTURE

When Calhoun resigned from the vice-presidency after the nullification crisis of 1832 and returned to the Senate it was as the representative of a minority. Henceforth he was to see in the increasing population of the North, in its rapidly developing industrial potential, in its increasing financial control, in its extension of domination over the expanding West, not the development of the American Nation, but rather a threat to the agrarian society of the South. His purpose became the protection of the South against the developing power of the Northern financial and industrial culture. The means to the achievement of this purpose were his opposition to any centralization of power in the Federal Government, where it must fall into the control of the Northern majority, and his attempts to keep the influx of new states into the union from giving the balance of legal power to the North. His opposition to the Bank Bills, to the tariff, to increasing the powers of the executive and to the admission of new states was well carried out. This effective opposition constitutes more than adequate refutation of Jackson, who had written to Van Buren, "You may rest assured Duff Green, Calhoun & Co. are politically dead."[10]

The course Calhoun pursued deviated from the stream of American history in his time, and it cost him an intensity of effort and concentration which has rarely been equalled. He became, because of his devotion to his sectional cause, an almost legendary figure. Harriet Martineau described him well as "the cast iron man who looks as if he had never been born, and could never be extinguished."[11] The force of his effort made him the man whom Henry Clay pictures at the White House the night the first Bank Bill was vetoed: "There, I say, I can imagine, stood the Senator from South Carolina,—tall, careworn, with furrowed brow, haggard, and intensely gazing, looking as if he were dissecting the last abstraction from a metaphysician's brain, and muttering to himself, in half-uttered tones, 'This is indeed a real crisis'."[12]

The crisis which Calhoun perpetually envisioned was theoretical as well as practical. His awareness of the plight of the South led him to see the growing sectional, regional and cultural differences in American social life; induced him to notice the diversities and structural differences which constitute society, compelled him to observe the social realities behind the accepted gloss of national feeling and solidarity. It became his crucial theoretical problem to discuss the relation of these social realities to the political order.

Indeed, Calhoun had replied to an earlier criticism of Clay's, that metaphysical faculties were precisely those needed to grasp social realities:

> I cannot retort on the Senator the charge of being metaphysical. I cannot accuse him of possessing the powers of analysis and generalization, those higher faculties of the mind (called metaphysical by those who do not possess them) which decompose and resolve into their elements the complex masses of ideas that exist in the world of mind . . . and without which those deep and hidden causes which are in constant action, and producing such mighty changes in the condition of society, would operate unseen and undetected. The absence of these higher qualities of mind is conspicuous throughout the whole course of the Senator's public life. To this may be traced that he prefers the specious to the solid, and the plausible to the true.[13]

The often unseen and undetected causes which work deep within society became Calhoun's concern. He conceived his theoretical problem to be the understanding of the relation of political order to these often hidden social causes. Undoubtedly Calhoun's political theory serves to explain and justify, to rationalize, his practical efforts on behalf of the South. It is also, we must not forget, a rational construction which deals with an aspect of society often neglected in political thought. His acute observation of social facts extended beyond the harsh conflicts of sectional patterns to the "tendency to conflict in North, between labor and capital, which is constantly on the increase,"[14] to the conflict produced by banking and financial interests, to the realities of social life in frontier communities, mining towns and eastern cities—indeed, to all the "different interests, orders, classes, or portions, into which the community may be divided."[15] Thus his understanding of the complex tissue of minority relations which actually structured society, an understanding stimulated by his allegiance to the cultural minority of the South, provided the fundamental theme in his restatement of political theory.

To note the threat of the growing Northern majority to the Southern minority was, after all, to observe the obvious. To deal with this threat as effectively as Calhoun did against the tide of circumstances was a political achievement. To point out that this was potentially a threat to all minorities, rooted in a misidentification of the political order with a part of the social order, and to suggest, moreover, a conception of political order which, in principle, might recognize minority groups was a primary intellectual achievement. Calhoun says, concerning his claim of the North's usurpation of political prerogatives, "What was once a constitutional federal republic [The United States], is now converted, in reality, into one as absolute as that of the Autocrat of Russia, and as despotic in its tendency as any absolute government that ever existed."[16] In his allegation Calhoun defended the South, but he also suggested a theoretical lesson to those who would learn what he, himself, had learned. He read the lesson which the succeeding one hundred years of history were to teach again and again, that those apparent political unities which in fact mask the dominance of a single regional pattern or any portion of the social order—even the majority, as such—could assume dictatorial power and become totalitarian in their exaction of conformity. A true political unity, on the contrary, must be one able "to cause the different interests, portions, or orders,—as the case may be—to desist from attempting to adopt any measure calculated to promote the prosperity of one, or more, by sacrificing that of others; and thus to force them to unite in such measures only as would promote the prosperity of all."[17]

Calhoun, thus, came to conceive the function of political order as "intended to protect and preserve society" in all its aspects.[18] He could not regard as true a conception of political order impotent to deal with the real diversity of American social life unless imposed despotically upon some of its elements.[19] And he accepted the responsibility of his dissent from the simple political unity of nationalistic tradition. He formulated and offered to the American people a political philosophy which sought to relate political unity to the diverse productions of human force and aspiration, the complex of contrary and conflicting movements and intentions which in fact constituted American life. He sought to incorporate these realities into an expression of American political meaning; he argued for the uniqueness of regions, for the rights of sections, for the integrity of diverse classes and groups, for the sanctity of the individual, and, through these only, for the attainment of political unity. Calhoun urged that the various aspects of society be made the mechanism for the expression of the political significance of life in America. He envisioned the ideal unity of a nation incorporating a diversity of individualistic motive, a complexity of sectional aspiration, a variety of parties and group interests bound together so that "every interest will be truly and fully represented."[20]

POWER AND PRINCIPLE

Calhoun's belief in the possibility of a political order based on principle remained with him until his death; his hope for The Union did not. Some days before his death on March 31, 1850, he told a friend, "The Union is doomed to dissolution; there is no mistaking the signs. I am satisfied in my judgment even were the questions which now agitate Congress settled to the satisfaction and with the concurrence of the Southern States, it would not avert, or materially delay, the catastrophe. I fix its probable occurrence within twelve years or three Presidential terms. You and others of your age will probably live to see it; I shall not. The mode by which it will be done is not so clear; it may be brought about in a manner that none now foresee. But the probability is it will explode in a Presidential election."[21] The signs which could not be mistaken were in his view those assaults on the integrity of the Southern minority which could not be met by the South within the framework of existing national political structure. This inadequacy of the existing political structure Calhoun emphasized in his last major speech on the floor of the Senate by conceding that the protection of the Southern minority in the end devolved not upon the principles of existing political order but upon the *power* of the North. Could a settlement of the issues between North and South be reached? "Yes, easily; not by the weaker party, for it can of itself do nothing—not even protect itself—but by the stronger. The North has only to will it to accomplish it—to do justice by conceding the South an equal right . . . which will restore to the South, in substance, the power she possessed of protecting herself, before the equilibrium between the sections was destroyed by the action of this Government."[22] In the end Calhoun asked for the restoration of political principle through the generous exercise of power by those who possessed it. Such a generous exercise of power, he thought as late as 1849, might avert open conflict if the new political order it could establish were designed to deal with the complex tissue of individuals, groups and classes which constituted American society. The nationalism accepted by the North had failed to do this. True national unity, however, could still be conceived in the terms of a political theory which recognized the full self-orientation of individuals and the restricted perspectives of those many social groups which were so necessary to the very existence of the individual.

Political order, Calhoun thus argued, must be doubly rooted in realism. First, true political order depends for its initial establishment upon the use of power by those who control it for the ends of principle. Second, true political order depends for its continued existence upon a recognition of the rights of finite individuals and diverse groups and upon the relation of these two important factors. Even though men do use the power they have for the ends of political principle, these ends cannot be made to endure should the order so established ignore the demand finite men make for the right to satisfy their own wants and desires. So far as individuals are concerned, "each . . . has a greater regard for his own safety and happiness, than for the safety or happiness of others; and, where these come in opposition, is ready to sacrifice the interests of others to his own. And hence, the tendency to a universal state of conflict, between individual and individual; accompanied by the connected passions of suspicion, jealousy, anger and revenge,—followed by insolence, fraud, and cruelty . . ."[23] As Calhoun adds, there are, of course, exceptions to this generalization; habit and education, all the circumstances of social life, modify this human trait. The typical picture, none the less, remains true. Nor could a political order endure which failed to deal explicitly with the diversity of groups, with the fact "that the human race is not comprehended in a single society or community. The limited faculties of man, the great diversity of language, customs, pursuits, situation and complexion, and the difficulty of intercourse . . . have . . . formed a great many separate communities acting independently of each other. Between these there is the same tendency to conflict,—and from the same constitution of our nature,—as between men individually; and even stronger . . . Self-preservation is the supreme law, as well with communities as individuals."[24] There are exceptions here as well; but if man never existed in a state of nature independently of society, this does not establish society as that organizing principle which resolves conflicts. Society, of itself, is shot through with the conflict of class and group.

An enduring political order, Calhoun realistically argues, must be built upon the facts of man's self-oriented wants and desires, upon the circumstances of the diversity and conflict of social groups and, further, upon the complex dependence of the individual on society. Man finds himself, as an individual, in pursuit of wants and desires. The successful attainment of these individual interests, however, depends upon social order. Man's "inclinations and wants, physical and moral, irresistibly impel him to associate with his kind; and he has, accordingly, never been found . . . in any state other than the social . . ."[25] Yet, despite this need, man often pursues his individual interests in such a way as to destroy the very social order upon which he is dependent. Man finds himself, as a social being, Calhoun observes, to be a member of society. Yet the inherent conflict of this society often deprives him of the goals to which he might attain through social order.

In view of these facts, as Calhoun saw them, the need for political order is clear. It is needed, first, to supplant with the benefits of unity the discord and confusion produced by the diversity of individuals and their motives. Second, it is required to replace group bias and conflicts by social harmony. And, finally, political order is essential for relating man to society in such a way that his dependence upon it for his very existence and progress may be maintained. Calhoun saw the need for political order in his realistic observation that the disparate motivation of individuals in relation to society and the diversity of group purposes in society tend to produce that anarchy and conflict which may destroy man and the possibility of his achievements. Given these facts, Calhoun regarded the initial establishment of a political order not only as necessary but as inevitable. "There is no difficulty in forming government . . . Necessity will force it on all communities in some one form or another."[26] The appeal from society to government, that is, to political principle, will be made. Those with power will and must use it in part for the ends of the state. Man finds himself in a position where he has no recourse but an appeal to the ideal. Since his nature is such that he can appeal to principle, since he must do so, he inevitably does make this appeal. What can be and must be, is. ". . . government is of Divine ordination."[27]

Calhoun believed that the anarchy of conflicting forces which man faces in his individual and social life inevitably forces an appeal to principle. In such circumstances, man's essential relation to the ideal is a matter of necessity, not of choice. Human power must be put at the disposal of the political order which such an appeal to principle establishes, because man has no other recourse in the circumstances of his life. Yet Calhoun had no illusion that the exercise of power in this way would as inevitably tend toward actual justice. Quite the contrary, the power placed at the disposal of the government will, he argued, normally be suborned to the ends of some individuals and groups at the expense of others. The appeal to political principle will not prevail and the established political order will not endure and be effective, unless both are rooted deep in the realistic circumstances of their origin. An enduring political order must be so constituted as to accord to the individual his rights, and to protect those social groups, minority and majority, which make it possible for the individual to live and progress. Enduring justice, he says, can be maintained only when men come to understand that the true principle of political order is a unity which preserves the integrity of the individual and the minority, and only when men will accept the full responsibility of their understanding. Then and then only will ideal principle prevail and become a living and enduring part of reality.

The events which culminated in the Civil War make too patent for explicit statement Calhoun's failure in his quest for true political unity. He knew, at the end of his life, that he had failed, and suspected that every man must fail. He had sought to bridge the gap between the ideal and the actual stream of historical events with political theory and practical devices such as the concurrent voice, the referendum, and nullification. These devices remained but the deficient expressions of his conception of a law above men's distorting and destructive motivations. In terms of these human embodiments of a supra-human law he had thought to idealize the power needed for social control, to unite the diverse courses of American development, to integrate the stream of industry and expansion with the life of the human spirit, and to avoid Civil War. In the end his principles of constitutional government remained abstract. He might struggle to make them real so that his colleagues said, "There is no *relaxation* in him";[28] his faith and his hope might remain unwavering; yet finally, as Harriet Martineau said, he was only "possessed" by his principles. His principles remained, for all their realistic emphasis, the statement of a vision—ineffectual and unreal.

RESPONSIBILITY AND FREEDOM

"I wish you would have him lodged in jail for one week, to be fed on bread and water, and to employ some one for me to give him 30 lashes well laid on . . ."[29] Calhoun's runaway slave, Aleck, had been captured. Concerning slavery in general, that "peculiar institution," as he called it, Calhoun spoke openly and favorably. He was the first leading Southerner to refer, upon the floor of Congress, to slavery as "a positive good." Indeed, he regarded slavery as a good in two senses. First, slavery was the condition of the cultural achievements of the South. It had fostered and was the condition, he claimed, of the development of one of the best of human societies. "The relation which now exists between the two races in the slave-holding States has existed for two centuries. It has grown with our growth, and strengthened with our strength. It has entered into and modified all our institutions, civil and political. No other can be substituted. We will not, cannot permit it to be destroyed. If we were base enough to do so, we would be traitors to our section, to ourselves; our families, and to posterity."[30] Second, he regarded slavery as a good for the slaves themselves. Slavery had fostered the development of their society from a state of savagery. "It may, indeed, be safely asserted, that there is no example in history in which a savage people, such as their ancestors were when brought into the country, have ever advanced in the same period so rapidly in numbers and improvement . . ."[31] With so much progress already achieved, Calhoun saw no need or desirability for radically changing existing social relations to equalize the condition of freedom. Indeed, it must be admitted, he saw no reason for any basic change at all. "A Mysterious Providence has brought the black and the white people together from different parts of the globe, and no human power could now separate them. The whites are an European race, being masters; and the Africans are the inferior race, and slaves . . . they could exist among us peaceably enough, if undisturbed, for all time."[32] An unequal distribution of freedom, Calhoun said, is in fact the condition of maximum progress for all.

Certainly Calhoun's views on the slavery question are unsatisfactory even when one takes into account the extent to which the pressure of circumstances emphasized the inherent social conservatism of his theoretical position. In his political philosophy Calhoun argues that the ultimate end of political control is to promote the perpetuation in progress of the human race. The function of political order is ultimately the preservation of man's existence and his development, for ". . . government is necessary to the existence of society, and society to . . . [man's] existence, and the perfection of his faculties."[33] Here Calhoun's conservatism is epitomized in his insistence that the security of social order is absolutely necessary to progress. Man cannot exist without society, and even further, "the existence of the race is of greater moment than its improvement."[34] Such a view seems, *prima facie*, sound enough. It suggests that in moments of great social crisis the freedom requisite to progress must be temporarily sacrificed to the greater need of protection. Yet, can this mean, however great the crisis, that the freedom of a group of men must be sacrificed, possibly for all time, to the protection of existing social patterns? To Calhoun it could and did. Calhoun believed both that the unequal distribution of freedom was a condition of maximum progress and that in moments of crisis human freedom could be sacrificed to the preservation of the social order. Neither belief was acceptable in terms of the developing American tradition.

Calhoun's deviation from the developing American political tradition was not limited to his considered suggestion that a strongly nationalist form of government be replaced by a more complex political order which could effectively protect minorities. Had his deviation been so limited his ultimate failure, although probable, would have been much less clear-cut and his impact upon the development of American political philosophy would have been much greater. Calhoun's practical political efforts were unsuccessful, in part, because they ran counter to the trend of developing nationalistic feeling. To say this alone, however, is to miss a more important sense in which Calhoun was deficient, a sense beside which this lack of success in practice is in fact secondary. Calhoun was also unable to convince the American people of his fundamental interest in mankind, and that he spoke for them. He failed in this because he deviated from the American tradition of man's essential nature, which holds that men are created free and equal, and because, once again, he failed to convince the American people of his beliefs.[35]

Both Calhoun and the American people believed that the mainspring of human progress was "the desire of individuals to better their condition."[36] Both Calhoun and the American people believed that freedom from restraint was essential to such progress. But where Calhoun saw freedom from restraint as the distant goal of progress, the American people viewed it as a primary condition of achievement, which all men should possess equally. Calhoun understood freedom from restraint to be ". . . a reward to be earned, not a blessing to be gratuitously lavished on all alike;—a reward reserved for the intelligent, the patriotic, the virtuous and deserving;—and not a boon to be bestowed on a people too ignorant, degraded and vicious, to be capable either of appreciating or enjoying it . . . the noblest and highest reward for the development of our faculties, moral and intellectual."[37] He also believed that too much freedom could interfere with progress, for to grant equal freedom to the talented and the untalented would reduce those most capable of aiding progress to the level of those least competent and would "destroy the desire [of the talented] of bettering their condition."[38]

Calhoun's insistence that freedom from restraint be bestowed only on responsible individuals and groups who have demonstrated their capacity to use such freedom for the promotion of human perfection carried no great conviction to the American people. They believed that men should be free from restriction because mankind was essentially free. Their demand for equality of freedom rested upon their belief in their own existence as free men. They refused, in general, to judge the achievements of their culture in terms of a goal *for* which they were free. Rather, they judged self-reliant action under the spur of the new continent to be good in itself because it was the expression of free men. They were willing to wager their future upon the conviction that the eventualities of free action would be good as well. Their trust, but not Calhoun's, was in originally free mankind. Caught by the thrust of their lives across the continent and into the future, the American people saw man's true character emergent from free effort, as a product of his unrestrained march across the wilderness. The American people found the evidences of man's activity good because these revealed his essential freedom as inherent in his universal nature.

It is this passionate affirmation of the individual, as expressed in the anarchy and confusion of freedom from restraint, that constitutes, in our reading of American history, a major theme in the developing American tradition. In the light of this affirmation the American people rejected Calhoun's political philosophy. In the years prior to the Civil War it was not Calhoun but Emerson who was acclaimed as the interpreter of American belief. Far from regarding, with Calhoun, government as necessary to ensure progress, they preferred to view freedom from restriction as sufficient and to regard the state as ideally unnecessary. They said, with Emerson, "The idea after which each community is aiming to make and mend its law, is the will of the wise man . . . All forms of government symbolize an immortal government . . . perfect where two men exist, perfect where there is only one man."[39] The ideal state, thus dissolved into human character, "the less government we have the better

. . . the appearance of character makes the state unnecessary. The wise man is the state."[40]

The American people believed, as Emerson said for them, in a beneficent necessity which shone through all things and which justified "a reliance on the moral sentiment and a sufficient belief in the unity of things, to persuade them that society can be maintained without artificial restraints, as well as the solar system."[41] In this they were certainly wrong, as Calhoun well knew. But behind this rejection of artificial restraints was their belief, even more vaguely expressed, that man was essentially free, that he had been created free and must remain free. They then declared, buoyed up by the hope of the frontier, that no commitment to principle, no hope of achievement could exact of them this freedom or prevent them from wishing to extend it to other peoples.

Calhoun's failure to convince the American people of his authentic interest in mankind would thus appear to be due to his failure to recognize and trust an autonomous man. Yet, Calhoun cannot be superficially convicted of ignoring the issues of man's freedom. He spoke, it must be remembered, from a position which the American people did not then and have never yet occupied. Calhoun spoke from the perspective of a losing minority. He spoke, thus, always with a sense of impending and disastrous crisis. His words were those of a prophet who saw in the signs of the times the omens of a developing human acceptance of power to be inevitably expressed in social conflict. In this losing position, in the face of the irrepressible conflicts of the future, as he saw them, Calhoun observed that man is his own enemy. He argued that man's misuse of his freedom stands between him and the preservation and progress of the human race. He noted that man's continual appeal to political principle is as continually frustrated by the egoism of his free acts. In this position and under these circumstances Calhoun would wish, protectively, to exact of man responsibility for his freedom. He thought that man must be permitted only that freedom which he could responsibly devote to the preservation of the race and its progress. And he wished to distribute freedom on the basis of demonstrated responsibility. "Man is left to perfect what the wisdom of the Infinite ordained, as necessary to preserve the race."[42]

How then did Calhoun fail? He failed, of course, to persuade the American people of his belief that freedom must always be balanced with responsibility. Yet why were they not convinced? The American tradition, it is true, could never find acceptable the thesis that human freedom should be sacrificed to a specific goal, a single principle, or a particular hope. Calhoun, however, did not urge this thesis. As Calhoun understood responsibility it was not a bondage to principle nor enslavement to the allurements of utopian expectation. He did not suggest that human freedom should ever be sacrificed to these false hopes. The responsibility of which he spoke was to the human race, the preservation and continued progress of mankind. Was this not acceptable? Should not individual freedom be balanced by responsibility to a common humanity?

Perhaps Calhoun's practical position on the question of slavery, his acceptance of this "peculiar institution," possibly "for all time," suggested to the American people that the mankind to which he referred was not that common humanity of which they felt themselves to be a part. Certainly Calhoun's understanding of mankind was based upon his realistic observations of human egotism and social partisanship. There is little in his writings to suggest that his insight extended beyond the fact of diverse human character and the pattern of class and group structure in society to a concrete grasp of man's universal nature. There is much in his thought which confirms the belief that he understood mankind only as an abstraction referring to the complex social pattern of the individual in his relation to other persons. Viewing man merely as an actual individual and a social being, Calhoun could and did interpret his conservative principle of the need to preserve the race to mean the need to preserve existing social forms. Surely the American people were right in rejecting this. For if, as Calhoun knew, there are circumstances in which freedom must be sacrificed to responsibility, then, as the American people knew, this responsibility must be to a common humanity. Man's universal nature is to be found in his freedom and in his capacity to idealize. The creative action which expresses this nature can be restrained, in principle, only in the interests of humanity. Certainly human freedom, in principle, cannot be sacrificed to what merely is; even though that should be, as Calhoun thought it was, a complex and cultured society.

Yet, if Calhoun's conception of the brotherhood of man is limited to the pattern of individual and social relations, within the limits of his perspective his plea is for the preservation of human creativity. Calhoun has left to us a fundamental body of thought including an incisive analysis of the problem of minority rights. His thought is well worth study in the light of the problems of today or, indeed, of any time. The issues with which he deals are the perennial issues of human political life. He points out clearly that an appeal to principle in the establishment of political order is not of itself enough. He argues, in terms of a social analysis well in advance of his times, that the vision of ideal political unity must be supplemented by a realistic analysis of human life. The appeal men make to the principle of political order in the face of individual and social conflict can not be given enduring realization in this world, Calhoun insists, without a realistic protection of both individual and minority rights. Perhaps Calhoun's treatment of the issues of human freedom would have been more satisfactory had he noted that man's inevitable appeal to political order in the face of anarchy and confusion is an appeal not only to the ideal of unity but to a sense of primal freedom as well. From this slightly different perspective it is possible that Calhoun's insistence upon the preservation of social order might have been less a doctrine urging the preservation of existing human achievements. It might have been restated, in different terms, as a part of the realistic problem of establishing the enduring fellowship of a free humanity. But if this is a correction of Calhoun's thought, it is also a lesson which has not yet been learned.

ON GOVERNMENT

ON GOVERNMENT

Calhoun said of his own work in June 1849:

"I devote all the time left me, to finishing the work I commenced three years ago, or more; but which I had to suspend the last two years. I ought not delay its execution any longer, and aim to put it in press, if I can finish it in the recess, next Spring or Summer. I finished yesterday the preliminary work [the Disquisition] which treats of the elementary principles of the Science of Government, except reading it over and making final corrections, previous to copying and publishing. It takes 125 pages of large foolscap closely written for me. I am pretty well satisfied with its execution. It will be nearly throughout new territory, and, I hope, lay a solid foundation for political Science. I have written, just as I thought, and told the truth without fear, favor or affection."[1]

Calhoun's A Disquisition on Government was written shortly before his death and probably never finally corrected. The present text is that of Cralle's edition of 1851, which was taken, with very few changes, from the copy Calhoun had made of his manuscript for publication.

In order to have a clear and just conception of the nature and object of government, it is indispensable to understand correctly what that constitution or law of our nature is, in which government originates; or, to express it more fully and accurately,—that law, without which government would not, and with which, it must necessarily exist. Without this, it is as impossible to lay any solid foundation for the science of government, as it would be to lay one for that of astronomy, without a like understanding of that constitution or law of the material world, according to which the several bodies composing the solar system mutually act on each other, and by which they are kept in their respective spheres. The first question, accordingly, to be considered is,—What is that constitution or law of our nature, without which government would not exist, and with which its existence is necessary?

In considering this, I assume, as an incontestable fact, that man is so constituted as to be a social being. His inclinations and wants, physical and moral, irresistibly impel him to associate with his kind; and he has, accordingly, never been found, in any age or country, in any state other than the social. In no other, indeed, could he exist; and in no other,—were it possible for him to exist,—could he attain to a full development of his moral and intellectual faculties, or raise himself, in the scale of being, much above the level of the brute creation.

I next assume, also, as a fact not less incontestable, that, while man is so constituted as to make the social state necessary to his existence and the full development of his faculties, this state itself cannot exist without government. The assumption rests on universal experience. In no age or country has any society or community ever been found, whether enlightened or savage, without government of some description.

Having assumed these, as unquestionable phenomena of our nature, I shall, without further remark, proceed to the investigation of the primary and important question,—What is that constitution of our nature, which, while it impels man to associate with his kind, renders it impossible for society to exist without government?

The answer will be found in the fact, (not less incontestable than either of the others,) that, while man is created for the social state, and is accordingly so formed as to feel what affects others, as well as what affects himself, he is, at the same time, so constituted as to feel more intensely what affects him directly, than what affects him indirectly through others; or, to express it differently, he is so constituted, that his direct or individual affections are stronger than his sympathetic or social feelings. I intentionally avoid the expression, *selfish* feelings, as applicable to the former; because, as commonly used, it implies an unusual excess of the individual over the social feelings, in the person to whom it is applied; and, consequently, something depraved and vicious. My object is, to exclude such inference, and to restrict the inquiry exclusively to facts in their bearings on the subject under consideration, viewed as mere phenomena appertaining to our nature,—constituted as it is; and which are as unquestionable as is that of gravitation, or any other phenomenon of the material world.

In asserting that our individual are stronger than our social feelings, it is not intended to deny that there are instances, growing out of peculiar relations,—as that of a mother and her infant,—or resulting from the force of education and habit over peculiar constitutions, in which the latter have overpowered the former; but these instances are few, and always regarded as something extraordinary. The deep impression they make, whenever they occur, is the strongest proof that they are regarded as exceptions to some general and well understood law of our nature; just as some of the minor powers of the material world are apparently to gravitation.

I might go farther, and assert this to be a phenomenon, not of our nature only, but of all animated existence, throughout its entire range, so far as our knowledge extends. It would, indeed, seem to be essentially connected with the great law of self-preservation which pervades all that feels, from man down to the lowest and most insignificant reptile or insect. In none is it stronger than in man. His social feelings may, indeed, in a state of safety and abundance, combined with high intellectual and moral culture, acquire great expansion and force; but not so great as to overpower this all-pervading and essential law of animated existence.

But that constitution of our nature which makes us feel more intensely what affects us directly than what affects us indirectly through others, necessarily leads to conflict between individuals. Each, in consequence, has a greater regard for his own safety or happiness, than for the safety or happiness of others; and, where these come in opposition, is ready to sacrifice the interests of others to his own. And hence, the tendency to a universal state of conflict, between individual and individual; accompanied by the connected passions of suspicion, jealousy, anger and revenge,—followed by insolence, fraud and cruelty;—and, if not prevented by some controlling power, ending in a state of universal discord and confusion, destructive of the social state and the ends for which it is ordained. This controlling power, wherever vested, or by whomsoever exercised, is GOVERNMENT.

It follows, then, that man is so constituted, that government is necessary to the existence of society, and society to his existence, and the perfection of his faculties. It follows, also, that government has its origin in this twofold constitution of his nature; the sympathetic or social feelings constituting the remote,—and the individual or direct, the proximate cause.

If man had been differently constituted in either particular; —if, instead of being social in his nature, he had been created without sympathy for his kind, and independent of others for his safety and existence; or if, on the other hand, he had been so created, as to feel more intensely what affected others than what affected himself, (if that were possible,) or, even, had this supposed interest been equal,—it is manifest that, in either case, there would have been no necessity for government, and that none would ever have existed. But, although society and government are thus intimately connected with and dependent on each other,—of the two society is the greater. It is the first in the order of things, and in the dignity of its object; that of society being primary,—to preserve and perfect our race; and that of government secondary and subordinate, to preserve and perfect society. Both are, however, necessary to the existence and well-being of our race, and equally of Divine ordination.

I have said,—if it were possible for man to be so constituted, as to feel what affects others more strongly than what affects himself, or even as strongly,—because, it may be well doubted, whether the stronger feeling or affection of individuals for themselves, combined with a feebler and subordinate feeling or affection for others, is not, in beings of limited reason and faculties, a constitution necessary to their preservation and existence. If reversed,—if their feelings and affections were stronger for others than for themselves, or even as strong, the necessary result would seem to be, that all individuality would be lost; and boundless and remediless disorder and confusion would ensue. For each, at the same moment, intensely participating in all the conflicting emotions of those around him, would, of course, forget himself and all that concerned him immediately, in his officious intermeddling with the affairs of all others; which, from his limited reason and faculties, he could neither properly understand nor manage. Such a state of things would, as far as we can see, lead to endless disorder and confusion, not less destructive to our race than a state of anarchy. It would, besides, be remediless,—for government would be impossible; or, if it could by possibility exist, its object would be reversed. Selfishness would have to be encouraged, and benevolence discouraged. Individuals would have to be encouraged, by rewards, to become more selfish, and deterred, by punishments, from being too benevolent; and this, too, by a government, administered by those who, on the supposition, would have the greatest aversion for selfishness and the highest admiration for benevolence.

To the Infinite Being, the Creator of all, belongs exclusively the care and superintendence of the whole. He, in his infinite wisdom and goodness, has allotted to every class of animated beings its condition and appropriate functions; and has endowed each with feelings, instincts, capacities, and faculties, best adapted to its allotted condition. To man, he has assigned the social and political state, as best adapted to develop the great capacities and faculties, intellectual and moral, with which he has endowed him; and has, accordingly, constituted him so as not only to impel him into the social state, but to make government necessary for his preservation and well-being.

But government, although intended to protect and preserve society, has itself a strong tendency to disorder and abuse of its powers, as all experience and almost every page of history testify. The cause is to be found in the same constitution of our nature which makes government indispensable. The powers which it is necessary for government to possess, in order to repress violence and preserve order, cannot execute themselves. They must be administered by men in whom, like others, the individual are stronger than the social feelings. And hence, the powers vested in them to prevent injustice and oppression on the part of others, will, if left unguarded, be by them converted into instruments to oppress the rest of the community. That, by which this is prevented, by whatever name called, is what is meant by CONSTITUTION, in its most comprehensive sense, when applied to GOVERNMENT.

Having its origin in the same principle of our nature, *constitution* stands to *government*, as *government* stands to *society;* and, as the end for which society is ordained, would be defeated without government, so that for which government is ordained would, in a great measure, be defeated without constitution. But they differ in this striking particular. There is no difficulty in forming government. It is not even a matter of choice, whether there shall be one or not. Like breathing, it is not permitted to depend on our volition. Necessity will force it on all communities in some one form or another. Very different is the case as to constitution. Instead of a matter of necessity, it is one of the most difficult tasks imposed on man to form a constitution worthy of the name; while, to form a perfect one,—one that would completely counteract the tendency of government to oppression and abuse, and hold it strictly to the great ends for which it is ordained,—has thus far exceeded human wisdom, and possibly ever will. From this, another striking difference results. Constitution is the contrivance of man, while government is of Divine ordination. Man is left to perfect what the wisdom of the Infinite ordained, as necessary to preserve the race.

With these remarks, I proceed to the consideration of the important and difficult question: How is this tendency of government to be counteracted? Or, to express it more fully,—How can those who are invested with the powers of government be prevented from employing them, as the means of aggrandizing themselves, instead of using them to protect and preserve society? It cannot be done by instituting a higher power to control the government, and those who administer it. This would be but to change the seat of authority, and to make this higher power, in reality, the government; with the same tendency, on the part of those who might control its powers, to pervert them into instruments of aggrandizement. Nor can it be done by limiting the powers of government, so as to make it too feeble to be made an instrument of abuse; for, passing by the difficulty of so limiting its powers, without creating a power higher than the government itself to enforce the observance of the limitations, it is a sufficient objection that it would, if practicable, defeat the end for which government is ordained, by making it too feeble to protect and preserve society. The powers necessary for this purpose will ever prove sufficient to aggrandize those who control it, at the expense of the rest of the community.

In estimating what amount of power would be requisite to secure the objects of government, we must take into the reckoning, what would be necessary to defend the community against external, as well as internal dangers. Government must be able to repel assaults from abroad, as well as to repress violence and disorders within. It must not be overlooked, that the human race is not comprehended in a single society or community. The limited reason and faculties of man, the great diversity of language, customs, pursuits, situation and complexion, and the difficulty of intercourse, with various other causes, have, by their operation, formed a great many separate communities, acting independently of each other. Between these there is the same tendency to conflict,—and from the same constitution of our nature,—as between men individually; and even stronger,—because the sympathetic or social feelings are not so strong between different communities, as between individuals of the same community. So powerful, indeed, is this tendency, that it has led to almost incessant wars between contiguous communities for plunder and conquest, or to avenge injuries, real or supposed.

So long as this state of things continues, exigencies will occur, in which the entire powers and resources of the community will be needed to defend its existence. When this is at stake, every other consideration must yield to it. Self-preservation is the supreme law, as well with communities as individuals. And hence the danger of withholding from government the full command of the power and resources of the state; and the great difficulty of limiting its powers consistently with the protection and preservation of the community. And hence the question recurs, —By what means can government, without being divested of the full command of the resources of the community, be prevented from abusing its powers?

The question involves difficulties which, from the earliest ages, wise and good men have attempted to overcome;—but hitherto with but partial success. For this purpose many devices have been resorted to, suited to the various stages of intelligence and civilization through which our race has passed, and to the different forms of government to which they have been applied. The aid of superstition, ceremonies, education, religion, organic arrangements, both of the government and the community, has been, from time to time, appealed to. Some of the most remarkable of these devices, whether regarded in reference to their wisdom and the skill displayed in their application, or to the permanency of their effects, are to be found in the early dawn of civilization;—in the institutions of the Egyptians, the Hindoos, the Chinese, and the Jews. The only materials which that early age afforded for the construction of constitutions, when intelligence was so partially diffused, were applied with consummate wisdom and skill. To their successful application may be fairly traced the subsequent advance of our race in civilization and intelligence, of which we now enjoy the benefits. For, without a constitution,—something to counteract the strong tendency of government to disorder and abuse, and to give stability to political institutions,—there can be little progress or permanent improvement.

In answering the important question under consideration, it is not necessary to enter into an examination of the various contrivances adopted by these celebrated governments to counteract this tendency to disorder and abuse, nor to undertake to treat of constitution in its most comprehensive sense. What I propose is far more limited,—to explain on what principles government must be formed, in order to resist, by its own interior structure, —or, to use a single term, *organism*,—the tendency to abuse of power. This structure, or organism, is what is meant by constitution, in its strict and more usual sense; and it is this which distinguishes, what are called, constitutional governments from absolute. It is in this strict and more usual sense that I propose to use the term hereafter.

How government, then, must be constructed, in order to counteract, through its organism, this tendency on the part of those who make and execute the laws to oppress those subject to their operation, is the next question which claims attention.

There is but one way in which this can possibly be done; and that is, by such an organism as will furnish the ruled with the means of resisting successfully this tendency on the part of the rulers to oppression and abuse. Power can only be resisted by power,—and tendency by tendency. Those who exercise power and those subject to its exercise,—the rulers and the ruled,—stand in antagonistic relations to each other. The same constitution of our nature which leads rulers to oppress the ruled,—regardless of the object for which government is ordained,—will, with equal strength, lead the ruled to resist, when possessed of the means of making peaceable and effective resistance. Such an organism, then, as will furnish the means by which resistance may be systematically and peaceably made on the part of the ruled, to oppression and abuse of power on the part of the rulers, is the first and indispensable step towards *forming* a constitutional government. And as this can only be effected by or through the right of suffrage,—(the right on the part of the ruled to choose their rulers at proper intervals, and to hold them thereby responsible for their conduct,)—the responsibility of the rulers to the ruled, through the right of suffrage, is the indispensable and primary principle in the *foundation* of a constitutional government. When this right is properly guarded, and the people sufficiently enlightened to understand their own rights and the interests of the community, and duly to appreciate the motives and conduct of those appointed to make and execute the laws, it is all-sufficient to give to those who elect, effective control over those they have elected.

I call the right of suffrage the indispensible and primary principle; for it would be a great and dangerous mistake to suppose, as many do, that it is, of itself, sufficient to form constitutional governments. To this erroneous opinion may be traced one of the causes, why so few attempts to form constitutional governments have succeeded; and why, of the few which have, so small a number have had durable existence. It has led, not only to mistakes in the attempts to form such governments, but to their overthrow, when they have, by some good fortune, been correctly formed. So far from being, of itself, sufficient,—however well guarded it might be, and however enlightened the people,—it would, unaided by other provisions, leave the government as absolute, as it would be in the hands of irresponsible rulers; and with a tendency, at least as strong, towards oppression and abuse of its powers; as I shall next proceed to explain.

The right of suffrage, of itself, can do no more than give complete control to those who elect, over the conduct of those they have elected. In doing this, it accomplishes all it possibly can accomplish. This is its aim,—and when this is attained, its end is fulfilled. It can do no more, however enlightened the people, or however widely extended or well guarded the right may be. The sum total, then, of its effects, when most successful, is, to make those elected, the true and faithful representatives of those who elected them,—instead of irresponsible rulers,—as they would be without it; and thus, by converting it into an agency, and the rulers into agents, to divest government of all claims to sovereignty, and to retain it unimpaired to the community. But it is manifest that the right of suffrage, in making these changes, transfers, in reality, the actual control over the government, from those who make and execute the laws, to the body of the community; and, thereby, places the powers of the government as fully in the mass of the community, as they would be if they, in fact, had assembled, made, and executed the laws themselves, without the intervention of representatives or agents. The more perfectly it does this, the more perfectly it accomplishes its ends; but in doing so, it only changes the seat of authority, without counteracting, in the least, the tendency of the government to oppression and abuse of its powers.

If the whole community had the same interests, so that the interests of each and every portion would be so affected by the action of the government, that the laws which oppressed or impoverished one portion, would necessarily oppress and impoverish all others,—or the reverse,—then the right of suffrage, of itself, would be all-sufficient to counteract the tendency of the government to oppression and abuse of its powers; and, of course, would form, of itself, a perfect constitutional government. The interest of all being the same, by supposition, as far as the action of the government was concerned, all would have like interests as to what laws should be made, and how they should be executed. All strife and struggle would cease as to who should be elected to make and execute them. The only question would be, who was most fit; who the wisest and most capable of understanding the common interest of the whole. This decided, the election would pass off quietly, and without party discord; as no one portion could advance its own peculiar interest without regard to the rest, by electing a favorite candidate.

But such is not the case. On the contrary, nothing is more difficult than to equalize the action of the government, in reference to the various and diversified interests of the community; and nothing more easy than to pervert its powers into instruments to aggrandize and enrich one or more interests by oppressing and impoverishing the others; and this too, under the operation of laws, couched in general terms;—and which, on their face, appear fair and equal. Nor is this the case in some particular communities only. It is so in all; the small and the great,—the poor and the rich,—irrespective of pursuits, productions, or degrees of civilization;—with, however, this difference, that the more extensive and populous the country, the more diversified the condition and pursuits of its population, and the richer, more luxurious, and dissimilar the people, the more difficult it is to equalize the action of the government,—and the more easy for one portion of the community to pervert its powers to oppress, and plunder the other.

Such being the case, it necessarily results, that the right of suffrage, by placing the control of the government in the community must, from the same constitution of our nature which makes government necessary to preserve society, lead to conflict among its different interests,—each striving to obtain possession of its powers, as the means of protecting itself against the others; —or of advancing its respective interests, regardless of the interests of others. For this purpose, a struggle will take place between the various interests to obtain a majority, in order to control the government. If no one interest be strong enough, of itself, to obtain it, a combination will be formed between those whose interests are most alike;—each conceding something to the others, until a sufficient number is obtained to make a majority. The process may be slow, and much time may be required before a compact, organized majority can be thus formed; but formed it will be in time, even without preconcert or design, by the sure workings of that principle or constitution of our nature in which government itself originates. When once formed, the community will be divided into two great parties,—a major and minor,— between which there will be incessant struggles on the one side to retain, and on the other to obtain the majority,—and, thereby, the control of the government and the advantages it confers.

So deeply seated, indeed, is this tendency to conflict between the different interests or portions of the community, that it would result from the action of the government itself, even though it were possible to find a community, where the people were all of the same pursuits, placed in the same condition of life, and in every respect, so situated, as to be without inequality of condition or diversity of interests. The advantages of possessing the control of the powers of the government, and, thereby, of its honors and emoluments, are, of themselves, exclusive of all other considerations, ample to divide even such a community into two great hostile parties.

In order to form a just estimate of the full force of these advantages,—without reference to any other consideration,—it must be remembered, that government,—to fulfill the ends for which it is ordained, and more especially that of protection against external dangers,—must, in the present condition of the world, be clothed with powers sufficient to call forth the resources of the community, and be prepared, at all times, to command them promptly in every emergency which may possibly arise. For this purpose large establishments are necessary, both civil and military, (including naval, where, from situation, that description of force may be required,) with all the means necessary for prompt and effective action,—such as fortifications, fleets, armories, arsenals, magazines, arms of all descriptions, with well-trained forces, in sufficient numbers to wield them with skill and energy, whenever the occasion requires it. The administration and management of a government with such vast establishments must necessarily require a host of employees, agents, and officers;—of whom many must be vested with high and responsible trusts, and occupy exalted stations, accompanied with much influence and patronage. To meet the necessary expenses, large sums must be collected and disbursed; and, for this purpose, heavy taxes must be imposed, requiring a multitude of officers for their collection and disbursement. The whole united must necessarily place under the control of government an amount of honors and emoluments, sufficient to excite profoundly the ambition of the aspiring and the cupidity of the avaricious; and to lead to the formation of hostile parties, and violent party conflicts and struggles to obtain the control of the government. And what makes this evil remediless, through the right of suffrage of itself, however modified or carefully guarded, or however enlightened the people, is the fact that, as far as the honors and emoluments of the government and its fiscal action are concerned, it is impossible to equalize it. The reason is obvious. Its honors and emoluments, however great, can fall to the lot of but a few, compared to the entire number of the community, and the multitude who will seek to participate in them. But, without this, there is a reason which renders it impossible to equalize the action of the government, so far as its fiscal operation extends,—which I shall next explain.

Few, comparatively, as they are, the agents and employees of of the government constitute that portion of the community who are the exclusive recipients of the proceeds of the taxes. Whatever amount is taken from the community, in the form of taxes, if not lost, goes to them in the shape of expenditures or disbursements. The two,—disbursement and taxation,—constitute the fiscal action of the government. They are correlatives. What the one takes from the community, under the name of taxes, is transferred to the portion of the community who are the recipients, under that of disbursements. But, as the recipients constitute only a portion of the community, it follows, taking the two parts of the fiscal process together, that its action must be unequal between the payers of the taxes and the recipients of their proceeds. Nor can it be otherwise, unless what is collected from each individual in the shape of taxes, shall be returned to him, in that of disbursements; which would make the process nugatory and absurd. Taxation may, indeed, be made equal, regarded separately from disbursement. Even this is no easy task; but the two united cannot possibly be made equal.

Such being the case, it must necessarily follow, that some one portion of the community must pay in taxes more than it receives back in disbursements; while another receives in disbursements more than it pays in taxes. It is, then, manifest, taking the whole process together, that taxes must be, in effect, bounties to that portion of the community which receives more in disbursements than it pays in taxes; while, to the other which pays in taxes more than it receives in disbursements, they are taxes in reality,—burthens, instead of bounties. This consequence is unavoidable. It results from the nature of the process, be the taxes ever so equally laid, and the disbursements ever so fairly made, in reference to the public service.

It is assumed, in coming to this conclusion, that the disbursements are made within the community. The reasons assigned would not be applicable if the proceeds of the taxes were paid in tribute, or expended in foreign countries. In either of these cases, the burthen would fall on all, in proportion to the amount of taxes they respectively paid.

Nor would it be less a bounty to the portion of the community which received back in disbursements more than it paid in taxes, because received as salaries for official services; or payments to persons employed in executing the works required by the government; or furnishing it with its various supplies; or any other description of public employment,—instead of being bestowed gratuitously. It is the disbursements which give additional, and, usually, very profitable and honorable employments to the portion of the community where they are made. But to create such employments, by disbursements, is to bestow on the portion of the community to whose lot the disbursements may fall, a far more durable and lasting benefit,—one that would add much more to its wealth and population,—than would the bestowal of an equal sum gratuitously: and hence, to the extent that the disbursements exceed the taxes, it may be fairly regarded as a bounty. The very reverse is the case in reference to the portion which pays in taxes more than it receives in disbursements. With them, profitable employments are diminished to the same extent, and population and wealth correspondingly decreased.

The necessary result, then, of the unequal fiscal action of the government is, to divide the community into two great classes; one consisting of those who, in reality, pay the taxes, and, of course, bear exclusively the burthen of supporting the government; and the other, of those who are the recipients of their proceeds, through disbursements, and who are, in fact, supported by the government; or, in fewer words, to divide it into tax-payers and tax-consumers.

But the effect of this is to place them in antagonistic relations, in reference to the fiscal action of the government, and the entire course of policy therewith connected. For, the greater the taxes and disbursements, the greater the gain of the one and the loss of the other,—and *vice versa;* and consequently, the more the policy of the government is calculated to increase taxes and disbursements, the more it will be favored by the one and opposed by the other.

The effect, then, of every increase is, to enrich and strengthen the one, and impoverish and weaken the other. This, indeed, may be carried to such an extent, that one class or portion of the community may be elevated to wealth and power, and the other depressed to abject poverty and dependence, simply by the fiscal action of the government; and this too, through disbursements only,—even under a system of equal taxes imposed for revenue only. If such may be the effect of taxes and disbursements, when confined to their legitimate objects,—that of raising revenue for the public service,—some conception may be formed, how one portion of the community may be crushed, and another elevated on its ruins, by systematically perverting the power of taxation and disbursement, for the purpose of aggrandizing and building up one portion of the community at the expense of the other.

That it *will* be so used, unless prevented, is, from the constitution of man, just as certain as that it *can* be so used; and that, if not prevented, it must give rise to two parties, and to violent conflicts and struggles between them, to obtain the control of the government, is, for the same reason, not less certain.

Nor is it less certain, from the operation of all these causes, that the dominant majority, for the time, would have the same tendency to oppression and abuse of power, which, without the right of suffrage, irresponsible rulers would have. No reason, indeed, can be assigned, why the latter would abuse their power, which would not apply, with equal force, to the former. The dominant majority, for the time, would, in reality, through the right of suffrage, be the rulers—the controlling, governing, and irresponsible power; and those who make and execute the laws would, for the time, be, in reality, but *their* representatives and agents.

Nor would the fact that the former would constitute a majority of the community, counteract a tendency originating in the constitution of man; and which, as such, cannot depend on the number by whom the powers of the government may be wielded. Be it greater or smaller, a majority or minority, it must equally partake of an attribute inherent in each individual composing it; and, as in each the individual is stronger than the social feelings, the one would have the same tendency as the other to oppression and abuse of power. The reason applies to government in all its forms,—whether it be that of the one, the few, or the many. In each there must, of necessity, be a governing and governed,—a ruling and a subject portion. The one implies the other; and in all, the two bear the same relation to each other;—and have, on the part of the governing portion, the same tendency to oppression and abuse of power. Where the majority is that portion, it matters not how its powers may be exercised;—whether directly by themselves, or indirectly, through represenatives or agents. Be it which it may, the minority, for the time, will be as much the governed or subject portion, as are the people in an aristocracy, or the subjects in a monarchy. The only difference in this respect is, that in the government of a majority, the minority may become the majority, and the majority the minority, through the right of suffrage; and thereby change their relative positions, without the intervention of force and revolution. But the duration, or uncertainity of the tenure, by which power is held, cannot, of itself, counteract the tendency inherent in government to oppression and abuse of power. On the contrary, the very uncertainty of the tenure, combined with the violent party warfare which must ever precede a change of parties under such governments, would rather tend to increase than diminish the tendency to oppression.

As, then, the right of suffrage, without some other provision, cannot counteract this tendency of government, the next question for consideration is—What is that other provision? This demands the most serious consideration; for of all the questions embraced in the science of government, it involves a principle, the most important, and the least understood; and when understood, the most difficult of application in practice. It is, indeed, emphatically, that principle which *makes* the constitution, in its strict and limited sense.

From what has been said, it is manifest, that this provision must be of a character calculated to prevent any one interest, or combination of interests, from using the powers of government to aggrandize itself at the expense of the others. Here lies the evil: and just in proportion as it shall prevent, or fail to prevent it, in the same degree it will effect, or fail to effect the end intended to be accomplished. There is but one certain mode in which this result can be secured; and that is, by the adoption of some restriction or limitation, which shall so effectually prevent any one interest, or combination of interests, from obtaining the exclusive control of the government, as to render hopeless all attempts directed to that end. There is, again, but one mode in which this can be effected; and that is, by taking the sense of each interest or portion of the community, which may be unequally and injuriously affected by the action of the government, separately, through its own majority, or in some other way by which its voice may be fairly expressed; and to require the consent of each interest, either to put or to keep the government in action. This, too, can be accomplished only in one way,—and that is, by such an organism of the government,—and, if necessary for the purpose, of the community also,—as will, by dividing and distributing the powers of government, give to each division or interest, through its appropriate organ, either a concurrent voice in making and executing the laws, or a veto on their execution. It is only by such an organism, that the assent of each can be made necessary to put the government in motion; or the power made effectual to arrest its action, when put in motion;—and it is only by the one or the other that the different interests, orders, classes, or portions, into which the community may be divided, can be protected, and all conflict and struggle between them prevented,—by rendering it impossible to put or to keep it in action, without the concurrent consent of all.

Such an organism as this, combined with the right of suffrage, constitutes, in fact, the elements of constitutional government. The one, by rendering those who make and execute the laws responsible to those on whom they operate, prevents the rulers from oppressing the ruled; and the other, by making it impossible for any one interest or combination of interests or class, or order, or portion of the community, to obtain exclusive control, prevents any one of them from oppressing the other. It is clear, that oppression and abuse of power must come, if at all, from the one or the other quarter. From no other can they come. It follows, that the two, suffrage and proper organism combined, are sufficient to counteract the tendency of government to oppression and abuse of power; and to restrict it to the fulfilment of the great ends for which it is ordained.

In coming to this conclusion, I have assumed the organism to be perfect, and the different interests, portions, or classes of the community, to be sufficiently enlightened to understand its character and object, and to exercise, with due intelligence, the right of suffrage. To the extent that either may be defective, to the same extent the government would fall short of fulfilling its end. But this does not impeach the truth of the principles on which it rests. In reducing them to proper form, in applying them to practical uses, all elementary principles are liable to difficulties; but they are not, on this account, the less true, or valuable. Where the organism is perfect, every interest will be truly and fully represented, and of course the whole community must be so. It may be difficult, or even impossible, to make a perfect organism,—but, although this be true, yet even when, instead of the sense of each and of all, it takes that of a few great and prominent interests only, it would still, in a great measure, if not altogether, fulfil the end intended by a constitution. For, in such case, it would require so large a portion of the community, compared with the whole, to concur, or acquiesce in the action of the government, that the number to be plundered would be too few, and the number to be aggrandized too many, to afford adequate motives to oppression and the abuse of its powers. Indeed, however imperfect the organism, it must have more or less effect in diminishing such tendency.

It may be readily inferred, from what has been stated, that the effect of organism is neither to supersede nor diminish the importance of the right of suffrage; but to aid and perfect it. The object of the latter is, to collect the sense of the community. The more fully and perfectly it accomplishes this, the more fully and perfectly it fulfils its end. But the most it can do, of itself, is to collect the sense of the greater number; that is, of the stronger interests, or combination of interests; and to assume this to be the sense of the community. It is only when aided by a proper organism, that it can collect the sense of the entire community,—of each and all its interests; of each, through its appropriate organ, and of the whole, through all of them united. This would truly be the sense of the entire community; for whatever diversity each interest might have within itself,—as all would have the same interest in reference to the action of the government, the individuals composing each would be fully and truly represented by its own majority or appropriate organ, regarded in reference to the other interests. In brief, every individual of every interest might trust, with confidence, its majority or appropriate organ, against that of every other interest.

It results, from what has been said, that there are two different modes in which the sense of the community may be taken; one, simply by the right of suffrage, unaided; the other, by the right through a proper organism. Each collects the sense of the majority. But one regards numbers only, and considers the whole community as a unit, having but one common interest throughout; and collects the sense of the greater number of the whole, as that of the community. The other, on the contrary, regards interests as well as numbers;—considering the community as made up of different and conflicting interests, as far as the action of the government is concerned; and takes the sense of each, through its majority or appropriate organ, and the united sense of all, as the sense of the entire community. The former of these I shall call the numerical, or absolute majority; and the latter, the concurrent, or constitutional majority. I call it the constitutional majority, because it is an essential element in every constitutional government,—be its form what it may. So great is the difference, politically speaking, between the two majorities, that they cannot be confounded, without leading to great and fatal errors; and yet the distinction between them has been so entirely overlooked, that when the term *majority* is used in political discussions, it is applied exclusively to designate the numerical,—as if there were no other. Until this distinction is recognized, and better understood, there will continue to be great liability to error in properly constructing constitutional governments, especially of the popular form, and of preserving them when properly constructed. Until then, the latter will have a strong tendency to slide, first, into the government of the numerical majority, and, finally, into absolute government of some other form. To show that such must be the case, and at the same time to mark more strongly the difference between the two, in order to guard against the danger of overlooking it, I propose to consider the subject more at length.

The first and leading error which naturally arises from overlooking the distinction referred to, is, to confound the numerical majority with the people; and this so completely as to regard them as identical. This is a consequence that necessarily results from considering the numerical as the only majority. All admit, that a popular government, or democracy, is the government of the people; for the terms imply this. A perfect government of the kind would be one which would embrace the consent of every citizen or member of the community; but as this is impracticable, in the opinion of those who regard the numerical as the only majority, and who can perceive no other way by which the sense of the people can be taken,—they are compelled to adopt this as the only true basis of popular government, in contradistinction to governments of the aristocratical or monarchical form. Being thus constrained, they are, in the next place, forced to regard the numerical majority, as, in effect, the entire people; that is, the greater part as the whole; and the government of the greater part as the government of the whole. It is thus the two come to be confounded, and a part made identical with the whole. And it is thus, also, that all the rights, powers, and immunities of the whole people come to be attributed to the numerical majority;

and, among others, the supreme, sovereign authority of establishing and abolishing governments at pleasure.

This radical error, the consequence of confounding the two, and of regarding the numerical as the only majority, has contributed more than any other cause, to prevent the formation of popular constitutional governments,—and to destroy them even when they have been formed. It leads to the conclusion that, in their formation and establishment nothing more is necessary than the right of suffrage,—and the attotment to each division of the community a representation in the government, in proportion to numbers. If the numerical majority were really the people; and if, to take its sense truly, were to take the sense of the people truly, a government so constituted would be a true and perfect model of a popular constitutional government; and every departure from it would detract from its excellence. But, as such is not the case,—as the numerical majority, instead of being the people, is only a portion of them,—such a government, instead of being a true and perfect model of the people's government, that is, a people self-governed, is but the government of a part, over a part,—the major over the minor portion.

But this misconception of the true elements of constitutional government does not stop here. It leads to others equally false and fatal, in reference to the best means of preserving and perpetuating them, when, from some fortunate combination of circumstances, they are correctly formed. For they who fall into these errors regard the restrictions which organism imposes on the will of the numerical majority as restrictions on the will of the people, and, therefore, as not only useless, but wrongful and mischievous. And hence they endeavor to destroy organism, under the delusive hope of making government more democratic.

Such are some of the consequences of confounding the two, and of regarding the numerical as the only majority. And in this may be found the reason why so few popular governments have been properly constructed, and why, of these few, so small a number have proved durable. Such must continue to be the result, so long as these errors continue to be prevalent.

There is another error, of a kindred character, whose influence contributes much to the same results: I refer to the prevalent opinion, that a written constitution, containing suitable restrictions on the powers of government, is sufficient, of itself, without the aid of any organism,—except such as is necessary to separate its several departments, and render them independent of each other,—to counteract the tendency of the numerical majority to oppression and the abuse of power.

A written constitution certainly has many and considerable advantages; but it is a great mistake to suppose, that the mere insertion of provisions to restrict and limit the powers of the government, without investing those for whose protection they are inserted with the means of enforcing their observance, will be sufficient to prevent the major and dominant party from abusing its powers. Being the party in possession of the government, they will, from the same constitution of man which makes government necessary to protect society, be in favor of the powers granted by the constitution, and opposed to the restrictions intended to limit them. As the major and dominant party, they will have no need of these restrictions for their protection. The ballot-box, of itself, would be ample protection to them. Needing no other, they would come, in time, to regard these limitations as unnecessary and improper restraints;—and endeavor to elude them, with the view of increasing their power and influence.

The minor, or weaker party, on the contrary, would take the opposite direction;—and regard them as essential to their protection against the dominant party. And, hence, they would endeavor to defend and enlarge the restrictions, and to limit and contract the powers. But where there are no means by which they could compel the major party to observe the restrictions, the only resort left them would be, a strict construction of the constitution,—that is, a construction which would confine these powers to the narrowest limits which the meaning of the words used in the grant would admit.

To this the major party would oppose a liberal construction,—one which would give to the words of the grant the broadest meaning of which they were susceptible. It would then be construction against construction; the one to contract, and the other to enlarge the powers of the government to the utmost. But of what possible avail could the strict construction of the minor party be, against the liberal interpretation of the major, when the one would have all the powers of the government to carry its construction into effect,—and the other be deprived of all means of enforcing its construction? In a contest so unequal, the result would not be doubtful. The party in favor of the restrictions would be overpowered. At first, they might command some respect, and do something to stay the march of encroachment; but they would, in the progress of the contest, be regarded as mere abstractionists; and, indeed, deservedly, if they should indulge the folly of supposing that the party in possession of the ballot-box and the physical force of the country, could be successfully resisted by an appeal to reason, truth, justice, or the obligations imposed by the constitution. For when these, of themselves, shall exert sufficient influence to stay the hand of power, then government will be no longer necessary to protect society, nor constitutions needed to prevent government from abusing its powers. The end of the contest would be the subversion of the constitution, either by the undermining process of construction, —where its meaning would admit of possible doubt,—or by substituting in practice what is called party-usage, in place of its provisions;—or, finally, when no other contrivance would subserve the purpose, by openly and boldly setting them aside. By the one or the other, the restrictions would ultimately be annulled, and the government be converted into one of unlimited powers.

Nor would the division of government into separate, and, as it regards each other, independent departments, prevent this result. Such a division may do much to facilitate its operations, and to secure to its administration greater caution and deliberation; but as each and all the departments,—and, of course, the entire government,—would be under the control of the numerical majority, it is too clear to require explanation, that a mere distribution of its powers among its agents or representatives, could do little or nothing to counteract its tendency to oppression and abuse of power. To effect this, it would be necessary to go one step further, and make the several departments the organs of the distinct interests or portions of the community; and to clothe each with a negative on the others. But the effect of this would be to change the government from the numerical into the concurrent majority.

Having now explained the reasons why it is so difficult to form and preserve popular constitutional government, so long as the distinction between the two majorities is overlooked, and the opinion prevails that a written constitution, with suitable restrictions and a proper division of its powers, is sufficient to counteract the tendency of the numerical majority to the abuse of its power,—I shall next proceed to explain, more fully, why the concurrent majority is an indispensable element in forming constitutional governments; and why the numerical majority, of itself, must, in all cases, make governments absolute.

The necessary consequence of taking the sense of the community by the concurrent majority is, as has been explained, to give to each interest or portion of the community a negative on the others. It is this mutual negative among its various conflicting interests, which invests each with the power of protecting itself;—and places the rights and safety of each, where only they can be securely placed, under its own guardianship. Without this there can be no systematic, peaceful, or effective resistance to the natural tendency of each to come into conflict with the others: and without this there can be no constitution. It is this negative power,—the power of preventing or arresting the action of the government,—be it called by what term it may,—veto, interposition, nullification, check, or balance of power,—which, in fact, forms the constitution. They are all but different names for the negative power. In all its forms, and under all its names, it results from the concurrent majority. Without this there can be no negative; and, without a negative, no constitution. The assertion is true in reference to all constitutional governments, be their forms what they may. It is, indeed, the negative power which makes the constitution,—and the positive which makes the government. The one is the power of acting;—and the other the power of preventing or arresting action. The two, combined, make constitutional governments.

But, as there can be no constitution without the negative power, and no negative power without the concurrent majority; —it follows, necessarily, that where the numerical majority has the sole control of the government, there can be no constitution; as constitution implies limitation or restriction,—and, of course, is inconsistent with the idea of sole or exclusive power. And hence, the numerical, unmixed with the concurrent majority, necessarily forms, in all cases, absolute government.

It is, indeed, the single, or *one power*, which excludes the negative, and constitutes absolute government; and not the *number* in whom the power is vested. The numerical majority is as truly a *single power*, and excludes the negative as completely as the absolute government of one, or of the few. The former is as much the absolute government of the democratic, or popular form, as the latter of the monarchical or aristocratical. It has, accordingly, in common with them, the same tendency to oppression and abuse of power.

Constitutional governments, of whatever form, are, indeed, much more similar to each other, in their structure and character, than they are, respectively, to the absolute governments, even of their own class. All constitutional governments, of whatever class they may be, take the sense of the community by its parts, —each through its appropriate organ; and regard the sense of all its parts, as the sense of the whole. They all rest on the right of suffrage, and the responsibility of rulers, directly or indirectly. On the contrary, all absolute governments, of whatever form, concentrate power in one uncontrolled and irresponsible individual or body, whose will is regarded as the sense of the community. And, hence, the great and broad distinction between governments is,—not that of the one, the few, or the many,—but of the constitutional and the absolute.

From this there results another distinction, which, although secondary in its character, very strongly marks the difference between these forms of government. I refer to their respective conservative principle;—that is, the principle by which they are upheld and preserved. This principle, in constitutional governments, is *compromise;*—and in absolute governments, is *force;*—as will be next explained.

It has been already shown, that the same constitution of man which leads those who govern to oppress the governed,—if not prevented,—will, with equal force and certainty, lead the latter to resist oppression, when possessed of the means of doing so peaceably and successfully. But absolute governments, of all forms, exclude all other means of resistance to their authority, than that of force; and, of course, leave no other alternative to the governed, but to acquiesce in oppression, however great it may be, or to resort to force to put down the government. But the dread of such a resort must necessarily lead the government to prepare to meet force in order to protect itself; and hence, of necessity, force becomes the conservative principle of all such governments.

On the contrary, the government of the concurrent majority,

where the organism is perfect, excludes the possibility of oppression, by giving to each interest, or portion, or order,—where there are established classes,—the means of protecting itself, by its negative, against all measures calculated to advance the peculiar interests of others at its expense. Its effect, then, is, to cause the different interests, portions, or orders,—as the case may be,—to desist from attempting to adopt any measure calculated to promote the prosperity of one, or more, by sacrificing that of others; and thus to force them to unite in such measures only as would promote the prosperity of all, as the only means to prevent the suspension of the action of the government;—and, thereby, to avoid anarchy, the greatest of all evils. It is by means of such authorized and effectual resistance, that oppression is prevented, and the necessity of resorting to force superseded, in governments of the concurrent majority;—and, hence, compromise, instead of force, becomes their conservative principle.

It would, perhaps, be more strictly correct to trace the conservative principle of constitutional governments to the necessity which compels the different interests, or portions, or orders, to compromise,—as the only way to promote their respective prosperity, and to avoid anarchy,—rather than to the compromise itself. No necessity can be more urgent and imperious, than that of avoiding anarchy. It is the same as that which makes government indispensable to preserve society; and is not less imperative than that which compels obedience to superior force. Traced to this source, the voice of a people,—uttered under the necessity of avoiding the greatest of calamities, through the organs of a government so constructed as to suppress the expression of all partial and selfish interests, and to give a full and faithful utterance to the sense of the whole community, in reference to its common welfare,—may, without impiety, be called *the voice of God*. To call any other so, would be impious.

In stating that force is the conservative principle of absolute, and compromise of constitutional governments, I have assumed both to be perfect in their kind; but not without bearing in mind, that few or none, in fact, have ever been so absolute as not to be under some restraint, and none so perfectly organized as to represent fully and perfectly the voice of the whole community. Such being the case, all must, in practice, depart more or less from the principles by which they are respectively upheld and preserved; and depend more or less for support, on force, or compromise, as the absolute or the constitutional form predominates in their respective organizations.

Nor, in stating that absolute governments exclude all other means of resistance to its authority than that of force, have I overlooked the case of governments of the numerical majority, which form, apparently, an exception. It is true that, in such governments, the minor and subject party, for the time, have the right to oppose and resist the major and dominant party, for the time, through the ballot-box; and may turn them out, and take their place, if they can obtain a majority of votes. But, it is no less true, that this would be a mere change in the relations of the two parties. The minor and subject party would become the major and dominant party, with the same absolute authority and tendency to abuse power; and the major and dominant party would become the minor and subject party, with the same right to resist through the ballot-box; and, if successful, again to change relations, with like effect. But such a state of things must necessarily be temporary. The conflict between the two parties must be transferred, sooner or later, from an appeal to the ballot-box to an appeal to force;—as I shall next proceed to explain.

The conflict between the two parties, in the government of the numerical majority, tends necessarily to settle down into a struggle for the honors and emoluments of the government; and each, in order to obtain an object so ardently desired, will, in the process of the struggle, resort to whatever measure may seem best calculated to effect this purpose. The adoption, by the one, of any measure, however objectionable, which might give it an advantage, would compel the other to follow its example. In such case, it would be indispensable to success to avoid division and keep united;—and hence, from a necessity inherent in the nature of such governments, each party must be alternately forced, in order to insure victory, to resort to measures to concentrate the control over its movements in fewer and fewer hands, as the struggle became more and more violent. This, in process of time, must lead to party organization, and party caucuses and discipline; and these, to the conversion of the honors and emoluments of the government into means of rewarding partisan services, in order to secure the fidelity and increase the zeal of the members of the party. The effect of the whole combined, even in the earlier stages of the process, when they exert the least pernicious influence, would be to place the control of the two parties in the hands of their respective majorities; and the government itself, virtually, under the control of the majority of the dominant party, for the time, instead of the majority of the whole community;—where the theory of this form of government vests it. Thus, in the very first stage of the process, the government becomes the government of a minority instead of a majority;—a minority, usually, and under the most favorable circumstances, of not much more than one-fourth of the whole community.

But the process, as regards the concentration of power, would not stop at this stage. The government would gradually pass from the hands of the majority of the party into those of its leaders; as the struggle became more intense, and the honors and emoluments of the government the all-absorbing objects. At this stage, principles and policy would lose all influence in the elections; and cunning, falsehood, deception, slander, fraud, and gross appeals to the appetites of the lowest and most worthless portions of the community, would take the place of sound reason and wise debate. After these have thoroughly debased and corrupted the community, and all the arts and devices of party have been exhausted, the government would vibrate between the two factions (for such will parties have become) at each successive election. Neither would be able to retain power beyond some fixed term; for those seeking office and patronage would become too numerous to be rewarded by the offices and patronage at the disposal of the government; and these being the sole objects of pursuit, the disappointed would, at the next succeeding election, throw their weight into the opposite scale, in the hope of better success at the next turn of the wheel. These vibrations would continue until confusion, corruption, disorder, and anarchy, would lead to an appeal to force;—to be followed by a revolution in the form of the government. Such must be the end of the government of the numerical majority; and such, in brief, the process through which it must pass, in the regular course of events, before it can reach it.

This transition would be more or less rapid, according to circumstances. The more numerous the population, the more extensive the country, the more diversified the climate, productions, pursuits and character of the people, the more wealthy, refined, and artificial their condition,—and the greater the amount of revenues and disbursements,—the more unsuited would the community be to such a government, and the more rapid would be the passage. On the other hand, it might be slow in its progress amongst small communities, during the early stages of their existence, with inconsiderable revenues and disbursements, and a population of simple habits; provided the people are sufficiently intelligent to exercise properly, the right of suffrage, and sufficiently conversant with the rules necessary to govern the deliberations of legislative bodies. It is, perhaps, the only form of popular government suited to a people, while they remain in such a condition. Any other would be not only too complex and cumbersome, but unnecessary to guard against oppression, where the motive to use power for that purpose would be so feeble. And hence, colonies, from countries having constitutional governments, if left to themselves, usually adopt governments based on the numerical majority. But as population increases, wealth accumulates, and, above all, the revenues and expenditures become large,—governments of this form must become less and less suited to the condition of society; until, if not in the mean time changed into governments of the concurrent majority, they must end in an appeal to force, to be followed by a radical change in its structure and character; and, most probably, into monarchy in its absolute form,— as will be next explained.

Such, indeed, is the repugnance between popular governments and force,—or, to be more specific,—military power,—that the almost necessary consequence of a resort to force, by such governments, in order to maintain their authority, is, not only a change of their form, but a change into the most opposite,—that of absolute monarchy. The two are the opposites of each other. From the nature of popular governments, the control of its powers is vested in the many; while military power, to be efficient, must be vested in a single individual. When, then, the two parties, in governments of the numerical majority, resort to force, in their struggle for supremancy, he who commands the successful party will have the control of the government itself. And, hence, in such contests, the party which may prevail, will usually find, in the commander of its forces, a master, under whom the great body of the community will be glad to find protection against the incessant agitation and violent struggles of two corrupt factions, —looking only to power as the means of securing to themselves the honors and emoluments of the government.

From the same cause, there is a like tendency in aristocratical to terminate in absolute governments of the monarchical form; but by no means as strong, because there is less repugnance between military power and aristocratical, than between it and democratical governments.

A broader position may, indeed, be taken; viz., that there is a tendency, in constitutional governments of every form, to degenerate into their respective absolute forms; and, in all absolute governments, into that of the monarchical form. But the tendency is much stronger in constitutional governments of the democratic form to degenerate into their respective absolute forms, than in either of the others; because, among other reasons, the distinction between the constitutional and absolute forms of aristocratical and monarchical governments, is far more strongly marked than in democratic governments. The effect of this is, to make the different orders or classes in an aristocracy, or monarchy, far more jealous and watchful of encroachment on their respective rights; and more resolute and persevering in resisting attempts to concentrate power in any one class or order. On the contrary, the line between the two forms, in popular governments, is so imperfectly understood, that honest and sincere friends of the constitutional form not unfrequently, instead of jealously watching and arresting their tendency to degenerate into their absolute forms, not only regard it with approbation, but employ all their powers to add to its strength and to increase its impetus, in the vain hope of making the government more perfect and popular. The numerical majority, perhaps, should usually be one of the elements of a constitutional democracy; but to make it the sole element, in order to perfect the constitution and make the government more popular, is one of the greatest and most fatal of political errors.

Among the other advantages which governments of the concurrent have over those of the numerical majority,—and which strongly illustrates their more popular character, is,—that they admit, with safety, a much greater extension of the right of suffrage. It may be safely extended in such governments to universal suffrage: that is,—to every male citizen of mature age, with few ordinary exceptions; but it cannot be so far extended in those of the numerical majority, without placing them ultimately under the control of the more ignorant and dependent portions of the community. For, as the community becomes populous, wealthy, refined, and highly civilized, the difference between the rich and the poor will become more strongly marked; and the number of the ignorant and dependent greater in proportion to the rest of the community. With the increase of this difference, the tendency to conflict between them will become stronger; and, as the poor and dependent become more numerous in proportion, there will be, in governments of the numerical majority, no want of leaders among the wealthy and ambitious, to excite and direct them in their efforts to obtain the control.

The case is different in governments of the concurrent majority. There, mere numbers have not the absolute control; and the wealthy and intelligent being identified in interest with the poor and ignorant of their respective portions or interests of the community, become their leaders and protectors. And hence, as the latter would have neither hope nor inducement to rally the former in order to obtain the control, the right of suffrage, under such a government, may be safely enlarged to the extent stated, without incurring the hazard to which such enlargement would expose governments of the numerical majority.

In another particular, governments of the concurrent majority have greatly the advantage. I allude to the difference in their respective tendency, in reference to dividing or uniting the community. That of the concurrent, as has been shown, is to unite the community, let its interests be ever so diversified or opposed; while that of the numerical is to divide it into two conflicting portions, let its interests be, naturally, ever so united and identified.

That the numerical majority will divide the community, let it be ever so homogeneous, into two great parties, which will be engaged in perpetual struggles to obtain the control of the government, has already been established. The great importance of the object at stake, must necessarily form strong party attachments and party antipathies;—attachments on the part of the members of each to their respective parties, through whose efforts they hope to accomplish an object dear to all; and antipathies to the opposite party, as presenting the only obstacle to success.

In order to have a just conception of their force, it must be taken into consideration, that the object to be won or lost appeals to the strongest passions of the human heart,—avarice, ambition, and rivalry. It is not then wonderful, that a form of government, which periodically stakes all its honors and emoluments, as prizes to be contended for, should divide the community into two great hostile parties; or that party attachments, in the progress of the strife, should become so strong among the members of each respectively, as to absorb almost every feeling of our nature, both social and individual; or that their mutual antipathies should be carried to such an excess as to destroy, almost entirely, all sympathy between them, and to substitute in its place the strongest aversion. Nor is it surprising, that under their joint influence, the community should cease to be the common centre of attachment, or that each party should find that centre only in itself. It is thus, that, in such governments, devotion to party becomes stronger than devotion to country;—the promotion of the interests of party more important than the promotion of the common good of the whole, and its triumph and ascendency, objects of far greater solicitude, than the safety and prosperity of the community. It is thus, also, that the numerical majority, by regarding the community as a unit, and having, as such, the same interests throughout all its parts, must, by its necessary operation, divide it into two hostile parts, waging, under the forms of law, incessant hostilities against each other.

The concurrent majority, on the other hand, tends to unite the most opposite and conflicting interests, and to blend the whole in one common attachment to the country. By giving to each interest, or portion, the power of self-protection, all strife and struggle between them for ascendency, is prevented; and, thereby, not only every feeling calculated to weaken the attachment to the whole is suppressed, but the individual and the social feelings are made to unite in one common devotion to country. Each sees and feels that it can best promote its own prosperity by conciliating the good-will, and promoting the prosperity of the others. And hence, there will be diffused throughout the whole community kind feelings between its different portions; and, instead of antipathy, a rivalry amongst them to promote the interests of each other, as far as this can be done consistently with the interest of all. Under the combined influence of these causes, the interests of each would be merged in the common interests of the whole; and thus, the community would become a unit, by becoming the common centre of attachment of all its parts. And hence, instead of faction, strife, and struggle for party ascendency, there would be patriotism, nationality, harmony, and a struggle only for supremacy in promoting the common good of the whole.

But the difference in their operation, in this respect, would not end here. Its effects would be as great in a moral, as I have attempted to show they would be in a political point of view. Indeed, public and private morals are so nearly allied, that it would be difficult for it to be otherwise. That which corrupts and debases the community, politically, must also corrupt and debase it morally. The same cause, which, in governments of the numerical majority, gives to party attachments and antipathies such force, as to place party triumph and ascendency above the safety and prosperity of the community, will just as certainly give them sufficient force to overpower all regard for truth, justice, sincerity, and moral obligations of every description. It is, accordingly, found that, in the violent strifes between parties for the high and glittering prize of governmental honors and emoluments,—falsehood, injustice, fraud, artifice, slander, and breach of faith, are freely resorted to, as legitimate weapons;—followed by all their corrupting and debasing influences.

In the government of the concurrent majority, on the contrary, the same cause which prevents such strife, as the means of obtaining power, and which makes it the interest of each portion to conciliate and promote the interests of the others, would exert a powerful influence towards purifying and elevating the character of the government and the people, morally, as well as politically. The means of acquiring power,—or, more correctly, influence,—in such governments, would be the reverse. Instead of the vices, by which it is acquired in that of the numerical majority, the opposite virtues—truth, justice, integrity, fidelity, and all others, by which respect and confidence are inspired, would be the most certain and effectual means of acquiring it.

Nor would the good effects resulting thence be confined to those who take an active part in political affairs. They would extend to the whole community. For of all the causes which contribute to form the character of a people, those by which power, influence, and standing in the government are most certainly and readily obtained, are, by far, the most powerful. These are the objects most eagerly sought of all others by the talented and aspiring; and the possession of which commands the greatest respect and admiration. But, just in proportion to this respect and admiration will be their appreciation by those, whose energy, intellect, and position in society, are calculated to exert the greatest influence in forming the character of a people. If knowledge, wisdom, patriotism, and virtue, be the most certain means of acquiring them, they will be most highly appreciated and assiduously cultivated; and this would cause them to become prominent traits in the character of the people. But if, on the contrary, cunning, fraud, treachery, and party devotion be the most certain, they will be the most highly prized, and become marked features in their character. So powerful, indeed, is the operation of the concurrent majority, in this respect, that, if it were possible for a corrupt and degenerate community to establish and maintain a well-organized government of the kind, it would of itself purify and regenerate them; while, on the other hand, a government based wholly on the numerical majority, would just as certainly corrupt and debase the most patriotic and virtuous people. So great is their difference in this respect, that, just as the one or the other element predominates in the construction of any government, in the same proportion will the character of the government and the people rise or sink in the scale of patriotism and virtue. Neither religion nor education can counteract the strong tendency of the numerical majority to corrupt and debase the people.

If the two be compared, in reference to the ends for which government is ordained, the superiority of the government of the concurrent majority will not be less striking. These, as has been stated, are twofold; to protect, and to perfect society. But to preserve society, it is necessary to guard the community against injustice, violence, and anarchy within, and against attacks from without. If it fail in either, it would fail in the primary end of government, and would not deserve the name.

To perfect society, it is necessary to develop the faculties, intellectual and moral, with which man is endowed. But the main spring to their development, and, through this, to progress, improvement and civilization, with all their blessings, is the desire of individuals to better their condition. For, this purpose, liberty and security are indispensable. Liberty leaves each free to pursue the course he may deem best to promote his interest and happiness, as far as it may be compatible with the primary end for which government is ordained;—while security gives assurance to each, that he shall not be deprived of the fruits of his exertions to better his condition. These combined, give to this desire the strongest impulse of which it is susceptible. For, to extend liberty beyond the limits assigned, would be to weaken the government and to render it incompetent to fulfil its primary end,—the protection of society against dangers, internal and external. The effect of this would be, insecurity; and, of insecurity, —to weaken the impulse of individuals to better their condition, and thereby retard progress and improvement. On the other hand, to extend the powers of the government, so as to contract the sphere assigned to liberty, would have the same effect, by disabling individuals in their efforts to better their condition.

Herein is to be found the principle which assigns to power and liberty their proper spheres, and reconciles each to the other under all circumstances. For, if power be necessary to secure to liberty the fruits of its exertions, liberty, in turn, repays power with interest, by increased population, wealth, and other advantages, which progress and improvement bestow on the community. By thus assigning to each its appropriate sphere, all conflicts between them cease; and each is made to co-operate with and assist the other, in fulfilling the great ends for which government is ordained.

But the principle, applied to different communities, will assign to them different limits. It will assign a larger sphere to power and a more contracted one to liberty, or the reverse, according to circumstances. To the former, there must ever be allotted, under all circumstances, a sphere sufficiently large to protect the community against danger from without and violence and anarchy within. The residuum belongs to liberty. More cannot be safely or rightly allotted to it.

But some communities require a far greater amount of power than others to protect them against anarchy and external dangers; and, of course, the sphere of liberty in such, must be proportionally contracted. The causes calculated to enlarge the one and contract the other, are numerous and various. Some are physical;—such as open and exposed frontiers, surrounded by powerful and hostile neighbors. Others are moral;—such as the different degrees of intelligence, patriotism, and virtue among the mass of the community, and their experience and proficiency in the art of self-government. Of these, the moral are, by far, the most influential. A community may possess all the necessary moral qualifications, in so high a degree, as to be capable of self-government under the most adverse circumstances; while, on the other hand, another may be so sunk in ignorance and vice, as to be incapable of forming a conception of liberty, or of living, even when most favored by circumstances, under any other than an absolute and despotic government.

The principle, in all communities, according to these numerous and various causes, assigns to power and liberty their proper spheres. To allow to liberty, in any case, a sphere of action more extended than this assigns, would lead to anarchy; and this, probably, in the end, to a contraction instead of an enlargement of its sphere. Liberty, then, when forced on a people unfit for it, would, instead of a blessing, be a curse; as it would, in its reaction, lead directly to anarchy,—the greatest of all curses. No people, indeed, can long enjoy more liberty than that to which their situation and advanced intelligence and morals fairly entitle them. If more than this be allowed, they must soon fall into confusion and disorder,—to be followed, if not by anarchy and despotism, by a change to a form of government more simple and absolute; and, therefore, better suited to their condition. And hence, although it may be true, that a people may not have as much liberty as they are fairly entitled to, and are capable of enjoying,—yet the reverse is unquestionably true,—that no people can long possess more than they are fairly entitled to.

Liberty, indeed, though among the greatest of blessings, is not so great as that of protection; inasmuch, as the end of the former is the progress and improvement of the race,—while that of the latter is its preservation and perpetuation. And hence, when the two come into conflict, liberty must, and ever ought, to yield to protection; as the existence of the race is of greater moment than its improvement.

It follows, from what has been stated, that it is a great and dangerous error to suppose that all people are equally entitled to liberty. It is a reward to be earned, not a blessing to be gratuitously lavished on all alike;—a reward reserved for the intelligent, the patriotic, the virtuous and deserving;—and not a boon to be bestowed on a people too ignorant, degraded and vicious, to be capable either of appreciating or of enjoying it. Nor is it any disparagement to liberty, that such is, and ought to be the case. On the contrary, its greatest praise,—its proudest distinction is, that an all-wise Providence has reserved it, as the noblest and highest reward for the development of our faculties, moral and intellectual. A reward more appropriate than liberty could not be conferred on the deserving;—nor a punishment inflicted on the undeserving more just, than to be subject to lawless and despotic rule. This dispensation seems to be the result of some fixed law;—and every effort to disturb or defeat it, by attempting to elevate a people in the scale of liberty, above the point to which they are entitled to rise, must ever prove abortive, and end in disappointment. The progress of a people rising from a lower to a higher point in the scale of liberty, is necessarily slow;—and by attempting to precipitate, we either retard, or permanently defeat it.

There is another error, not less great and dangerous, usually associated with the one which has just been considered. I refer to the opinion, that liberty and equality are so intimately united, that liberty cannot be perfect without perfect equality.

That they are united to a certain extent,—and that equality of citizens, in the eyes of the law, is essential to liberty in a popular government, is conceded. But to go further, and make equality of *condition* essential to liberty, would be to destroy both liberty and progress. The reason is, that inequality of condition, while it is a necessary consequence of liberty, is, at the same time, indispensable to progress. In order to understand why this is so, it is necessary to bear in mind, that the main spring to progress is, the desire of individuals to better their condition; and that the strongest impulse which can be given to it is, to leave individuals free to exert themselves in the manner they may deem best for that purpose, as far at least as it can be done consistently with the ends for which government is ordained,—and to secure to all the fruits of their exertions. Now, as individuals differ greatly from each other, in intelligence, sagacity, energy, perseverance, skill, habits of industry and economy, physical power, position and opportunity,—the necessary effect of leaving all free to exert themselves to better their condition, must be a corresponding inequality between those who may possess these qualities and advantages in a high degree, and those who may be deficient in them. The only means by which this result can be prevented are, either to impose such restrictions on the exertions of those who may possess them in a high degree, as will place them on a level with those who do not; or to deprive them of the fruits of their exertions. But to impose such restrictions on them would be destructive of liberty,—while, to deprive them of the fruits of their exertions, would be to destroy the desire of bettering their condition. It is, indeed, this inequality of condition between the front and rear ranks, in the march of progress, which gives so strong an impulse to the former to maintain their position, and to the latter to press forward into their files. This gives to progress its greatest impulse. To force the front rank back to the rear, or attempt to push forward the rear into line with the front, by the interposition of the government, would put an end to the impulse, and effectually arrest the march of progress.

These great and dangerous errors have their origin in the prevalent opinion that all men are born free and equal;—than which nothing can be more unfounded and false. It rests upon the assumption of a fact, which is contrary to universal observation, in whatever light it may be regarded. It is, indeed, difficult to explain how an opinion so destitute of all sound reason, ever could have been so extensively entertained, unless we regard it as being confounded with another, which has some semblance of truth;—but which, when properly understood, is not less false and dangerous. I refer to the assertion, that all men are equal in the state of nature; meaning, by a state of nature, a state of individuality, supposed to have existed prior to the social and political state; and in which men lived apart and independent of each other. If such a state ever did exist, all men would have been, indeed, free and equal in it; that is, free to do as they pleased, and exempt from the authority or control of others—as, by supposition, it existed anterior to society and government. But such a state is purely hypothetical. It never did, nor can exist; as it is inconsistent with the preservation and perpetuation of the race. It is, therefore, a great misnomer to call it *the state of nature*. Instead of being the natural state of man, it is, of all conceivable states, the most opposed to his nature—most repugnant to his feelings, and most incompatible with his wants. His natural state is, the social and political—the one for which his Creator made him, and the only one in which he can preserve and perfect his race. As, then, there never was such a state as the, so called, state of nature, and never can be, it follows, that men, instead of being born in it, are born in the social and political state; and of course, instead of being born free and equal, are born subject, not only to parental authority, but to the laws and institutions of the country where born, and under whose protection they draw their first breath. With these remarks, I return from this digression, to resume the thread of the discourse.

It follows, from all that has been said, that the more perfectly a government combines power and liberty,—that is, the greater its power and the more enlarged and secure the liberty of individuals, the more perfectly it fulfils the ends for which government is ordained. To show, then, that the government of the concurrent majority is better calculated to fulfil them than that of the numerical, it is only necessary to explain why the former is better suited to combine a higher degree of power and a wider scope of liberty than the latter. I shall begin with the former.

The concurrent majority, then, is better suited to enlarge and secure the bounds of liberty, because it is better suited to prevent government from passing beyond its proper limits, and to restrict it to its primary end,—the protection of the community. But in doing this, it leaves, necessarily, all beyond it open and free to individual exertions; and thus enlarges and secures the sphere of liberty to the greatest extent which the condition of the community will admit, as has been explained. The tendency of government to pass beyond its proper limits is what exposes liberty to danger, and renders it insecure; and it is the strong counteraction of governments of the concurrent majority to this tendency which makes them so favorable to liberty. On the contrary, those of the numerical, instead of opposing and counteracting this tendency, add to it increased strength, in consequence of the violent party struggles incident to them, as has been fully explained. And hence their encroachments on liberty, and the danger to which it is exposed under such governments.

So great, indeed, is the difference between the two in this

respect, that liberty is little more than a name under all governments of the absolute form, including that of the numerical majority; and can only have a secure and durable existence under those of the concurrent or constitutional form. The latter, by giving to each portion of the community which may be unequally affected by its action, a negative on the others, prevents all partial or local legislation, and restricts its action to such measures as are designed for the protection and the good of the whole. In doing this, it secures, at the same time, the rights and liberty of the people, regarded individually; as each portion consists of those who, whatever may be the diversity of interests among themselves, have the same interest in reference to the action of the government.

Such being the case, the interest of each individual may be safely confided to the majority, or voice of his portion, against that of all others, and, of course, the government itself. It is only through an organism which vests each with a negative, in some one form or another, that those who have like interests in preventing the government from passing beyond its proper sphere, and encroaching on the rights and liberty of individuals, can co-operate peaceably and effectually in resisting the encroachments of power, and thereby preserve their rights and liberty. Individual resistance is too feeble, and the difficulty of concert and co-operation too great, unaided by such an organism, to oppose, successfully, the organized power of government, with all the means of the community at its disposal; especially in populous countries of great extent, where concert and co-operation are almost impossible. Even when the oppression of the government comes to be too great to be borne, and force is resorted to in order to overthrow it, the result is rarely ever followed by the establishment of liberty. The force sufficient to overthrow an oppressive government is usually sufficient to establish one equally, or more, oppressive in its place. And hence, in no governments, except those that rest on the principle of the concurrent or constitutional majority, can the people guard their liberty against power; and hence, also, when lost, the great difficulty and uncertainty of regaining it by force.

It may be further affirmed, that, being more favorable to the enlargement and security of liberty, governments of the concurrent, must necessarily be more favorable to progress, development, improvement, and civilization,—and, of course, to the increase of power which results from, and depends on these, than those of the numerical majority. That it is liberty which gives to them their greatest impulse, has already been shown; and it now remains to show, that these, in turn, contribute greatly to the increase of power.

In the earlier stages of society, numbers and individual prowess constituted the principle elements of power. In a more advanced stage, when communities had passed from the barbarous to the civilized state, discipline, strategy, weapons of increased power, and money,—as the means of meeting increased expense, —became additional and important elements. In this stage, the effects of progress and improvement on the increase of power, began to be disclosed; but still numbers and personal prowess were sufficient, for a long period, to enable barbarous nations to contend successfully with the civilized,—and, in the end, to overpower them,—as the pages of history abundantly testify. But a more advanced progress, with its numerous inventions and improvements, has furnished new and far more powerful and destructive implements of offence and defence, and greatly increased the intelligence and wealth, necessary to engage the skill and meet the increased expense required for their construction and application to purposes of war. The discovery of gunpowder, and the use of steam as an impelling force, and their application to military purposes, have for ever settled the question of ascendency between civilized and barbarous communities, in favor of the former. Indeed, these, with other improvements, belonging to the present state of progress, have given to communities the most advanced, a superiority over those the least so, almost as great as that of the latter over the brute creation. And among the civilized, the same causes have decided the question of superiority, where other circumstances are nearly equal, in favor of those whose governments have given the greatest impulse to development, progress, and improvement; that is, to those whose liberty is the largest and best secured. Among these, England and the United States afford striking examples, not only of the effects of liberty in increasing power, but of the more perfect adaptation of governments founded on the principle of the concurrent, or constitutional majority, to enlarge and secure liberty. They are both governments of this description, as will be shown hereafter.

But in estimating the power of a community, moral, as well as physical causes, must be taken into the calculation; and in estimating the effects of liberty on power, it must not be overlooked, that it is, in itself, an important agent in augmenting the force of moral, as well as of physical power. It bestows on a people elevation, self-reliance, energy, and enthusiasm; and these combined, give to physical power a vastly augmented and almost irresistible impetus.

These, however, are not the only elements of moral power. There are others, and among them harmony, unanimity, devotion to country, and a disposition to elevate to places of trust and power, those who are distinguished for wisdom and experience. These, when the occasion requires it, will, without compulsion, and from their very nature, unite and put forth the entire force of the community in the most efficient manner, without hazard to its institutions or its liberty.

All these causes combined, give to a community its maximum of power. Either of them, without the other, would leave it comparatively feeble. But it cannot be necessary, after what has been stated, to enter into any further explanation or argument in order to establish the superiority of governments of the concurrent majority over the numerical, in developing the great elements of moral power. So vast is this superiority, that the one, by its operation, necessarily leads to their development, while the other as necessarily prevents it,—as has been fully shown.

Such are the many and striking advantages of the concurrent over the numerical majority. Against the former but two objections can be made. The one is, that it is difficult of construction, which has already been sufficiently noticed; and the other, that it would be impracticable to obtain the concurrence of conflicting interests, where they were numerous and diversified; or, if not, that the process for this purpose, would be too tardy to meet, with sufficient promptness, the many and dangerous emergencies, to which all communities are exposed. This objection is plausible; and deserves a fuller notice than it has yet received.

The diversity of opinion is usually so great, on almost all questions of policy, that it is not surprising, on a slight view of the subject, it should be thought impracticable to bring the various conflicting interests of a community to unite on any one line of policy;—or, that a government, founded on such a principle, would be too slow in its movements and too weak in its foundation to succeed in practice. But, plausible as it may seem at the first glance, a more deliberate view will show, that this opinion is erroneous. It is true, that, when there is no urgent necessity, it is difficult to bring those who differ, to agree on any one line of action. Each will naturally insist on taking the course he may think best;—and, from pride of opinion, will be unwilling to yield to others. But the case is different when there is an urgent necessity to unite on some common course of action; as reason and experience both prove. When something *must* be done,—and when it can be done only by the united consent of all,—the necessity of the case will force to a compromise;—be the cause of that necessity what it may. On all questions of acting, necessity, where it exists, is the overruling motive; and where, in such cases, compromise among the parties is an indispensable condition to acting, it exerts an overruling influence in predisposing them to acquiesce in some one opinion or course of action. Experience furnishes many examples in confirmation of this important truth. Among these, the trial by jury is the most familiar, and on that account, will be selected for illustration.

In these, twelve individuals, selected without discrimination, must unanimously concur in opinion,—under the obligations of an oath to find a true verdict, according to law and evidence; and this, too, not unfrequently under such great difficulty and doubt, that the ablest and most experienced judges and advocates differ in opinion, after careful examination. And yet, as impracticable as this mode of trial would seem to a superficial observer, it is found, in practice, not only to succeed, but to be the safest, the wisest and the best that human ingenuity has ever devised. When closely investigated, the cause will be found in the necessity, under which the jury is placed, to agree unanimously, in order to find a verdict. This necessity acts as the predisposing cause of concurrence in some common opinion; and with such efficacy, that a jury rarely fails to find a verdict.

Under its potent influence, the jurors take their seats with the disposition to give a fair and impartial hearing to the arguments on both sides,—meet together in the jury-room,—not as disputants, but calmly to hear the opinions of each other, and to compare and weigh the arguments on which they are founded;—and, finally, to adopt that which, on the whole, is thought to be true. Under the influence of this *disposition to harmonize*, one after another falls into the same opinion, until unanimity is obtained. Hence its practicability;—and hence, also, its peculiar excellence. Nothing, indeed, can be more favorable to the success of truth and justice, than this predisposing influence caused by the necessity of being unanimous. It is so much so, as to compensate for the defect of legal knowledge, and a high degree of intelligence on the part of those who usually compose juries. If the necessity of unanimity were dispensed with, and the finding of a jury made to depend on a bare majority, jury-trial, instead of being one of the greatest improvements in the judicial department of government, would be one of the greatest evils that could be inflicted on the community. It would be, in such case, the conduit through which all the factious feelings of the day would enter and contaminate justice at its source.

But the same cause would act with still greater force in predisposing the various interests of the community to agree in a well organized government, founded on the concurrent majority. The necessity for unanimity, in order to keep the government in motion, would be far more urgent, and would act under circumstances still more favorable to secure it. It would be superfluous, after what has been stated, to add other reasons in order to show that no necessity, physical or moral, can be more imperious than that of government. It is so much so that, to suspend its action altogether, even for an inconsiderable period, would subject the community to convulsions and anarchy. But in governments of the concurrent majority such fatal consequences can only be avoided by the unanimous concurrence or acquiescence of the various portions of the community. Such is the imperious character of the necessity which impels to compromise under governments of this description.

But to have a just conception of the overpowering influence it would exert, the circumstances under which it would act must be taken into consideration. These will be found, on comparison, much more favorable than those under which juries act. In the latter case there is nothing besides the necessity of unanimity in finding a verdict, and the inconvenience to which they might be subjected in the event of division, to induce juries to agree, except the love of truth and justice, which, when not counteracted by some improper motive or bias, more or less influences all, not excepting the most depraved. In the case of governments of the concurrent majority, there is, besides these, the love of country, than which, if not counteracted by the unequal and oppressive action of government, or other causes, few motives exert a greater sway. It comprehends, indeed, within itself, a large portion both of our individual and social feelings; and, hence, its almost boundless control when left free to act. But the government of the concurrent majority leaves it free, by preventing abuse and oppression, and, with them, the whole train of feelings and passions which lead to discord and conflict between different portions of the community. Impelled by the imperious necessity of preventing the suspension of the action of government, with the fatal consequences to which it would lead, and by the strong additional impulse derived from an ardent love of country, each portion would regard the sacrifice it might have to make by yielding its peculiar interests to secure the common interest and safety of all, including its own, as nothing compared to the evils that would be inflicted on all, including its own, by pertinaciously adhering to a different line of action. So powerful, indeed, would be the motives for concurring, and, under such circumstances, so weak would be those opposed to it, the wonder would be, not that there should, but that there should not be a compromise.

But to form a juster estimate of the full force of this impulse to compromise, there must be added that, in government of the concurrent majority, each portion, in order to advance its own peculiar interests, would have to conciliate all others, by showing a disposition to advance theirs; and, for this purpose, each would select those to represent it, whose wisdom, patriotism, and weight of character, would command the confidence of the others. Under its influence,—and with representatives so well qualified to accomplish the object for which they were selected, —the prevailing desire would be, to promote the common interests of the whole; and, hence, the competition would be, not which should yield the least to promote the common good, but which should yield the most. It is thus, that concession would cease to be considered a sacrifice,—would become a free-will offering on the altar of the country, and lose the name of compromise. And herein is to be found the feature, which distinguishes governments of the concurrent majority so strikingly from those of the numerical. In the latter, each faction, in the struggle to obtain the control of the government, elevates to power the designing, the artful, and unscrupulous, who, in their devotion to party,—instead of aiming at the good of the whole,—aim exclusively at securing the ascendency of party.

When traced to its source, this difference will be found to originate in the fact, that, in governments of the concurrent majority, individual feelings are, from its organism, necessarily enlisted on the side of the social, and made to unite with them in promoting the interests of the whole, as the best way of promoting the separate interests of each; while, in those of the numerical majority, the social are necessarily enlisted on the side of the individual, and made to contribute to the interest of parties, regardless of that of the whole. To effect the former,—to enlist the individual on the side of the social feelings to promote the good of the whole, is the greatest possible achievement of the science of government; while, to enlist the social on the side of the individual to promote the interest of parties at the expense of the good of the whole, is the greatest blunder which ignorance can possibly commit.

To this, also, may be referred the greater solidity of foundation on which governments of the concurrent majority repose. Both, ultimately, rest on necessity; for force, by which those of the numerical majority are upheld, is only acquiesced in from necessity; a necessity not more imperious, however, than that which compels the different portions, in governments of the concurrent majority, to acquiesce in compromise. There is, however, a great difference in the motive, the feeling, the aim, which characterize the act in the two cases. In the one, it is done with that reluctance and hostility ever incident to enforced submission to what is regarded as injustice and oppression; accompanied by the desire and purpose to seize on the first favorable opportunity for resistance:—but in the other, willingly and cheerfully, under the impulse of an exalted patriotism, impelling all to acquiesce in whatever the common good requires.

It is, then, a great error to suppose that the government of the concurrent majority is impracticable;—or that it rests on a feeble foundation. History furnishes many examples of such governments;—and among them, one, in which the principle was carried to an extreme that would be thought impracticable, had it never existed. I refer to that of Poland. In this it was carried to such an extreme that, in the election of her kings, the concurrence or acquiescence of every individual of the nobles and gentry present, in an assembly numbering usually from one hundred and fifty to two hundred thousand, was required to make a choice; thus giving to each individual a veto on his election. So, likewise, every member of her Diet, (the supreme legislative body,) consisting of the king, the senate, bishops and deputies of the nobility and gentry of the palatinates, possessed a veto on all its proceedings;—thus making an unanimous vote necessary to enact a law, or to adopt any measure whatever. And, as if to carry the principle to the utmost extent, the veto of a single member not only defeated the particular bill or measure in question, but prevented all others, passed during the session, from taking effect. Further, the principle could not be carried. It, in fact, made every individual of the nobility and gentry, a distinct element in the organism;—or, to vary the expression, made him an *Estate of the kingdom.* And yet this government lasted, in this form, more than two centuries; embracing the period of Poland's greatest power and renown. Twice, during its existence, she protected Christendom, when in great danger, by defeating the Turks under the walls of Vienna, and permanently arresting thereby the tide of their conquests westward.

It is true her government was finally subverted, and the people subjugated, in consequence of the extreme to which the principle was carried; not, however, because of its tendency to dissolution *from weakness*, but from the facility it afforded to powerful and unscrupulous neighbors to control, by their intrigues, the election of her kings. But the fact, that a government, in which the principle was carried to the utmost extreme, not only existed, but existed for so long a period, in great power and splendor, is proof conclusive both of its practicability and its compatibility with the power and permanency of government.

Another example, not so striking indeed, but yet deserving notice, is furnished by the government of a portion of the aborigines of our own country. I refer to the Confederacy of the Six Nations, who inhabited what now is called the western portion of the State of New-York. One chief delegate, chosen by each nation,—associated with six others of his own selection,—making, in all, forty-two members,—constituted their federal, or general government. When met, they formed the council of the union,—and discussed and decided all questions relating to the common welfare. As in the Polish Diet, each member possessed a veto on its decision; so that nothing could be done without the united consent of all. But this, instead of making the Confederacy weak, or impracticable, had the opposite effect. It secured harmony in council and action, and with them a great increase of power. The Six Nations, in consequence, became the most powerful of all the Indian tribes within the limits of our country. They carried their conquest and authority far beyond the country they originally occupied.

I pass by, for the present, the most distinguished of all these examples;—the Roman Republic;—where the veto, or negative power, was carried, not indeed to the same extreme as in the Polish government, but very far, and with great increase of power and stability;—as I shall show more at large hereafter.

It may be thought,—and doubtless many have supposed, that the defects inherent in the government of the numerical majority may be remedied by a free press, as the organ of public opinion, —especially in the more advanced stage of society,—so as to supersede the necessity of the concurrent majority to counteract its tendency to oppression and abuse of power. It is not my aim to detract from the importance of the press, nor to underestimate the great power and influence which it has given to public opinion. On the contrary, I admit these are so great, as to entitle it to be considered a new and important political element. Its influence is, at the present day, on the increase; and it is highly probable that it may, in combination with the causes which have contributed to raise it to its present importance, effect, in time, great changes,—social and political. But, however important its present influence may be, or may hereafter become,—or, however great and beneficial the changes to which it may ultimately lead, it can never counteract the tendency of the numerical majority to the abuse of power,—nor supersede the necessity of the concurrent, as an essential element in the formation of constitutional governments. These it cannot effect for two reasons, either of which is conclusive.

The one is, that it cannot change that principle of our nature, which makes constitutions necessary to prevent government from abusing its powers,—and government necessary to protect and perfect society.

Constituting, as this principle does, an essential part of our nature,—no increase of knowledge and intelligence, no enlargement of our sympathetic feelings, no influence of education, or modification of the condition of society can change it. But so long as it shall continue to be an essential part of our nature, so long will government be necessary; and so long as this continues to be necessary, so long will constitutions, also, be necessary to counteract its tendency to the abuse of power,—and so long must the concurrent majority remain an essential element in the formation of constitutions. The press may do much,—by giving impulse to the progress of knowledge and intelligence, to aid the cause of education, and to bring about salutary changes in the condition of society. These, in turn may do much to explode political errors,—to teach how governments should be constructed in order to fulfil their ends; and by what means they can be best preserved, when so constructed. They may, also, do much to enlarge the social, and to restrain the individual feelings;—and thereby to bring about a state of things, when far less power will be required by governments to guard against internal disorder and violence, and external danger; and when, of course, the sphere of power may be greatly contracted and that of liberty proportionally enlarged. But all this would not change the nature of man; nor supersede the necessity of government. For so long as government exists, the possession of its control, as the means of directing its action and dispensing its honors and emoluments, will be an object of desire. While this continues to be the case, it must, in governments of the numerical majority, lead to party struggles; and, as has been shown, to all the consequences, which necessarily follow in their train, and, against which, the only remedy is the concurrent majority.

The other reason is to be found in the nature of the influence, which the press politically exercises.

It is similar, in most respects, to that of suffrage. They are, indeed, both organs of public opinion. The principle difference is, that the one has much more agency in forming public opinion, while the other gives a more authentic and authoritative expression to it. Regarded in either light, the press cannot, of itself, guard any more against the abuse of power, than suffrage; and for the same reason.

If what is called public opinion were always the opinion of the whole community, the press would, as its organ, be an effective guard against the abuse of power, and supersede the necessity of the concurrent majority; just as the right of suffrage would do, where the community, in reference to the action of government, had but one interest. But such is not the case. On the contrary, what is called public opinion, instead of being the united opinion of the whole community, is, usually, nothing more than the opinion or voice of the strongest interest, or combination of interests; and, not unfrequently, of a small, but energetic and active portion of the whole. Public opinion, in relation to government and its policy, is as much divided and diversified, as are the interests of the community; and the press, instead of being the organ of the whole, is usually but the organ of these various and diversified interests respectively; or, rather, of the parties growing out of them. It is used by them as the mean of controlling public opinion, and of so moulding it, as to promote their peculiar interests, and to aid in carrying on the warfare of party. But as the organ and instrument of parties, in governments of the numerical majority, it is as incompetent as suffrage itself, to counteract the tendency to oppression and abuse of power;—and can, no more than that, supersede the necessity of the concurrent majority. On the contrary, as the instrument of party warfare, it contributes greatly to increase party excitement, and the violence and virulence of party struggles; and, in the same degree, the tendency to oppression and abuse of power. Instead, then, of superseding the necessity of the concurrent majority, it increases it, by increasing the violence and force of party feelings,—in like manner as party caucuses and party machinery; of the latter of which, indeed, it forms an important part.

In one respect, and only one, the government of the numerical majority has the advantage over that of the concurrent, if, indeed, it can be called an advantage. I refer to its simplicity and facility of construction. It is simple indeed, wielded, as it is, by a single power—the will of the greater number—and very easy of construction. For this purpose, nothing more is necessary than universal suffrage, and the regulation of the manner of voting, so as to give to the greater number the supreme control over every department of government.

But, whatever advantages simplicity and facility of construction may give it, the other forms of absolute government possess them in a still higher degree. The construction of the government of the numerical majority, simple as it is, requires some preliminary measures and arrangements; while the others, especially the monarchical, will, in its absence, or where it proves incompetent, force themselves on the community. And hence, among other reasons, the tendency of all governments is, from the more complex and difficult of construction, to the more simple and easily constructed; and, finally, to absolute monarchy, as the most simple of all. Complexity and difficulty of construction, as far as they form objections, apply, not only to governments of the concurrent majority of the popular form, but to constitutional governments of every form. The least complex, and the most easily constructed of them, are much more complex and difficult of construction than any one of the absolute forms. Indeed, so great has been this difficulty, that their construction has been the result, not so much of wisdom and patriotism, as of favorable combinations of circumstances. They have, for the most part, grown out of the struggles between conflicting interests, which, from some fortunate turn, have ended in a compromise, by which both parties have been admitted, in some one way or another, to have a separate and distinct voice in the government. Where this has not been the case, they have been the product of fortunate circumstances, acting in conjunction with some pressing danger, which forced their adoption, as the only means by which it could be avoided. It would seem that it has exceeded human sagacity deliberately to plan and construct constitutional governments, with a full knowledge of the principles on which they were formed; or to reduce them to practice without the pressure of some immediate and urgent necessity. Nor is it surprising that such should be the case; for it would seem almost impossible for any man, or body of men, to be so profoundly and thoroughly acquainted with the people of any community which has made any considerable progress in civilization and wealth, with all the diversified interests ever accompanying them, as to be able to organize constitutional governments suited to their condition. But, even were this possible, it would be difficult to find any community sufficiently enlightened and patriotic to adopt such a government, without the compulsion of some pressing necessity. A constitution, to succeed, must spring from the bosom of the community, and be adapted to the intelligence and character of the people, and all the multifarious relations, internal and external, which distinguish one people from another. If it do not, it will prove, in practice, to be, not a constitution, but a cumbrous and useless machine, which must be speedily superseded and laid aside, for some other more simple, and better suited to their condition.

It would thus seem almost necessary that governments should commence in some one of the simple and absolute forms, which, however well suited to the community in its earlier stages, must, in its progress, lead to oppression and abuse of power, and, finally, to an appeal to force,—to be succeeded by a military despotism,—unless the conflicts to which it leads should be fortunately adjusted by a compromise, which will give to the respective parties a participation in the control of the government; and thereby lay the foundation of a constitutional government, to be afterwards matured and perfected. Such governments have been, emphatically, the product of circumstances. And hence, the difficulty of one people imitating the government of another. And hence, also, the importance of terminating all civil conflicts by a compromise, which shall prevent either party from obtaining complete control, and thus subjecting the other.

Of the different forms of constitutional governments, the popular is the most complex and difficult of construction. It is, indeed, so difficult, that ours, it is believed, may with truth be said to be the only one of a purely popular character, of any considerable importance, that ever existed. The cause is to be found in the fact, that, in the other two forms, society is arranged in artificial orders or classes. Where these exist, the line of distinction between them is so strongly marked as to throw into shade, or, otherwise, to absorb all interests which are foreign to them respectively. Hence, in an aristocracy, all interests are, politically, reduced to two,—the nobles and the people; and in a monarchy, with a nobility, into three,—the monarch, the nobles, and the people. In either case, they are so few that the sense of each may be taken separately, through its appropriate organ, so as to give to each a concurrent voice, and a negative on the other, through the usual departments of the government, without making it too complex, or too tardy in its movements to perform, with promptness and energy, all the necessary functions of government.

The case is different in constitutional governments of the popular form. In consequence of the absence of these artificial distinctions, the various natural interests, resulting from diversity of pursuits, condition, situation and character of different portions of the people,—and from the action of the government itself,—rise into prominence, and struggle to obtain the ascendency. They will, it is true, in governments of the numerical majority, ultimately coalesce, and form two great parties; but not so closely as to lose entirely their separate character and existence. These they will ever be ready to re-assume, when the objects for which they coalesced are accomplished. To overcome the difficulties occasioned by so great a diversity of interests, an organism far more complex is necessary.

Another obstacle, difficult to be overcome, opposes the formation of popular constitutional governments. It is much more difficult to terminate the struggles between conflicting interests, by compromise, in absolute popular governments, than in an aristocracy or monarchy.

In an aristocracy, the object of the people, in the ordinary struggle between them and the nobles, is not, at least in its early stages, to overthrow the nobility and revolutionize the government,—but to participate in its powers. Notwithstanding the oppression to which they may be subjected, under this form of government, the people commonly feel no small degree of respect for the descendants of a long line of distinguished ancestors; and do not usually aspire to more,—in opposing the authority of the nobles,—than to obtain such a participation in the powers of the government, as will enable them to correct its abuses and to lighten their burdens. Among the nobility, on the other hand, it sometimes happens that there are individuals of great influence with both sides, who have the good sense and patriotism to interpose, in order to effect a compromise by yielding to the reasonable demands of the people; and, thereby, to avoid the hazard of a final and decisive appeal to force. It is thus, by a judicious and timely compromise, the people, in such governments, may be raised to a participation in the administration sufficient for their protection, without the loss of authority on the part of the nobles.

In the case of a monarchy, the process is somewhat different. Where it is military despotism, the people rarely have the spirit or intelligence to attempt resistance; or, if otherwise, their resistance must almost necessarily terminate in defeat, or in a mere change of dynasty,—by the elevation of their leader to the throne. It is different, where the monarch is surrounded by an hereditary nobility. In a struggle between him and them, both (but especially the monarch) are usually disposed to court the people, in order to enlist them on their respective sides,—a state of things highly favorable to their elevation. In this case, the struggle, if it should be long continued without decisive results, would almost necessarily raise them to political importance, and to a participation in the powers of the government.

The case is different in an absolute Democracy. Party conflicts between the majority and minority, in such governments, can hardly ever terminate in compromise.—The object of the opposing minority is to expel the majority from power; and of the majority to maintain their hold upon it. It is, on both sides, a struggle for the whole,—a struggle that must determine which shall be the governing, and which the subject party;—and, in character, object and result, not unlike that between competitors for the sceptre in absolute monarchies. Its regular course, as has been shown, is, excessive violence,—an appeal to force,—followed by revolution,—and terminating at last, in the elevation to supreme power of the general of the successful party. And hence, among other reasons, aristocracies and monarchies more readily assume the constitutional form than absolute popular governments.

Of the three different forms, the monarchical has heretofore been much the most prevalent, and, generally, the most powerful and durable. This result is doubtless to be attributed principally to the fact that, in its absolute form, it is the most simple and easily constructed. And hence, as government is indispensable, communities having too little intelligence to form or preserve the others, naturally fall into this. It may also, in part, be attributed to another cause, already alluded to; that, in its organism and character, it is much more closely assimilated than either of the other two, to military power; on which all absolute governments depend for support. And hence, also, the tendency of the others, and of constitutional governments which have been so badly constructed or become so disorganized as to require force to support them,—to pass into military despotism,—that is, into monarchy in its most absolute and simple form. And hence, again, the fact, that revolutions in absolute monarchies, end, almost invariably, in a change of dynasty,—and not of the forms of the government; as is almost universally the case in the other systems.

But there are, besides these, other causes of a higher character, which contribute much to make monarchies the most prevalent, and, usually, the most durable governments. Among them, the leading one is, they are the most susceptible of improvement;—that is, they can be more easily and readily modified, so as to prevent, to a limited extent, oppression and abuse of power, without assuming the constitutional form, in its strict sense. It slides, almost naturally, into one of the most important modifications. I refer to hereditary descent. When this becomes well defined and firmly established, the community or kingdom, comes to be regarded by the sovereign as the hereditary possession of his family,—a circumstance which tends strongly to identify his interests with those of his subjects, and thereby, to mitigate the rigor of the government. It gives, besides, great additional security to his person; and prevents, in the same degree, not only the suspicion and hostile feelings incident to insecurity,—but invites all those kindly feelings which naturally spring up on both sides, between those whose interests are indentified,—when there is nothing to prevent it. And hence the strong feelings of paternity on the side of the sovereign,—and of loyalty on that of his subjects, which are often exhibited in such governments.

There is another improvement of which it is readily susceptible, nearly allied to the preceding. The hereditary principle not unfrequently extends to other families,—especially to those of the distinguished chieftains, by whose aid the monarchy was established, when it originates in conquest. When this is the case,—and a powerful body of hereditary nobles surround the sovereign, they oppose a strong resistance to his authority, and he to theirs,—tending to the advantage and security of the people. Even when they do not succeed in obtaining a participation in the powers of the government, they usually acquire sufficient weight to be felt and respected. From this state of things, such governments usually, in time, settle down on some fixed rules of action, which the sovereign is compelled to respect, and by which increased protection and security are acquired by all. It was thus the enlightened monarchies of Europe were formed, under which the people of that portion of the globe have made such great advances in power, intelligence, and civilization.

To these may be added the greater capacity, which governments of the monarchical form have exhibited, to hold under subjection a large extent of territory, and a numerous population; and which has made them more powerful than others of a different form, to the extent, that these constitute an element of power. All these causes combined, have given such great and decisive advantages, as to enable them, heretofore, to absorb, in the progress of events, the few governments which have, from time to time, assumed different forms;—not excepting even the mighty Roman Republic, which, after attaining the highest point of power, passed, seemingly under the operation of irresistible causes, into a military despotism. I say, heretofore,—for it remains to be seen whether they will continue to retain their advantages, in these respects, over the others, under the great growing influence of public opinion, and the new and imposing form which popular government has assumed with us.

These have already effected great changes, and will probably effect still greater,—adverse to the monarchical form; but, as yet, these changes have tended rather to the absolute, than to the constitutional form of popular government,—for reasons which have been explained. If this tendency should continue permanently in the same direction, the monarchical form must still retain its advantages, and continue to be the most prevalent. Should this be the case, the alternative will be between monarchy and popular government, in the form of the numerical majority, —or absolute democracy; which, as has been shown, is not only the most fugitive of all the forms, but has the strongest tendency of all others to the monarchical. If, on the contrary, this tendency, or the changes referred to, should incline to the constitutional form of popular government,—and a proper organism come to be regarded as not less indispensable than the right of suffrage to the establishment of such governments,—in such case, it is not improbable that, in the progress of events, the monarchical will cease to be the prevalent form of government. Whether they will take this direction, at least for a long time, will depend on the success of our government,—and a correct understanding of the principles on which it is constructed.

To comprehend more fully the force and bearing of public opinion, and to form a just estimate of the changes to which, aided by the press, it will probably lead, politically and socially, —it will be necessary to consider it in connection with the causes that have given it an influence so great, as to entitle it to be regarded as a new political element. They will, upon investigation, be found in the many discoveries and inventions made in the last few centuries.

Among the more prominent of those of an earlier date, stand the practical application of the magnetic power to the purposes of navigation, by the invention of the mariner's compass; the discovery of the mode of making gunpowder, and its application to the art of war; and the invention of the art of printing. Among the more recent are, the numerous chemical and mechanical discoveries and inventions, and their application to the various arts of production; the application of steam to machinery of almost every description, especially to such as is designed to facilitate transportation and travel by land and water; and, finally, the invention of the magnetic telegraph.

All these have led to important results. Through the invention of the mariner's compass, the globe has been circumnavigated and explored, and all who inhabit it, with but few exceptions, brought within the sphere of an all-pervading commerce, which is daily diffusing over its surface the light and blessings of civilization. Through that of the art of printing, the fruits of observation and reflection, of discoveries and inventions, with all the accumulated stores of previously acquired knowledge, are preserved and widely diffused. The application of gunpowder to the art of war, has for ever settled the long conflict for ascendency between civilization and barbarism in favor of the former, and thereby guaranteed that, whatever knowledge in now accumulated, or may hereafter be added, shall never again be lost. The numerous discoveries and inventions, chemical and mechanical, and the application of steam to machinery, have increased, many-fold, the productive powers of labor and capital; and have, thereby, greatly increased the number, who may devote themselves to study and improvement,—and the amount of means necessary for commercial exchanges,—especially between the more and the less advanced and civilized portions of the globe,—to the great advantage of both, but particularly of the latter. The application of steam to the purposes of travel and transportation, by land and water, has vastly increased the facility, cheapness and rapidity of both;—diffusing, with them, information and intelligence almost as quickly and as freely as if borne by the winds; while the electrical wires outstrip them, in velocity—rivalling, in rapidity, even thought itself.

The joint effect of all has been, a great increase and diffusion of knowledge; and, with this, an impulse to progress and civilization heretofore unexampled in the history of the world,—accompanied by a mental energy and activity unprecedented.

To all these causes, public opinion, and its organ, the press, owe their origin and great influence. Already they have attained a force in the more civilized portions of the globe sufficient to be felt by all governments, even the most absolute and despotic. But, as great as they now are, they have as yet attained nothing like their maximum force. It is probable, that not one of the causes, which have contributed to their formation and influence, has yet produced its full effects; while several of the most powerful have just begun to operate; and many others, probably of equal or even greater force, yet remain to be brought to light.

When the causes now in operation have produced their full effect, and inventions and discoveries shall have been exhausted, —if that may ever be,—they will give a force to public opinion, and cause changes, political and social, difficult to be anticipated. What will be their final bearing, time only can decide with any certainty. That they will, however, greatly improve the condition of man ultimately,—it would be impious to doubt. It would be to suppose, that the all-wise and beneficent Being,—the Creator of all,—had so constituted man, as that the employment of the high intellectual faculties, with which He has been pleased to endow him, in order that he might develop the laws that control the great agents of the material world, and make them subservient to his use,—would prove to him the cause of permanent evil,—and not of permanent good. If, then, such a supposition be inadmissible, they must, in their orderly and full development, end in his permanent good. But this cannot be, unless the ultimate effect of their action, politically, shall be, to give ascendency to that form of government best calculated to fulfil the ends for which government is ordained. For, so completely does the well-being of our race depend on good government, that it is hardly possible any change, the ultimate effect of which should be otherwise, could prove to be a permanent good.

It is, however, not improbable, that many and great, but temporary evils, will follow the changes they have effected, and are destined to effect. It seems to be a law in the political, as well as in the material world, that great changes cannot be made, except very gradually, without convulsions and revolutions; to be followed by calamities, in the beginning, however beneficial they may prove to be in the end. The first effect of such changes, on long established governments, will be, to unsettle the opinions and principles in which they originated,—and which have guided their policy,—before those, which the changes are calculated to form and establish, are fairly developed and understood. The interval between the decay of the old and the formation and establishment of the new, constitutes a period of transition, which must always necessarily be one of uncertainty, confusion, error, and wild and fierce fanaticism.

The governments of the more advanced and civilized portions of the world are now in the midst of this period. It has proved, and will continue to prove a severe trial to existing political institutions of every form. Those governments which have not the sagacity to perceive what is truly public opinion,—to distinguish between it and the mere clamor of faction, or shouts of fanaticism,—and the good sense and firmness to yield, timely and cautiously, to the claims of the one,—and to resist, promptly and decidedly, the demands of the other,—are doomed to fall. Few will be able successfully to pass through this period of transition; and these, not without shocks and modifications, more or less considerable. It will endure until the governing and the governed shall better understand the ends for which government is ordained, and the form best adapted to accomplish them, under all the circumstances in which communities may be respectively placed.

I shall, in conclusion, proceed to exemplify the elementary

principles, which have been established, by giving a brief account of the origin and character of the governments of Rome and Great Britain; the two most remarkable and perfect of their respective forms of constitutional governments. The object is to show how these principles were applied, in the more simple forms of such governments; preparatory to an exposition of the mode in which they have been applied in our own more complex system. It will appear that, in each, the principles are the same; and that the difference in their application resulted from the different situation and social condition of the respective communities. They were modified, in each, so as to conform to these; and, hence, their remarkable success. They were applied to communities in which hereditary rank had long prevailed. Their respective constitutions originated in concession to the people; and, through them, they acquired a participation in the powers of government. But with us, they were applied to communities where all political rank and distinction between citizens were excluded; and where government had its origin in the will of the people.

But, however different their origin and character, it will be found that the object in each was the same,—to blend and harmonize the conflicting interests of the community; and the means the same,—taking the sense of each class or portion through its appropriate organ, and considering the concurrent sense of all as the sense of the whole community. Such being the fact, an accurate and clear conception how this was effected, in their more simple forms, will enable us better to understand how it was accomplished in our far more refined, artificial, and complex form.

It is well known to all, the least conversant with their history, that the Roman people consisted of two distinct orders, or classes,—the Patricians and the Plebeians; and that the line of distinction was so strongly drawn, that, for a long time, the right of intermarriage between them was prohibited. After the overthrow of the monarchy and the expulsion of the Tarquins, the government fell exclusively under the control of the patricians, who, with their clients and dependents, formed, at the time, a very numerous and powerful body. At first, while there was danger of the return of the exiled family, they treated the plebeians with kindness; but, after it had passed away, with oppression and cruelty.

It is not necessary, with the object in view, to enter into a minute account of the various acts of oppression and cruelty to which they were subjected. It is sufficient to state, that, according to the usages of war at the time, the territory of a conquered people became the property of the conquerors; and that the plebeians were harassed and oppressed by incessant wars, in which the danger and toil were theirs, while all the fruits of victory, (the lands of the vanquished, and the spoils of war,) accrued to the benefit of their oppressors. The result was such as might be expected. They were impoverished, and forced, from necessity, to borrow from the patricians, at usurious and exorbitant interest, funds which they had been enriched through their blood and toil; and to pledge their all for repayment at stipulated periods. In case of default, the pledge became forfeited; and, under the provisions of law in such cases, the debtors were liable to be seized, and sold or imprisoned by their creditors in private jails prepared and kept for the purpose. These savage provisions were enforced with the utmost rigor against the indebted and impoverished plebeians. They constituted, indeed, an essential part of the system through which they were plundered and oppressed by the patricians.

A system so oppressive could not be endured. The natural consequences followed. Deep hatred was engendered between the orders, accompanied by factions, violence, and corruption, which distracted and weakened the government. At length, an incident occurred which roused the indignation of the plebeians to the utmost pitch, and which ended in an open rupture between the two orders.

An old soldier, who had long served the country, and had fought with bravery in twenty-eight battles, made his escape from the prison of his creditor,—squalid, pale, and famished. He implored the protection of the plebeians. A crowd surrounded him; and his tale of service to the country, and the cruelty with which he had been treated by his creditor, kindled a flame, which continued to rage until it extended to the army. It refused to continue any longer in service,—crossed the Anio, and took possession of the sacred mount. The patricians divided in opinion as to the course which should be pursued. The more violent insisted on an appeal to arms, but, fortunately, the counsel of the moderate, which recommended concession and compromise, prevailed. Commissioners were appointed to treat with the army; and a formal compact was entered into between the orders, and ratified by the oaths of each, which conceded to the plebeians the right to elect two tribunes, as the protectors of their order, and made their persons sacred. The number was afterwards increased to ten, and their election by centuries changed to election by tribes;—a mode by which the plebeians secured a decided preponderance.

Such was the origin of the tribunate;—which, in process of time, opened all the honors of the government to the plebeians. They acquired the right, not only of vetoing the passage of all laws, but also their execution; and thus obtained, through their tribunes, a negative on the entire action of the government, without divesting the patricians of their control over the Senate. By this arrangement, the government was placed under the concurrent and joint voice of the two orders, expressed through separate and appropriate organs; the one possessing the positive, and the other the negative powers of the government. This simple change converted it from an absolute, into a constitutional government,—from a government of the patricians only, to that of the whole Roman people,—and from an aristocracy into a republic. In doing this, it laid the solid foundation of Roman liberty and greatness.

A superficial observer would pronounce a government, so organized, as that one order should have the power of making and executing the laws, and another, or the representatives of another, the unlimited authority of preventing their enactment and execution,—if not wholly impracticable, at least, too feeble to stand the shocks to which all governments are subject; and would, therefore, predict its speedy dissolution, after a distracted and inglorious career.

How different from the result! Instead of distraction, it proved to be the bond of concord and harmony; instead of weakness, of unequalled strength;—and, instead of a short and inglorious career, one of great length and immortal glory. It moderated the conflicts between the orders; harmonized their interests, and blended them into one; substituted devotion to country in the place of devotion to particular orders; called forth the united strength and energy of the whole, in the hour of danger; raised to power, the wise and patriotic; elevated the Roman name above all others; extended her authority and dominion over the greater part of the then known world, and transmitted the influence of her laws and institutions to the present day. Had the opposite counsel prevailed at this critical juncture; had an appeal been made to arms instead of to concession and compromise, Rome, instead of being what she afterwards became, would, in all probability, have been as inglorious, and as little known to posterity as the insignificant states which surrounded her, whose names and existence would have been long since consigned to oblivion, had they not been preserved in the history of her conquests of them. But for the wise course then adopted, it is not improbable, —whichever order might have prevailed,—that she would have fallen under some cruel and petty tyrant;—and, finally, been conquered by some of the neighboring states,—or by the Carthaginians, or the Gauls. To the fortunate turn which events then took, she owed her unbounded sway and imperishable renown.

It is true, that the tribunate, after raising her to a height of power and prosperity never before equalled, finally became one of the instruments by which her liberty was overthrown:—but it was not until she became exposed to new dangers, growing out of increase of wealth and the great extent of her dominions, against which the tribunate furnished no guards. Its original object was the protection of the plebeians against oppression and abuse of power on the part of the patricians. This, it thoroughly accomplished; but it had no power to protect the people of the numerous and wealthy conquered countries from being plundered by consuls and proconsuls. Nor could it prevent the plunderers from using the enormous wealth, which they extorted from the impoverished and ruined provinces, to corrupt and debase the people; nor arrest the formation of parties, (irrespective of the old division of patricians and plebeians,) having no other object than to obtain the control of the government for the purpose of plunder. Against these formidable evils, her constitution furnished no adequate security. Under their baneful influence, the possession of the government became the object of the most violent conflicts not between patricians and plebeians,—but between profligate and corrupt factions. They continued with increasing violence, until, finally, Rome sunk, as must every community under similar circumstances, beneath the strong grasp, the despotic rule of the chieftain of the successful party;—the sad, but only alternative which remained to prevent universal violence, confusion and anarchy. The Republic had, in reality, ceased to exist long before the establishment of the Empire. The interval was filled by the rule of ferocious, corrupt and bloody factions. There was, indeed, a small but patriotic body of eminent individuals, who struggled, in vain, to correct abuses, and to restore the government to its primitive character and purity;—and who sacrificed their lives in their endeavors to accomplish an object so virtuous and noble. But it can be no disparagement to the tribunate, that the great powers conferred on it for wise purposes, and which it had so fully accomplished, should be seized upon, during this violent and corrupt interval, to overthrow the liberty it had established, and so long nourished and supported.

In assigning such consequence to the tribunate, I must not overlook other important provisions of the Constitution of the Roman government. The Senate, as far as we are informed, seems to have been admirably constituted to secure consistency and steadiness of action. The power,—when the Republic was exposed to imminent danger,—to appoint a dictator,—vested, for a limited period, with almost boundless authority; the two consuls, and the manner of electing them; the auguries; the sibylline books; the priesthood, and the censorship;—all of which appertained to the patricians,—were, perhaps indispensable to withstand the vast and apparently irregular power of the tribunate;—while the possession of such great powers by the patricians, made it necessary to give proportionate strength to the only organ through which the plebeians could act on the government with effect. The government was, indeed, powerfully constituted; and, apparently, well proportioned both in its positive and negative organs. It was truly an iron government. Without the tribunate, it proved to be one of the most oppressive and cruel that ever existed; but with it, one of the strongest and best.

The origin and character of the British government are so well known, that a very brief sketch, with the object in view, will suffice.

The causes which ultimately moulded it into its present form, commenced with the Norman Conquest. This introduced the feudal system, with its necessary appendages, a hereditary monarchy and nobility; the former in the line of the chief, who led the invading army;—and the latter in that of his distinguished followers. They became his feudatories. The country,—both land and people,—(the latter as serfs,) was divided between them. Conflicts soon followed between the monarch and the nobles,—as must ever be the case under such systems. They were followed, in the progress of events, by efforts, on the part both of monarchs and nobles, to conciliate the favor of the people. They, in consequence, gradually rose to power. At every step of their ascent, they became more important,—and were more and more courted,—until at length their influence was so sensibly felt, that they were summoned to attend the meeting of parliament by delegates; not, however, as an estate of the realm, or constituent member of the body politic. The first summons came from the nobles; and was designed to conciliate their good feelings and secure their co-operation in the war against the king. This was followed by one from him; but his object was simply to have them present at the meeting of parliament, in order to be *consulted* by the crown, on questions relating to taxes and supplies; not, indeed, to discuss the right to lay the one, and to raise the other,—for the King claimed the arbitrary authority to do both,—but with a view to facilitate their collection, and to reconcile them to their imposition.

From this humble beginning, they, after a long struggle, accompanied by many vicissitudes, raised themselves to be considered one of the estates of the realm; and, finally, in their efforts to enlarge and secure what they had gained, overpowered, for a time, the other two estates; and thus concentrated all power in a single estate or body. This, in effect, made the government absolute, and led to consequences which, as by a fixed law, must ever result in popular governments of this form;—namely:—to organized parties, or, rather, factions, contending violently to obtain or retain the control of the government; and this, again, by laws almost as uniform, to the concentration of all the powers of government in the hands of the military commander of the successful party.

His heir was too feeble to hold the sceptre he had grasped; and the general discontent with the result of the revolution, led to the restoration of the old dynasty; without defining the limits between the powers of the respective estates.

After a short interval, another revolution followed, in which the lords and commons united against the king. This terminated in his overthrow; and the transfer of the crown to a collateral branch of the family, accompanied by a declaration of rights, which defined the powers of the several estates of the realm; and, finally, perfected and established the constitution. Thus, a feudal monarchy was converted, through a slow but steady process of many centuries, into a highly refined constitutional monarchy, without changing the basis of the original government.

As it now stands, the realm consists of three estates; the king; the lords temporal and spiritual; and the commons. The parliament is the grand council. It possesses the supreme power. It enacts laws, by the concurring assent of the lords and commons, —subject to the approval of the king. The executive power is vested in the monarch, who is regarded as constituting the first estate. Although irresponsible himself, he can only act through responsible ministers and agents. They are responsible to the other estates; to the lords, as constituting the high court before whom all the servants of the crown may be tried for malpractices, and crimes against the realm, or official delinquencies;—and to the commons, as possessing the impeaching power, and constituting the grand inquest of the kingdom. These provisions, with their legislative powers,—especially that of withholding supplies,—give them a controlling influence on the executive department, and, virtually, a participation in its powers;—so that the acts of the government, throughout its entire range, may be fairly considered as the result of the concurrent and joint action of the three estates;—and, as these embrace all the orders,—of the concurrent and joint action of the estates of the realm.

He would take an imperfect and false view of the subject who should consider the king, in his mere individual character, or even as the head of the royal family,—as constituting an estate. Regarded in either light, so far from deserving to be considered as the First Estate,—and the head of the realm, as he is,—he would represent an interest too inconsiderable to be an object of special protection. Instead of this, he represents what in reality is, habitually and naturally, the most powerful interest, all things considered, under every form of government in all civilized communities,—*the tax-consuming interest;* or, more broadly, the great interest which necessarily grows out of the action of the government, be its form what it may;—the interest that *lives by the government.* It is composed of the recipients of its honors and emoluments; and may be properly called, the government interest, or party;—in contradistinction to the rest of the community,—or, (as they must be properly called,) the people or commons. The one comprehends all who are supported by the government;—and the other all who support the government:—and it is only because the former are strongest, all things being considered, that they are enabled to retain, for any considerable time, advantages so great and commanding.

This great and predominant interest is naturally represented by a single head. For it is impossible, without being so represented, to distribute the honors and emoluments of the government among those who compose it, without producing discord and conflict:—and it is only by preventing these, that advantages so tempting can be long retained. And, hence, the strong tendency of this great interest to the monarchical form;—that is, to be represented by a single individual. On the contrary, the antagonistic interest,—that which supports the government, has the opposite tendency;—a tendency to be represented by many; because a large assembly can better judge, than one individual or a few, what burdens the community can bear;—and how it can be most equally distributed, and easily collected.

In the British government, the king constitutes an Estate, because he is the head and representative of this great interest. He is the conduit through which, all the honors and emoluments of the government flow;—while the House of Commons, according to the theory of the government, is the head and representative of the opposite—the great tax-paying interest, by which the government is supported.

Between these great interests, there is necessarily a constant and strong tendency to conflict; which, if not counteracted, must end in violence and an appeal to force,—to be followed by revolution, as has been explained. To prevent this, the House of Lords, as one of the estates of the realm, is interposed; and constitutes the conservative power of the government. It consists, in fact, of that portion of the community who are the principal recipients of the honors, emoluments, and other advantages derived from the government; and whose condition cannot be improved, but must be made worse by the triumph of either of the conflicting estates over the other; and, hence, it is opposed to the ascendency of either,—and in favor of preserving the equilibrium between them.

This sketch, brief as it is, is sufficient to show, that these two constitutional governments,—by far the most illustrious of their respective kinds,—conform to the principles that have been established, alike in their origin and in their construction. The constitutions of both originated in a pressure, occasioned by conflicts of interests between hostile classes or orders, and were intended to meet the pressing exigencies of the occasion; neither party, it would seem, having any conception of the principles involved, or the consequences to follow, beyond the immediate objects in contemplation. It would, indeed, seem almost impossible for constitutional governments, founded on orders or classes, to originate in any other manner. It is difficult to conceive that any people, among whom they did not exist, would, or could voluntarily institute them, in order to establish such governments; while it is not at all wonderful, that they should grow out of conflicts between different orders or classes when aided by a favorable combination of circumstances.

The constitutions of both rest on the same principle;—an organism by which the voice of each order or class is taken through its appropriate organ; and which requires the concurring voice of all to constitute that of the whole community. The effects, too, were the same in both;—to unite and harmonize conflicting interests;—to strengthen attachments to the whole community, and to moderate that to the respective orders or classes; to rally all, in the hour of danger, around the standard of their country; to elevate the feeling of nationality, and to develop power, moral and physical, to an extraordinary extent. Yet each has its distinguishing features, resulting from the difference of their organisms, and the circumstances in which they respectively originated.

In the government of Great Britian, the three orders are blended in the legislative department; so that separate and concurring act of each is necessary to make laws; while, on the contrary, in the Roman, one order had the power of making laws, and another of annulling them, or arresting their execution. Each had its peculiar advantages. The Roman developed more fully the love of country and the feelings of nationality. "*I am a Roman citizen*,"—was pronounced with a pride and elevation of sentiment, never, perhaps, felt before or since, by any citizen or subject of any community, in announcing the country to which he belonged.

It also developed more fully the power of the community. Taking into consideration their respective population, and the state of the arts at the different periods, Rome developed more power, comparatively, than Great Britian ever has,—vast as that is, and has been,—or, perhaps, than any other community ever did. Hence, the mighty control she acquired from a beginning so humble. But the British government is far superior to that of Rome, in its adaptation and capacity to embrace under its control extensive dominions, without subverting its constitution. In this respect, the Roman constitution was defective;—and, in consequence, soon began to exhibit marks of decay, after Rome had extended her dominions beyond Italy; while the British holds under its sway, without apparently impairing either, an empire equal to that, under the weight of which the constitution and liberty of Rome were crushed. This great advantage it derives from its different structure, especially that of the executive department; and the character of its conservative principle. The former is so constructed as to prevent, in consequence of its unity and hereditary character, the violent and factious struggles to obtain the control of the government,—and, with it, the vast patronage which distracted, corrupted, and finally subverted the Roman Republic. Against this fatal disease, the latter had no security whatever; while the British government,—besides the advantages it possesses, in this respect, from the structure of its executive department,—has, in the character of its conservative principle, another and powerful security against it. Its character is such, that patronage, instead of weakening, strengthens it:—For, the greater the patronage of the government, the greater will be the share which falls to the estate constituting the conservative department of the government; and the more eligible its condition, the greater its opposition to any radical change in its form. The two causes combined, give to the government a greater capacity of holding under subjection extensive dominions, without subverting the constitution or destroying liberty, than has ever been possessed by any other. It is difficult, indeed, to assign any limit to its capacity in this respect. The most probable which can be assigned is, its ability to bear increased burdens;—the taxation necessary to meet the expenses incident to the acquisition and government of such vast dominions, may prove, in the end, so heavy as to crush, under its weight, the laboring and productive portions of the population.

I have now finished the brief sketch I proposed, of the origin and character of these two renowned governments; and shall next proceed to consider the character, origin and structure of the Government of the United States.[2] It differs from the Roman and British, more than they differ from each other; and, although an existing government of recent origin, its character and structure are perhaps less understood than those of either.

SPEECHES

1 ON THE SECOND RESOLUTION OF THE COMMITTEE ON FOREIGN RELATIONS, DECEMBER 12, 1811

The Committee on Foreign Relations, of which Calhoun was a member, submitted a report on November 29, 1811, which reviewed relations with Great Britian and concluded by recommending adoption of a series of resolutions. Calhoun's strongly nationalist speech is a reply to John Randolph of Virginia, who had opposed the report on the floor of the House, and deals primarily with the second resolution, which was:

> "2. *Resolved, That an additional force of ten thousand regular troops ought to be immediately raised to serve for three years; and that a bounty in lands ought to be given to encourage enlistments.*"

The resolution was adopted.[1]

Mr. Speaker: I understood the opinion of the Committee of Foreign Relations differently from what the gentleman from Virginia (Mr. RANDOLPH) has stated to be his impression. I certainly understood that committee as recommending the measures now before the House as a preparation for war; and such in fact was its express resolve, agreed to, I believe, by every member except that gentleman. I do not attribute any wilful misstatement to him, but consider it the effect of inadvertency or mistake. Indeed, the report could mean nothing but war or empty menace. I hope no member of this House is in favor of the latter. A bullying, menacing system has everything to condemn and nothing to recommend it; in expense, it is almost as considerable as war; it excites contempt abroad, and destroys confidence at home. Menaces are serious things; and, if we expect any good from them, they ought to be resorted to with as much caution and seriousness as war itself, and should, if not successful, be invariably followed by it. It was not the gentleman from Tennessee (Mr. GRUNDY) that made this a war question. The resolve contemplates an additional regular force; a measure confessedly improper but as a preparation for war, but undoubtedly necessary in that event. Sir, I am not insensible of the weighty importance of this question, for the first time submitted to this House, as a redress of our long list of complaints against one of the belligerents; but, according to my mode of thinking on this subject, however serious the question, whenever I am on its affirmative side, my conviction must be strong and unalterable. War, in this country, ought never to be resorted to but when it is clearly justifiable and necessary; so much so, as not to require the aid of logic to convince our reason, nor the ardor of eloquence to inflame our passions. There are many reasons why this country should never resort to it but for causes the most urgent and necessary. It is sufficient that, under a Government like ours, none but such will justify it in the eye of the nation; and were I not satisfied that such is the present case, I certainly would be no advocate of the proposition now before the House.

Sir, I might prove the war, should it ensue, justifiable, by the express admission of the gentleman from Virginia; and necessary, by facts undoubted and universally admitted, such as that gentleman did not pretend to controvert. The extent, duration, and character of the injuries received; the failure of those peaceful means heretofore resorted to for the redress of our wrongs, is my proof that it is necessary. Why should I mention the impressment of our seamen; depredation on every branch of our commerce, including the direct export trade, continued for years, and made under laws which professedly undertake to regulate our trade with other nations; negotiation resorted to time after time, till it is become hopeless; the restrictive system persisted in to avoid war, and in the vain expectation of returning justice? The evil still grows, and in each succeeding year swells in extent and pretension beyond the preceding. The question, even in the opinion and admission of our opponents, is reduced to this single point—which shall we do, abandon or defend our own commercial and maritime rights, and the personal liberties of our citizens employed in exercising them? These rights are essentially attacked, and war is the only means of redress. The gentleman from Virginia has suggested none—unless we consider the whole of his speech as recommending patient and resigned submission as the best remedy. Sir, which alternative this House ought to embrace, it is not for me to say. I hope the decision is made already, by a higher authority than the voice of any man. It is not for the human tongue to instill the sense of independence and honor. This is the work of nature—a generous nature, that disdains tame submission to wrongs.

This part of the subject is so imposing, as to enforce silence even on the gentleman from Virginia. He dared not to deny his country's wrongs, or vindicate the conduct of her enemy.

Only one point of that gentleman's argument had any, the most remote, relation to this point. He would not say we had not a good cause of war, but insisted that it was our duty to define that cause. If he means that this House ought, at this stage of the proceeding, or any other, to enumerate such violations of our rights, as we are willing to contend for, he prescribes a course which neither good sense or the usage of nations warrants. When we contend, let us contend for all our rights; the doubtful and the certain, the unimportant and essential. It is as easy to struggle, or even more so, for the whole as a part. At the termination of the contest, secure all that our wisdom and valor and the fortune of the war will permit. This is the dictate of common sense; such also is the usage of nations. The single instance alluded to, the endeavor of Mr. Fox to compel Mr. Pitt to define the object of the war against France, will not support the gentleman from Virginia in his position. That was an extraordinary war for an extraordinary purpose, and could not be governed by the usual rules. It was not for conquest, or for redress of injury, but to impose a Government on France, which she refused to receive; an object so detestable, that an avowal dare not be made. Sir, here I might rest the question. The affirmative of the proposition is established. I cannot but advert, however, to the complaint of the gentleman from Virginia the first time he was up on this question. He said he found himself reduced to the necessity of supporting the negative side of the question, before the affirmative was established. Let me tell that gentleman, that there is no hardship in his case. It is not every affirmative that ought to be proved. Were I to affirm the House is now in session, would it be reasonable to ask for proof? He who would deny its truth, on him would be the proof of so extraordinary a negative. How, then, could the gentleman, after his admissions, with the facts before him and the nation, complain? The causes are such as to warrant, or rather make it indispensable in any nation not absolutely dependent to defend its rights by force. Let him, then, show the reasons why we ought not so to defend ourselves. On him, then, is the burden of proof. This he has attempted; he has endeavored to support his negative. Before I proceed to answer the gentleman particularly, let me call the attention of the House to one circumstance: that is, that almost the whole of his arguments consisted of an enumeration of evils always incident to war, however just and necessary; and that, if they have any force, it is calculated to produce unqualified submission to every species of insult and injury. I do not feel myself bound to answer arguments of the above description; and if I should touch on them, it will be only incidentally, and not for the purpose of serious refutation. The first argument of the gentleman which I shall notice, is the unprepared state of the country. Whatever weight this argument might have, in a question of immediate war, it surely has little in that of preparation for it. If our country is unprepared, let us remedy the evil as soon as possible. Let the gentleman submit his plan; and, if a reasonable one, I doubt not it will be supported by the House. But, sir, let us admit the fact and the whole force of the argument, I ask whose is the fault? Who has been a member for many years past, and has seen the defenceless state of his country even near home, under his own eyes, without a single endeavor to remedy so serious an evil? Let him not say "I have acted in a minority." It is no less the duty of the minority than a majority to endeavor to serve our country. For that purpose we are sent here, and not for that of opposition. We are next told of the expenses of the war, and that the people will not pay taxes. Why not? Is it a want of capacity? What, with one million tons of shipping, a trade of near $100,000,000, manufactures of $150,000,000, and agriculture of thrice that amount, shall we be told the country wants capacity to raise and support ten thousand or fifteen thousand additional regulars? No; it has the ability, that is admitted; but will it not have the disposition? Is not the course a just and necessary one? Shall we, then, utter this libel on the nation? Where will proof be found of a fact so disgraceful? It is said, in the history of the country twelve or fifteen years ago. The case is not parallel. The ability of the country is greatly increased since. The object of that tax was unpopular. But on this, as well as my memory and almost infant observation at that time serve me, the objection was not to the tax, or its amount, but the mode of collection. The eye of the nation was frightened by the number of officers; its love of liberty shocked with the multiplicity of regulations. We, in the vile spirit of imitation, copied from the most oppressive part of European laws on that subject, and imposed on a young and virtuous nation all the severe provisions made necessary by corruption and long growing chicane. If taxes should become necessary, I do not hesitate to say the people will pay cheerfully. It is for their Government and their cause, and would be their interest and duty to pay. But it may be, and I believe was said, that the nation will not pay taxes, because the rights violated are not worth defending, or that the defence will cost more than the profit. Sir, I here enter my solemn protest against this low and "calculating avarice" entering this hall of legislation. It is only fit for shops and counting-houses, and ought not to disgrace the seat of sovereignty by its squalid and vile appearance. Whenever it touches sovereign power, the nation is ruined. It is too short-sighted to defend itself. It is an unpromising spirit, always ready to yield a part to save the balance. It is too timid to have in itself the laws of self-preservation. It is never safe but under the shield of honor. Sir, I only know of one principle to make a nation great, to produce in this country not the form but real spirit of union, and that is, to protect every citizen in the lawful pursuit of his business. He will then feel that he is backed by the Government; that its arm is his arms; and will rejoice in its increased strength and prosperity. Protection and patriotism are reciprocal. This is the road that great nations have trod. Sir, I am not versed in this calculating policy; and will not, therefore, pretend to estimate in dollars and cents the value of national independence, or national affection. I cannot dare to measure, in shillings and pence, the misery, the stripes, and the slavery of our impressed seamen; nor even to value our shipping, commercial, and agricultural losses, under the Orders in Council and the British system of blockade. I hope I have not condemned any prudent estimate of the means of a country, before it enters on a war. This is wisdom, the other folly. Sir, the gentleman from Virginia has not failed to touch on the calamity of war; that fruitful source of declamation, by which pity becomes the advocate of cowardice; but I know not what we have to do with that subject. If the gentleman desires to repress the gallant ardor of our countrymen by such topics, let me inform him, that true courage regards only the cause—that it is just and necessary—and that it despises the pain and danger of war. If he really wishes to promote the cause of humanity, let his eloquence be addressed to Lord Wellesley or Mr. Percival and not the American Congress. Tell them, if they persist in such daring insult and injury to a neutral nation, that, however inclined to peace, it will be bound in honor and interest to resist; that their patience and benevolence, however great, will be exhausted; that the calamity of war will ensue; and that they, in the opinion of wounded humanity, will be answerable for all its devastation and misery. Let melting pity, a regard to the interest of humanity, stay the hand of injustice, and, my life on it, the gentleman will not find it difficult to call off his country from the bloody scenes of war.

We are next told of the danger of war! I believe we are all ready to acknowledge its hazard and accidents; but I cannot think we have any extraordinary danger to contend with, at least so much as to warrant an acquiescence in the injuries we have received. On the contrary, I believe no war can be less dangerous to internal peace, or national existence. But, we are told of the black population of the South. As far as the gentleman from Virginia speaks of his own personal knowledge, I will not pretend to contradict him; I only regret that such is the dreadful state of his particular part of the country. Of the Southern section, I too have some personal knowledge, and can say that, in South Carolina, no such fears in any part are felt. But, sir, admit the gentleman's statement; will a war with Great

Britian increase the danger? Will the country be less able to repress insurrection? Had we anything to fear from that quarter, which I sincerely disbelieve, in my opinion, the precise time of the greatest safety is during a war, in which we have no fear of invasion—then the country is most on its guard; our militia the best prepared; and standing force the greatest. Even in our Revolution no attempts were made by that portion of our population; and however, the gentleman may frighten himself with the disorganizing effects of French principles, I cannot think our ignorant blacks have felt much of their baneful influence. I dare say more than one-half of them never heard of the French Revolution. But, as great as is the danger from our slaves, the gentleman's fears end not there—the standing army is not less terrible to him. Sir, I think a regular force, raised for a period of actual hostilities, cannot be called a standing army. There is a just distinction between such a force, and one raised as a peace establishment. Whatever may be the composition of the latter, I hope the former will consist of some of the best materials of the country. The ardent patriotism of our young men, and the reasonable bounty in land, which is proposed to be given, will impel them to join their country's standard and to fight her battles; they will not forget the citizen in the soldier, and, in obeying their officer, learn to contemn their Constitution. In our officers and soldiers we will find patriotism no less pure and ardent than in the private citizen; but, if they should be depraved, as represented, what have we to fear from twenty-five or thirty thousand regulars? Where will be the boasted militia of the gentleman? Can one million of militia be over-powered by thirty thousand regulars? If so, how can we rely on them against a foe invading our country? Sir, I have no such contemptuous idea of our militia—their untaught bravery is sufficient to crush all foreign and internal attempts on their country's liberties. But we have not yet come to the end of the chapter of dangers. The gentleman's imagination, so fruitful on this subject, conceives that our Constitution is not calculated for war, and that it cannot stand its rude shock. This is rather extraordinary—we must depend upon the pity or contempt of other nations, for our existence. The Constitution, it seems, has failed in its essential part, "to provide for the common defense." No, says the gentleman from Virginia, it is competent for a defensive, but not an offensive war. It is not necessary for me to expose the error of this opinion. Why make the distinction in this instance? Will he pretend to say, that this is an offensive war; a war of conquest? Yes, the gentleman has dared to make this assertion; and for reasons no less extraordinary than the assertion itself. He says, our rights are violated on the ocean, and that these violations affect our shipping, and commercial rights, to which the Canadas have no relation. The doctrine of retaliation has been much abused of late by an unnatural extension; we have now to witness a new abuse. The gentleman from Virginia has limited it down to a point. By his system, if you receive a blow on the breast, you dare not return it on the head; you are obliged to measure and return it on the precise point on which it was received. If you do not proceed with mathematical accuracy, it ceases to be just self-defense; it becomes an unprovoked attack. In speaking of Canada, the gentleman from Virginia introduced the name of Montgomery with much feeling and interest. Sir, there is danger in that name to the gentleman's argument. It is sacred heroism! It is indignant of submission! This calls my memory back to the time of our Revolution; to the Congress of '74 and '75. Supposing a speaker of that day had risen and urged all the arguments which we have heard on this subject; had told that Congress, "your contest is about the right of laying a tax; and that the attempt on Canada had nothing to do with it: that the war would be expensive; that danger and devastation would overspread our country, and that the power of Great Britain was irresistible." With what sentiment, think you would such doctrines have been received? Happy for us, they had no force at that period of our country's glory. Had they been then acted on, this Hall would never have witnessed a great nation convened to deliberate for the general good; a mighty empire, with prouder prospects than any nation the sun ever shone on, would not have risen in the West. No; we would have been vile, subjected colonies; governed by that imperious rod which Great Britain holds over her distant provinces.

Sir, said Mr. C., the gentleman from Virginia attributes preparation for war to everything but its true cause. He endeavored to find it in the probable rise of the price of hemp. He represents the people of the Western States as willing to plunge our country into war for such base and precarious motives. I will not reason on this point. I see the cause of their ardor, not in such base motives, but in their known patriotism and disinterestedness. No less mercenary is the reason which he attributes to the Southern States. He says, that the non-importation act has reduced cotton to nothing, which has produced a feverish impatience. Sir, I acknowledge the cotton of our farms is worth but little; but not for the cause assigned by the gentleman from Virginia. The people of that section do not reason as he does; they do not attribute it to the efforts of their Government to maintain the peace and independence of their country; they see in the low price of the produce, the hand of foreign injustice; they know well, without the market to the Continent, the deep and steady current of supply will glut that of Great Britain; they are not prepared for the colonial state to which again that Power is endeavoring to reduce us. The manly spirit of that section of our country will not submit to be regulated by any foreign Power. The love of France and the hatred of England has also been assigned as the cause of the present measure. France has not done us justice, says the gentleman from Virginia, and how can we without partiality resist the aggressions of England? I know, sir, we have still cause of complaint against France; but it is of a different character from those against England. She professes now to respect our rights, and there cannot be a reasonable doubt but that the most objectionable parts of her decrees, as far as they respect us, are repealed. We have already formally acknowledged this to be a fact. I, however, protest against the whole of the principles on which this doctrine is founded. It is a novel doctrine, and nowhere to be found out of this House, that you cannot select your antagonist without being guilty of partiality. Sir, when two invade your rights you may resist both or either, at your pleasure. It is regulated by prudence and not by right. The stale imputation of partiality to France is better calculated for the columns of a newspaper than for the walls of this House. I ask, in this particular, of the gentleman from Virginia, but for the same measure which he claims for himself. That gentleman is at a loss to account for, what he calls, our hatred to England. He asks, how can we hate the country of Locke, of Newton, Hampden, and Chatham; a country having the same language and customs with ourselves, and descending from a common ancestry. Sir, the laws of human affections are uniform. If we have so much to attach us to that country, powerful indeed must be the cause which has overpowered it.

Yes, sir, there is a cause strong enough. Not that occult courtly affection which he has supposed to be entertained for France; but it is to be found in continued and unprovoked insult and injury. A cause so manifest that the gentleman from Virginia had to exert much ingenuity to overlook it. But, sir, here I think the gentleman, in his eager admiration of that country, has not been sufficiently guarded in his argument. Has he reflected on the cause of that admiration? Has he examined the reasons of our high regard for her Chatham? It is his ardent patriotism; the heroic courage of his mind that could not brook the least insult or injury offered to his country, but thought that her interest and honor ought to be vindicated at every hazard and expense.

I hope, when we are called on to admire, we shall also be asked to imitate. I hope the gentleman does not wish a monopoly of those great virtues to remain to that nation. The balance of power has also been introduced as an argument for submission. England is said to be a barrier against the military despotism of France. There is, sir, one great error in our legislation. We are ready enough to protect the interest of the States; and it should seem from this argument to watch over those of a foreign nation, while we grossly neglect our own immediate concerns. This argument of the balance of power is well calculated for the British Parliament, but not at all fitted to the American Congress. Tell them that they have to contend with a mighty Power, and that if they persist in insult and injury to the American people, they will compel them to throw the whole weight of their force into the scale of their enemy. Paint the danger to them, and if they desist from injury, we, I answer for it, will not disturb the balance. But it is absurd for us to talk of the balance of power, while they by their conduct smile with contempt at our simple good-natured policy. If, however, in the contest, it should be found that they underrate us, which I hope and believe, and that we can affect the balance of power, it will not be difficult for us to obtain such terms as our rights demand. I, sir, will now conclude by adverting to an argument of the gentleman from Virginia used in debate on a preceding day. He asked why not debate war immediately. The answer is obvious: because we are not yet prepared. But, says the gentleman, such language as is here held will provoke Great Britain to commence hostilities. I have no such fears. She knows well that such a course would unite all parties here; a thing which above all others she most dreads. Besides, such has been our past conduct, that she will still calculate on our patience and submission till war is actually commenced.

2 ON THE BILL TO ENCOURAGE ENLISTMENTS, JANUARY 15, 1814

Calhoun's speech is in favor of a bill to authorize the President, James Madison, to raise for five years' service, or during the war, 14 regiments of infantry. The speech develops the sense of his early nationalism in terms of his conception of a "defensive" war. Opposition to the war in general and this bill in particular was intense and sectional. In this speech Calhoun spoke for the majority against a New England minority. It is significant that the representatives of the New England minority, for example, Pickering, spoke against the war in terms of states' rights while Calhoun's views on the position of minority opposition as expressed in this speech might later have been used against the South.

Mr. CALHOUN did not rise, he said, to examine on what terms the President had assented to negotiate with the British Government; because he conceived it neither pertinent to the present question, nor proper at this time. He deemed it, however, his duty to state, that he wholly dissented from the construction which our oponents gave to the documents connected with this subject. If a proper opportunity should hereafter occur he would be happy to present the reasons for his opinion on this point.

He was induced to occupy the time of the Committee at present, to correct two essential errors, which gentlemen in the opposition have introduced into the discussion of this question; and, although not immediately connected with the merits of the bill, he thought it proper that they should be answered; because, from all that he had ever heard, as well on this as former occasions, it seemed to him that they constituted the basis on which the minority rested their justification. He alluded to the character which they gave to the war; and the claim set up in a political and Constitutional point of view to justify their opposition. Gentlemen contend that this is not a defensive but an offensive war; and under that character undertake its denunciation, without ever condescending to state what in their opinion constitutes the characteristic difference between them. He claimed the attention of the Committee while he examined this point; and he hoped that it would not be considered as a mere verbal criticism, since our opponents have made the distinction the foundation of so much declamation against the war. The inquiry, in another point of view, he believed, would be useful. The people of this country have an aversion to an offensive war; which he supposed interpreted the meaning of the vehemence of the Opposition on this subject; while they readily acknowledge the possible necessity and justice of one that is defensive. It is therefore proper, that our ideas on this point should be fixed with precision and certainty. He would lay it down as an universal criterion, that a war is offensive or defensive, not by the mode of carrying it on, which is an immaterial circumstance, but by the motive and cause which led to it. If it has its origin in ambition, avarice, or any of the like passions, then is it offensive; but if, on the contrary, to repel insult, injury, or oppression, it is of an opposite character, and is defensive. The truth of this position would not require much discussion. He conceived that it might safely rely on the authority of the best writers on the subject, or on its own internal evidence. It is only in this view that the prevalent feelings on this subject can be explained. If the distinction taken is a correct one; if the two species of war are distinguishable in their cause and motive, then our aversion to the one and approbation of the other is no longer a mystery—it is founded in the nature of things. But if, on the contrary, it is true that they are distinguished by the mere accidental circumstance of the mode of carrying them on, that the scene of action should make them the one or the other, then the feelings of this country, by which it condemns or approves of either species, is a profound mystery, never to be explained. In the view which he had presented, the difference between an offensive and defensive war is of the moral kind; and the American sense of justice accounts for their feelings. Their exemption from ambition and love of justice preserves them from the former, while their manly spirit and good sense will always make them cheerfully meet the other whenever it becomes necessary. What, then, is the character of the war in which we are now engaged? Was it dictated by avarice or love of conquest? He appealed to our opponents for a decision. They have already decided. When the resolutions of the gentleman from New Hampshire were under discussion, at the last session, it was repeated till the ear was fatigued, by every one on that side of the House who took any part in the debate, that if the repeal of the Berlin and Milan decrees had been communicated in time to the British Government, the Orders in Council would have been repealed; and, had the last event happened, the war would not have been declared. They then have acknowledged, that the Orders in Council, and not the conquest of Canada, as they now pretend, was the cause of the war; and it would be idle to inquire whether to resist them was in its nature offensive or defensive. It would be to inquire whether they were or were not an injury to our commerce; a point he had never heard denied by the most obstinate debater. It would be equally so to examine whether the cause of continuing the war, to protect our seamen from impressment, is of an offensive or defensive character.

Very few have the hardihood to deny that it is an injury of the most serious kind, both as it regards the Government, and the unhappy subjects of its operations. It involved the most sacred obligation which can bind the body politic to the citizen; he meant that of protection, due alike to all; to the beggar in the street—much more, if susceptible of degrees, to our sailors, that class of the community who have added so much to the wealth and renown of this country. Having thus established the character of the war in its origin and continuance, he would lay down as a rule not less clear, that a defensive war does not become offensive by being carried beyond the limits of our territory. The motive and cause will ever give character; all the rest are mere essential incidents. When once declared, the only question, even in a defensive war, is, how can it be carried on with the greatest effect. The reverse of this involves the most glaring absurdity. It supposes that we had determined to compel our enemy to respect our rights; and at the same time voluntarily renounced, what is acknowledged to be the best and most effectual mode of producing that effect. On this point, as well as the cause of the war, the opinion of our opponents may be arrayed against themselves. What have they advised as to the mode of carrying on the war? Withdraw your troops from Canada, reduce your army, and limit your operations to the ocean. What! to the ocean? Carry the war beyond our own territory! make it offensive! The gentlemen surely do not intend to support an offensive war. To use their own language, it is too immoral for a virtuous and religious people. It is then admitted, that it does not cease to be offensive by its being waged at sea; how then can the carrying it into Canada change its character?

Mr. C. again observed, that it was a mere question of expediency where and how the war ought to be prosecuted. For his part, so long as it continued, he thought no effort ought to be wanting to reduce Canada. Should success accompany our arms, we would be indemnified for the privations and expenses of the war, by the acquisition of an extensive and valuable territory, and the permanent peace and security which it would afford a large portion of our country; and even, in the worst event, should we fail of conquest, the attempt will not be without great advantages. The war in Canada is the best security to every part of our country. We have a very extended, and, from the thinness of the population, in many places weak seacoast. He did not believe that it had been neglected, as represented by the gentleman from New Hampshire; but he did believe that many points are, and must from necessity be, without efficient protection. He would, however, ask that gentleman, how did it happen that this coast, so easily assailed by a maritime Power, has sustained little or no damage in a war that has continued upwards of eighteen months? If he is at a loss for an answer, the scheme of his political friend from Virginia, (Mr. SHEFFEY,) to confine our troops to the defensive, should it succeed, would the next Summer amply explain the fact. The truth is, that the war in Canada is the security of the coast. It compels the enemy to concentrate the whole of his disposable force there for the defense of his own territory. Were the absurd policy to be adopted to confine the operation of our troops within our own limits, the whole of the enemy's force in Canada would be liberated from its defence, and the entire line of our seacoast menaced with destruction. The enemy, masters on the ocean, could act with such celerity, that it would be either impossible to defend ourselves, or it must be done at an expense greater than would be necessary to reduce his possessions. Thus, even under the limited view of defence, the most effectual mode is that which has been adopted—to carry the war into the enemy's country; and our opponents ought, according to their own distinction, to grant every aid in men and money.

Mr. C. said, that although not immediately in point, he could not refrain from observing that, of all the arguments he had ever heard since he had the honor of a seat in this House, those were by far the most extravagant which have been urged against the conquest of Canada. He had heard it characterized by every epithet which indicated vice or weakness. The advancers of such arguments surely did not reflect that, in their zeal to assail the majority, they were uttering libels on the founders of our liberty and empire. This scheme of conquest, this project of ambition, this product of folly and vice, as it has been liberally called, originated with those men to whom America owes so much, and whose wisdom and virtue is acknowledged by the world. It was by them thought an object worthy of the treasures and the best blood of the country; and, finally, relinquished by them with reluctance, and from necessity only.

Mr. C. said, it now remained to consider the defense which gentlemen have made for their opposition to the war and the policy of their country; a subject which he conceives is of the greatest importance, not only as affecting the result of the present contest, but the lasting peace and prosperity of our country. They assume as a fact, that opposition is in its nature harmless; and that the calamities which have afflicted free States have originated in the blunders and folly of the Government, and not from the perverseness of opposition. Opposition, say they, is a very convenient thing; a wicked and foolish Administration never fail to attribute all of their miscarriages to it; and, in confirmation of this doctrine, they appeal to Lord North's administration. He did not intend to examine the particular case to which gentlemen have with so much parade referred, as it did not fall in the course of his argument; but he thought that it could be easily proven to be essentially different, in character and consequence, from the opposition in this country. He conceived, however, that it would be proper, before he examined the general position taken over the way, to make a single remark, as it related to the British Government, on this subject. It struck him, that all arguments drawn from it on this point must be essentially erroneous. A more determined and vehement opposition there, is not only justifiable, but in some measure required. The difference in the two Governments, in this respect, results from a difference in the organization of their respective Executives. In England, such is its power, patronage, and consequent influence; such the veneration, which its hereditary quality and long descent possess over the subjects of that Empire, that her most enlightened statesmen have ever thought that it endangered the other branches of her Government, and have with much wisdom, ever since the dawn of liberty in that country, strenuously opposed its encroachments. Very different is the case here, under a Government purely Republican. It presents neither the cause to justify such vehemence of opposition, nor the means of restraining it when excited. But, even as applied to our Government, he would readily acknowledge there was a species of opposition, both innocent and useful. Opposition simply implies contrariety of opinion; and, when used in the abstract, it admitted neither censure nor praise. It cannot be said to be either good or bad; useful or pernicious. It is not from itself, but from the connected circumstances, that it derives its character. When it is simply the result of that diversity in the structure of our intellect, which conducts to different conclusions on the same subject, and is confined within those bounds which love of country and political honesty prescribe, it is one of the most useful guardians of liberty. It excites gentle collision, prompts to due vigilance, a quality so indispensable, and at the same time so opposite to our nature, and results in the establishment of an enlightened policy and useful laws. Such are its qualities when united with patriotism and moderation. But in many instances it assumes a far different character. Combined with faction and ambition, it bursts those limits, within which it may usefully act, and becomes the first of political evils. If, sir, the gentlemen on the other side of the House intended to include this last species of opposition, as he was warranted to infer from their expression, when they spoke of its harmless character, then have they made an assertion in direct contradiction to reason, experience, and all history. A factious opposition is compounded of such elements, that no reflecting man will ever consider it as harmless. The fiercest and most ungovernable passions of our nature, ambition, pride, rivalry, and hate, enter into its dangerous composition—made still more so by its power of delusion, by which its projects against Government are covered in most instances, even to the eyes of its victims, by the specious show of patriotism. Thus constituted, who can estimate its force? Where can benevolent and social feelings be found sufficiently strong to counteract its progress? Is love of country? Alas! the attachment to a party becomes stronger than that to our country. A factious opposition sickens at the sight of the prosperity and success of the country. Common adversity is its life; general prosperity its death. Nor is it only over our virtuous sentiments that this bane of freedom triumphs. Even the selfish passions of our nature, planted in our bosom for our individual safety, afford no obstacle to its progress. It is this opposition which gentlemen call harmless, and treat with so much respect; it is this moral treason, to use the language of his friend from Tennessee, (Mr. GRUNDY,) which has in all ages and countries ever proved the most deadly foe to freedom. Nor is it then only dangerous, when it breaks forth into open treason and rebellion. Without resort to violence, it is capable in a thousand ways to counteract and deaden all the motions of Government; to render its policy wavering, and to compel it to submit to schemes of aggrandizement on the part of other Governments; or, if resistance is determined on, to render it feeble and ineffectual. Do gentlemen ask for instances? Unhappily, they are but too numerous. Where shall they not be found? Admired and lamented Republics of antiquity!—Athens, Carthage, and Rome—you are the victims and witnesses of the fell spirit of factious opposition. Fatal fields of Zama and Chaeronea! you can attest its destructive cruelty. What is the history of Polybius, and that of the other historians of the free States of antiquity? What the political speeches of

Cicero, and the orations of Demosthenes, those models of eloquence and wisdom, but volumes of evidence, attesting that an opposition founded in faction, unrestrained by moderation and a regard to the general welfare, is the most dangerous of political evils. Nor does antiquity alone testify. The history of modern times is pregnant with examples. What, he would ask, have became of the free States of modern Italy, which once flourished in wealth and power—Florence, Genoa, Venice, and many others? What of the United Provinces and Switzerland? Gone; perished under the deadly feuds of opposition. Even England, with her deep-rooted and powerful Executive, has not been free from its pernicious effect. What arrested the war of Marlborough, when France was so humbled that, had it been continued, Europe might have been free from the danger which she has experienced from that Power? What staid the conquering hand of Chatham, when before his genius and power the throne of the Bourbons trembled to its centre? The spirit of factious opposition, that common cause of calamity, that without which liberty might be eternal, and free States irresistible.

Our country, as young as she is, also has her examples. In the war of the Revolution had she been united to a man; had there been no apologists of opposition; had no one opposed his will to the general determination, would the enemy ever had a hold in our country, or would that contest have lasted for a year, or would we have been indebted to foreign aid for the establishment of our independence? Even in this war, how much has it debilitated the energies of our country! The gentleman from New Hampshire, who spoke with ingenuity on this subject, told us that if we were united the Canadas would be reduced in thirty days; and that in consequence of our disasters, springing from our divisions, we had been disgraced. What more could he say on the fatal effect of opposition? Mr. C. appealed to that gentleman to state the cause of our divisions; and would ask him, whether, with the certain knowledge of its pernicious effect, every means that could excite opposition had not been unceasingly applied? To obviate the natural conclusion, the gentleman from New Hampshire was compelled to deny that the party now in power is a majority in this country; and to contend that the representation in this body furnishes no evidence of that fact. He argued, that many who are opposed to the war were from party motives induced to vote for those in favor of it. Even admitting the argument to be well founded, which he did not think, might it not be retorted? He would be glad to know why the rule does not apply to the minority in an equal degree? Until he assigned some reason why it did not, he must continue to consider the majority here, as representing a great majority of the nation; and the minority as opposing the will of that majority.

Mr. C. said, that the pretensions and declarations of the gentlemen on the other side of the House, had compelled him to make these general observations. He knew not how else they could be met, and he thought these arguments were fraught with doctrines so erroneous and dangerous, that it was his duty to present their falsity in the best manner in his power to this House and nation. From the same sense of duty, he felt bound to offer his sentiments on a subject of great delicacy; he meant on the character of the opposition which the Government has experienced since the commencement of the present difficulties in 1806, and to inquire under which of the two species of opposition, the moderate and useful, or factious and dangerous, it ought to be arranged. It was with pain he would make this inquiry. He took no pleasure in perceiving the faults of any part of our citizens, much less in presenting them to the public. His object was not to expose, but to reform; to admonish of a danger so natural to free States, to which all opposition, even of the most virtuous kind, so easily degenerates, if not incessantly watched; and to call on them, while yet possible, to arrest its fatal career. It is important to know, that there is a stage in the progress of opposition, which gentlemen consider as harmless, which when once attained, no power can arrest; not love of country; not even the certainty of being involved in the common destruction. Has it made any progress in this country to so dangerous a state? He feared there were appearances which would justify such a belief. One of its most natural symptoms, was a settled and fixed character, which, as its object was to embarrass and weaken Government, lost no opportunity to throw impediments in the way of every measure. It had two other concomitants; the one, a violence and vehemence not warranted by any considerations of expediency; and the other, urging of measures, which, if adopted, must lead to national ruin. It seemed to him that there were reasons to believe that the whole of these existed in the present Opposition. Is it not settled and fixed? In an unexampled state of national difficulties, from the first belligerent decree against our neutral commerce down to this day, he would ask which one of all the measures of our Government to resist this almost universal depredation, that has not, under one pretext or another, been opposed, ridiculed and weakened? Yes, opposed with a violence that would lead to a belief that the constituted authorities, instead of opposing the most gross and outrageous injustice, sought only the destruction of their country. Again, what have been the measures that the Opposition has virtually urged? What is it at this moment? Withhold the laws; withhold the loans; withhold the men who are to fight our battles; or, in other words, to destroy public faith, and deliver the country unarmed to the mercy of the enemy. Suppose all of their objects accomplished, and what would be the situation of the country? He appealed to the people for a decision. Nor are those morbid symptoms confined to this body. The contagion has gone forth into the community, and, wherever it has appeared, has exhibited the same dangerous appearances. The inquiry might be pushed much farther; but he would abstain from it, as it was to him by no means a pleasant task. But, say the gentlemen on the other side of the House, what right have we to object? the Constitution justifies and secures them in opposition to the measures of Government. They claim to be not only above laws, but beyond animadversion. It is in their eyes fair and proper that the majority, who act under the undoubted and express sanction of the Constitution, should be subjected to every species of abuse and impediment; but should any one question the right or the expediency of the opposition, we hear an immediate cry of oppression. For his part, he thought that a fair and moderate opposition ought at all times to be respected; but that our Constitution authorized that dangerous and vicious species, which he had attempted to describe, he utterly denied. He called on those who made the claim to so extravagant a power, to point out the article of that instrument which would warrant such a construction. Will they cite that which establishes the liberty of speech here? Its object was far different; and it furnishes not the shadow of such a power. Will they rely on its general spirit? It knows no object but the general good, and must forever condemn all fictitious opposition to measures emanating from its own authority. It is then not authorized either by the letter or the spirit of the Constitution. If then our opponents have the right, it is because it is not expressly forbidden. In this sense, there is no limitation to their Constitutional rights. A right might be thus derived to violate the whole decalogue. The Constitution forbids almost no crimes; nor ought it to be considered in the light of a voluminous penal code, whose object was the definition and prohibition of all acts injurious to society. Even had this been the case, the argument, that what is not forbid is justified, would be fallacious; for there are many acts of the most dangerous tendency, (of which an unprincipled opposition is one,) which in their very nature are not susceptible of that rigid definition necessary to subject them to punishment. How absurd, then, the argument, as applied to the Constitution, whose object is the mere enumeration, distribution, and organization of the powers of the body politic!

Mr. C. concluded by again observing, that he was compelled by the great and dangerous errors of the gentlemen on the other side, to take a view more general, than what was usually proper, of a subject on which it was so important to think correctly; and he could not take his seat without reiterating his admonition to this body and the country, to guard against the pernicious effect of a factious opposition. Universal experience and the history of all ages furnish ample testimony of its dangerous consequences, particularly in a state of war. Could any certain remedy be applied to restrain it within the bounds of moderation, then, indeed, might our liberty be immortal. He knew of none but the good sense and the virtue of the people. The triumph of a party can be nothing to them. They can have no interest but in the general welfare.

3 ON THE TARIFF BILL, APRIL 4, 1816

The breadth of Calhoun's early nationalism is evident in the favorable views of manufacturing expressed here which included the conception of a protective tariff. Indeed, his argument for the tariff bill of April, 1816, provided his later opponents, for example, Senator Wilkins of Pennsylvania, with the data they used in 1833 to charge Calhoun with inconsistency. His speech, as Calhoun said, was extemporaneous. He was called from work on a currency report to answer arguments, particularly those of John Randolph, concerning amendments to the bill. This speech, however, fairly represents his early beliefs and it stands in marked contrast to his later opinions as expressed in his speech "On the Revenue Collection (Force) Bill, February 15-16, 1833" reprinted below.

The debate heretofore on this subject, has been on the degree of protection which ought to be afforded to our cotton and woollen manufactures; all professing to be friendly to those infant establishments, and to be willing to extend to them adequate encouragement. The present motion assumes a new aspect. It is introduced professedly on the ground that manufactures ought not to receive any encouragement, and will, in its operation, leave our cotton establishments exposed to the competition of the cotton goods of the East Indies, which, it is acknowledged on all sides, they are not capable of meeting with success, without the proviso proposed to be stricken out by the motion now under discussion. Until the debate assumed this new form, he had determined to be silent; participating, as he largely did, in that general anxiety which is felt, after so long and laborious a session, to return to the bosom of our families. But on a subject of such vital importance, touching, as it does, the security and permanent prosperity of our country, he hoped that the House would indulge him in a few observations. He regretted much his want of preparation—he meant not a verbal preparation, for he had ever despised such, but that due and mature meditation and arrangement of thought, which the House is entitled to on the part of those who occupy any portion of their time. But whatever his arguments might want on that account in weight, he hoped might be made up in the disinterestedness of his situation. He was no manufacturer; he was not from that portion of our country supposed to be peculiarly interested. Coming, as he did, from the South, having, in common with his immediate constitutents, no interest but in the cultivation of the soil, in selling its products high, and buying cheap the wants and conveniences of life, no motive could be attributed to him but such as were disinterested.

He had asserted, that the subject before them was connected with the security of the country. It would, doubtless, by some be considered a rash assertion, but he conceived it to be susceptible of the clearest proof, and he hoped, with due attention, to establish it to the satisfaction of the House.

The security of a country mainly depends on its spirit and its means; and the latter principally on its moneyed resources. Modified as the industry of this country now is, combined with our peculiar situation, and want of a naval ascendency, whenever we have the misfortune to be involved in a war with a nation dominant on the ocean, and it is almost only with such we can at present be, the moneyed resources of the country, to a great extent, must fail. He took it for granted, that it was the duty of this body to adopt those measures of prudent foresight which the event of war made necessary. We cannot, he presumed, be indifferent to dangers from abroad, unless, indeed, the House is prepared to indulge in the phantom of eternal peace, which seemed to possess the dream of some of its members. Could such a state exist, no foresight or fortitude would be necessary to conduct the affairs of the Republic; but as it is the mere illusion of the imagination—as every people, who ever has or ever will exist, are subjected to the vicissitudes of peace and war, it must ever be considered as the plain dictate of wisdom, in peace to prepare for war. What, then, let us consider, constitute the resources of this country, and what are the effects of war on them? Commerce and agriculture, till lately, almost the only, still constitute the principle sources of our wealth. So long as these remain uninterrupted, the country prospers; but war, as we are now circumstanced, is equally destructive to both. They both depend on foreign markets, and our country is placed, as it regards them, in a situation strictly insular; a wide ocean rolls between. Our commerce neither is or can be protected by the present means of the country. What, then, are the effects of a war with a maritime Power—with England? Our commerce annihilated, spreading individual misery, and producing national poverty; our agriculture cut off from its accustomed markets, the surplus product of the farmer perishes on his hands; and he ceases to produce, because he cannot sell. His resources are dried up, while his expenses are greatly increased; as all manufactured articles, the necessaries as well as the conveniencies of life, rise to an extravagant price. The recent war fell with peculiar pressure on the growers of cotton and tobacco, and other great staples of the country; and the same state of things will recur in the event of another, unless prevented by the foresight of this body. If the mere statement of facts did not carry conviction to any mind, as he conceived it is calculated to do, additional arguments might be drawn from the general nature of wealth. Neither agriculture, manufactures, nor commerce, taken separately, is the cause of wealth; it flows from the three combined, and cannot exist without each. The wealth of any single nation, or any individual, it is true, may not immediately depend on the three, but such wealth always presupposes their existence. He viewed the words in the most enlarged sense. Without commerce, industry would have no stimulus; without manufactures, it would be without the means of production; and without agriculture, neither of the others can subsist. When separated entirely and permanently, they perish. War in this country produces, to a great extent, that effect; and hence the great embarrassments which follow in its train. The failure of the wealth and resources of the nation necessarily involved the ruin of its finances and its currency. It is admitted, by the most strenuous advocates on the other side, that no country ought to be dependent on another for its means of defence; that, at least, our musket and bayonet, our cannon and ball, ought to be of domestic manufacture. But what, he asked, is more necessary to the defence of a country than its currency and finance? Circumstanced as our country is, can these stand the shock of war? Behold the effect of the late war on them! When our manufactures are grown to a certain perfection, as they soon will under the fostering care of Government, we will no longer experience these evils. The farmer will find a ready market for his surplus produce; and, what is almost of equal consequence, a certain and cheap supply of all his wants. His prosperity will diffuse itself to every class in the community; and instead of that languor of industry, and individual distress now incident to a state of war and suspended commerce, the wealth and vigor of the community will not be materially impaired. The arm of Government will be nerved, and taxes in the hour of danger, when essential to the independence of the nation, may be greatly increased; loans, so uncertain and hazardous, may be less relied on; thus situated, the storm may beat without, but within all will be quiet and safe. To give perfection to this state of things it will be necessary to add, as soon as possible, a system of internal improvements, and at least such an extension of our navy as will prevent the cutting off our coasting trade. The advantage of each is so striking, as not to require illustration, especially after the experience of the recent war. It is thus the resources of this Government and people would be placed beyond the power of a foreign war materially to impair—But it may be said, that the derangement then experienced resulted, not from the cause assigned, but from the errors or the weakness of the Government. He admitted that many financial blunders were committed, for the subject was new to us; that the taxes were not laid sufficiently early or to as great an extent as they ought to have been; and that the loans were in some instances injudiciously made; but he ventured to affirm, that had the greatest foresight and fortitude been exerted, the embarrassment would have been still very great; and that even under the best management, the total derangement which was actually felt would not have been postponed eighteen months, had the war so long continued. How could it be otherwise? A war, such as this country was then involved in, in a great measure dries up the resources of individuals, as he had already proved; and the resources of the Government are no more than the aggregate of the surplus incomes of individuals, called into action by a system of taxation. It is certainly a great political evil, incident to the character of the industry of this country, that, however prosperous our situation when at peace, with uninterrupted commerce, and nothing then could exceed it, the moment that we were involved in war the whole is reversed. When resources are most needed; when indispensable to maintain the honor, yes, the very existence of the nation, then they desert us. Our currency is also sure to experience the shock, and becomes so deranged, as to prevent us from calling out fairly whatever of means is left to the country. The result of a war in the present state of our naval power, is the blockade of our seacoast, and consequent destruction of our trade. The wants and habits of the country, founded on the use of foreign articles, must be gratified; importation to a certain extent continues, through the policy of the enemy, or unlawful traffic; the exportation of our bulky articles is prevented, too; the specie of the country is drawn to pay the balance perpetually accumulating against us; and the final result is a total derangement of our currency.

To this distressing state of things there were two remedies, and only two; one in our power immediately, the other requiring much time and exertion; but both constituting, in his opinion, the essential policy of this country; he meant the Navy, and domestic manufactures. By the former, we could open the way to our markets; by the latter, we bring them from beyond the ocean, and naturalize them. Had we the means of attaining an immediate naval ascendency, he acknowledged that the policy recommended by this bill would be very questionable; but as this is not the fact—as it is a period remote, with any exertion, and will be probably more so, from that relaxation of exertion, so natural in peace, when necessity is not felt, it became the duty of this House to resort, to a considerable extent, at least as far as is proposed, to the only remaining remedy. But to this it has been objected, that the country is not prepared, and that the result of our premature exertion would be to bring distress on it, without effecting the intended object. Were it so, however urgent the reasons in its favor, we ought to desist, as it is folly to oppose the laws of necessity. But he could not for a moment yield to the assertion; on the contrary, he firmly believed that the country is prepared, even to maturity, for the introduction of manufactures. We have abundance of resources, and things naturally tend at this moment in that direction. A prosperous commerce has poured an immense amount of commercial capital into this country. This capital has, until lately, found occupation in commerce; but that state of the world which transferred it to this country, and gave it active employment, has passed away, never to return. Where shall we now find full employment for our prodigious amount of tonnage; where markets for the numerous and abundant products of our country? This great body of active capital, which for the moment has found sufficient employment in supplying our markets, exhausted by the war, and measures preceding it, must find a new direction; it will not be idle. What channel can it take but that of manufactures? This, if things continue as they are, will be its direction. It will introduce a new era in our affairs, in many respects highly advantageous, and ought to be countenanced by the Government. Besides, we have already surmounted the greatest difficulty that has ever been found in undertakings of this kind. The cotton and woollen manufactures are not to be introduced—they are already introduced to a great extent; freeing us entirely from the hazards, and, in a great measure, the sacrifices experienced in giving the capital of the country a new direction. The restrictive measures and the war, though not intended for that purpose, have, by the necessary operation of things, turned a large amount of capital to this new branch of industry. He had often heard it said, both in and out of Congress, that this effect alone would indemnify the country for all of its losses. So high was this tone of feeling, when the want of these establishments was practically felt, that he remembered, during the war, when some question was agitated respecting the introduction of foreign goods, that many then opposed it on the ground of injuring our manufactures. He then said that war alone furnished sufficient stimulus, and perhaps too much, as it would make their growth unnaturally rapid; but, that on the return of peace, it would then be time to show our affection for them. He at that time did not expect an apathy and aversion to the extent which is now seen. But it will no doubt be said, if they are so far established, and if the situation of the country is so favorable to their growth, where is the necessity of affording them protection? It is to put them beyond the reach of contingency. Besides, capital is not yet, and cannot, for some time, be adjusted to the new state of things. There is, in fact, from the operation of temporary causes, a great pressure on these establishments. They had extended so rapidly during the late war, that many, he feared, were without the requisite surplus capital or skill to meet the present crisis. Should such prove to be the fact, it would give a back set, and might, to a great extent, endanger their ultimate success. Should the present owners be ruined, and the workmen dispersed and turn to other pursuits, the country would sustain a great loss. Such would, no doubt, be the fact to a considerable extent, if not protected. Besides, cir-sumstances, if we act with wisdom, are favorable to attract to our country much skill and industry. The country in Europe having the most skilful workmen is broken up. It is to us, if wisely used, more valuable than the repeal of the Edict of Nantz was to England. She had the prudence to profit by it; let us not discover less political sagacity. Afford to ingenuity and industry immediate and ample protection, and they will not fail to give a preference to this free and happy country.

It has been objected to this bill, that it will injure our marine, and consequently impair our naval strength. How far it is fairly liable to this charge, he was not prepared to say. He hoped and believed it would not, at least to any alarming extent, have that effect immediately; and he firmly believed that its lasting operation would be highly beneficial to our commerce. The trade to the East Indies would certainly be much affected; but it was stated in debate that the whole of that trade employed but six hundred sailors. But whatever might be the loss in this, or other branches of our foreign commerce, he trusted it would be amply compensated in our coasting trade—a branch of navi-gation wholly in our own hands. It has at all times employed a great amount of tonnage, something more, he believed, than one-third of the whole; nor is it liable to the imputation thrown out by a member from North Carolina, (Mr. Gaston,) that it pro-duced inferior sailors. It required long and dangerous voyages; and, if his information was correct, no branch of trade made better or more skilful seamen. The fact that it is wholly in our own hands is a very important one, while every branch of our foreign trade must suffer from competition with other nations.

Other objections, of a political character, were made to the encouragement of manufactures. It is said they destroy the moral and physical power of the people. This might formerly have been true to a considerable extent, before the perfection of machinery, and when the success of the manufactures depended on the minute subdivision of labor. At that time it required a large portion of the population of a country to be engaged in them; and every minute subdivision of labor is undoubtedly unfavorable to the intellect; but the great perfection of machinery has in a considerable degree obviated these objections. In fact it has been stated that the manufacturing districts in England furnish the greatest number of recruits to her army, and that, as soldiers, they are not materially inferior to the rest of her population. It has been further asserted that manufactures are the fruitful cause of pauperism, and England has been referred to as furnishing conclusive evidence of its truth. For his part, he could perceive no such tendency in them, but the exact contrary, as they furnished new stimulus and means of subsistence to the laboring classes of the community. We ought not to look to the cotton and woollen establishments of Great Britain for the prodigious numbers of poor with which her population was disgraced. Causes much more efficient exist. Her poor laws, and statutes regulating the price of labor, with heavy taxes, were the real causes. But if it must be so; if the mere fact that England manufactured more than any other country, explained the cause of her having more beggars, it is just as reasonable to refer her courage, spirit, and all her masculine virtues, in which she excels all other nations, with a single exception—he meant our own—in which we might without vanity challenge a preeminence. Another objection had been made, which he must acknowledge was better founded, that capital employed in manufacturing produced a greater dependence on the part of the employed, than in commerce, navigation, or agriculture. It is certainly an evil, and to be regretted; but he did not think it a decisive objection to the system, especially when it had incidental political advantages which, in his opinion, more than counterpoised it. It produced an interest strictly American, as much so as agriculture; in which it had the decided advantage of commerce or navigation. The country will from this derive much advantage. Again, it is calculated to bind together more closely our widely-spread Republic. It will greatly increase our mutual dependence and intercourse; and will, as a necessary consequence, excite an increased attention to internal improvement—a subject every way so intimately connected with the ultimate attainment of national strength, and the perfection of our political institutions. He regarded the fact that it would make the parts adhere more closely; that it would form a new and most powerful cement, far outweighting any political objections that might be urged against the system. In his opinion the liberty and the union of the country were inseparably united. That as the destruction of the latter would most certainly involve the former, so its maintenance will with equal certainty preserve it. He did not speak lightly. He had often and long revolved it in his mind, and he had critically examined into the causes that destroyed the liberty of other States. There are none that apply to us, or apply with a force to alarm. The basis of our Republic is too broad, and its structure too strong to be shaken by them. Its extension and organization will be found to afford effectual security against their operation; but let it be deeply impressed on the heart of this House and country, that while they guarded against the old, they exposed us to a new and terrible danger—disunion. This single word comprehended almost the sum of our political dangers; and against it we ought to be perpetually guarded.

4 ON THE REVENUE COLLECTION (FORCE) BILL, FEBRUARY 15-16, 1833

After his break with Jackson during the Nullification crisis, Calhoun resigned the Vice-Presidency and went home. Returning to Washington as a Senator and as a defender of the South, he half expected to be arrested. He was not. He began his career as a Senator with the first of a series of debates with Webster, in which he expressed the sectional perspective of his thought in its relation to his previous views and to the future. His references in this speech to his previous views were chiefly those stated in "On the Tariff Bill, April 4, 1816," reprinted above.

He knew not, he said, which was most objectionable, the provision of the bill, or the temper in which its adoption had been urged. If the extraordinary powers with which the bill proposed to clothe the Executive, to the utter prostration of the constitution and the rights of the States, be calculated to impress our minds with alarm at the rapid progress of despotism in our country, the zeal with which every circumstance calculated to misrepresent or exaggerate the conduct of Carolina in the controversy was seized on, with a view to excite hostility against her, but too plainly indicated the deep decay of that brotherly feeling which once existed between these States, and to which we are indebted for our beautiful federal system. It was not his intention, he said, to advert to all these misrepresentations; but there were some so well calculated to mislead the mind as to the real character of the controversy, and to hold up the State in a light so odious, that he did not feel himself justified in permitting them to pass unnoticed.

Among them, one of the most prominent was the false statement that the object of South Carolina was to exempt herself from her share of the public burdens, while she participated in the advantages of the Government. If the charge were true, if the State were capable of being actuated by such low and unworthy motives, mother as he considered her, he would not stand up on this floor to vindicate her conduct. Among her faults, (and faults he would not deny she had,) no one had ever yet charged her with that low and most sordid of vices, avarice. Her conduct on all occasions had been marked with the very opposite quality. From the commencement of the revolution, from its first breaking out at Boston till this hour, no State had been more profuse of its blood in the cause of the country; nor had any contributed so largely to the common treasury, in proportion to her wealth and population. She had in that proportion contributed more to the exports of the Union, on the exchange of which, with the rest of the world, the greater portion of the public burden had been levied, than any other State. No, the controversy was not such as had been stated; the State did not seek to participate in the advantages of the Government without contributing her full share to the public treasury. Her object was far different. A deep constitutional question lay at the bottom of the controversy. The real question at issue is, has the Government a right to impose burdens on the capital and industry of one portion of the country, not with a view to revenue, but to benefit another? And he must be permitted to say that, after the long and deep agitation of this controversy, it was with surprise that he perceived so strong a disposition to misrepresent its real character. To correct the impressions which those misrepresentations were calculated to make, he would dwell on the point under consideration for a few moments longer.

The Federal Government has, by an express provision of the constitution, the right to lay duties on imports. The State has never denied or resisted this right, nor even thought of so doing. The Government has, however, not been contented with exercising this power as she had a right to do, but had gone a step beyond it, by laying imposts, not for revenue, but for protection. This the State considered as an unconstitutional exercise of power, highly injurious and oppressive to her and the other staple States, and had accordingly met it with the most determined resistance. He did not intend to enter, at this time, into the argument as to the unconstitutionality of the protective system. It was not necessary. It is sufficient that the power is no where granted; and that, from the journals of the convention which formed the constitution, it would seem that it had been refused. In support of the journals, he might cite the statement of Luther Martin, which had been already referred to, to show that the convention, so far from conferring the power on the Federal Government, had left to the State the right to impose duties on imports, with the express view of enabling the several States to protect their own manufactures. Notwithstanding this, Congress had assumed, without any warrant from the constitution, the right of exercising this most important power, and had so exercised it as to impose a ruinous burden on the labor and capital of the State, by which her resources were exhausted, the enjoyments of her citizens curtailed, the means of education contracted, and all her interests essentially and injuriously affected. We have been sneeringly told that she was a small State; that her population did not much exceed half a million of souls; and that more than one-half were not of the European race. The facts were so. He knew she never could be a great State, and that the only distinction to which she could aspire must be based on the moral and intellectual acquirements of her sons. To the development of these, much of her attention had been directed; but this restrictive system, which had so unjustly exacted the proceeds of her labor, to be bestowed on other sections, had so impaired the resources of the State, that, if not speedily arrested, it would dry up the means of education, and, with it, deprive her of the only source through which she could aspire to distinction.

There was another misstatement as to the nature of the controversy so frequently made in debate, and so well calculated to mislead, that he felt bound to notice it. It has been said that South Carolina claims the right to annul the constitution and laws of the United States; and to rebut this supposed claim, the gentleman from Virginia [Mr. RIVES] has gravely quoted the constitution, to prove that the constitution, and the laws made in pursuance thereof, are the supreme law of the land; as if the State claimed the right to act contrary to this provision of the constitution. Nothing can be more erroneous: her object is not to resist laws made in pursuance of the constitution, but those made without its authority, and which encroach on her reserved powers. She claims not even the right of judging of the delegated powers, but of those that are reserved; and to resist the former when they encroach upon the latter. He would pause to illustrate this important point.

All must admit that there are delegated and reserved powers; and that the powers reserved are reserved to the States respectively. The powers, then, of the Government are divided between the General and the State Governments; and the point immediately under consideration is, whether a State has any right to judge as to the extent of its reserved powers, and to defend them against the encroachments of the General Government. Without going deeply into this point, at this stage of the argument, or looking into the nature and origin of the Government, there was a simple view of the subject which he considered as conclusive. The very idea of a divided power implied the right, on the part of the State, for which he contended. The expression was metaphorical when applied to power. Every one readily understands that the division of matter consists in the separation of the parts. But, in this sense, it was not applicable to power. What, then, is meant by a division of power? He could not conceive of a division, without giving an equal right to each to judge of the extent of the power allotted to each. Such right he held to be essential to the existence of a division; and that to give to either party the conclusive right of judging, not only the share allotted to it, but of that allotted to the other, was to annul the division, and would confer the whole power on the party vested with such right. But it is contended that the constitution has conferred on the Supreme Court the right of judging between the States and the General Government. Those who make this objection overlooked, he conceived, an important provision of the constitution. By turning to the tenth amended article of the constitution, it will be seen that the reservation of power to the States is not only against the powers delegated to

Congress, but against the United States themselves; and extends, of course, as well to the Judiciary as to the other departments of the Government.

The article provides that all powers, not delegated to the United States, or prohibited by it to the States, are reserved to the States respectively, or to the people. This presents the inquiry, what powers are delegated to the United States? They may be classed under four divisions: First, those that are delegated by the States to each other, by virtue of which the constitution may be altered or amended by three-fourths of the States, when, without which, it would have required the unanimous vote of all. Next, the powers conferred on Congress; then those on the President; and, finally, those on the judicial department—all of which are particularly enumerated in the parts of the constitution which organize the respective departments. The reservation of powers to the States is, as he had said, against the whole, and is as full against the judicial as it is against the executive and legislative departments of the Government. It could not be claimed for the one without claiming it for the whole, and without, in fact, annulling this important provision of the constitution. Against this, as it appeared to him, conclusive view of the subject, it has been urged that this power is expressly conferred on the Supreme Court by that portion of the constitution which provides that the judicial power shall extend to all cases in law and equity arising under the constitution, the laws of the United States, and treaties made under their authority. He believed the assertion to be utterly destitute of any foundation. It obviously was the intenion of the constitution simply to make the judicial power commensurate with the law-making and treaty-making powers, and to vest it with the right of applying the constitution, the laws, and the treaties, to the cases which might arise under them; and not to make it the judge of the constitution, the laws, and the treaties themselves. In fact, the power of applying the laws to the facts of the case, and deciding upon such application, constitutes, in truth, the judicial power. The distinction between such power and that of judging of the laws would be perfectly apparent when we advert to what is the acknowledged power of the court in reference to treaties or compacts between sovereigns. It was perfectly established that the courts have no right to judge of the violation of treaties; and that, in reference to them, their power is limited to the right of judging simply of the violation of rights under them; and that the right of judging of infractions belongs exclusively to the parties themselves, and not to the courts; of which we have an example in the French treaty, which was declared by Congress null and void, in consequence of its violation by the Government of France. Without such declaration, had a French citizen sued a citizen of this country under the treaty, the court could have taken no cognizance of its infraction; nor, after such a declaration, would it have heard any argument or proof going to show that the treaty had not been violated.

The declaration, of itself, was conclusive on the court. But it would be asked, how the court obtained the power to pronounce a law or treaty unconstitutional, when they came in conflict with that instrument? He did not deny that it possesses the right, but he could by no means concede that it was derived from the constitution. It had its orgin in the necessity of the case. Where there were two or more rules established, one from a higher, and the other from a lower authority, which might come into conflict, in applying them to a particular case, the judge could not avoid pronouncing in favor of the superior against the inferior. It was from this necessity, and this alone, that the power which is now set up to overrule the rights of the States, against an express provision of the constitution, was derived. It had no other origin. That he had traced it to its true source, would be manifest from the fact, that it was a power which, so far from being conferred exclusively on the Supreme Court, as was insisted, belonged to every court, inferior and superior, State and general, and even to foreign courts.

But the Senator from Delaware [Mr. CLAYTON] relies on the journals of the convention to prove that it was the intention of that body to confer on the Supreme Court the right of deciding in the last resort between a State and the General Government. He would not follow him through the journals, as he did not deem that to be necessary to refute his argument. It was sufficient for this purpose to state, that Mr. Rutledge reported a resolution providing expressly that the United States and the States might be parties before the Supreme Court. If this proposition had been adopted, he would ask the Senator whether this very controversy between the United States and South Carolina might not have been brought before the court? He would also ask him, whether it could be brought before the court as the constitution now stands? If he answers the former in the affirmative, and the latter in the negative, as he must, then it is clear, his elaborate argument to the contrary notwithstanding, that the report of Mr. Rutledge was not in substance adopted, as he contended; and that the journals, so far from supporting, are in direct opposition to the position which he attempts to maintain. He might push the argument much further against the power of the court, but he did not deem it necessary, at least at this stage of the discussion. If the views which had already been presented be correct, and he did not see how they could be resisted, the conclusion was inevitable, that the reserved powers were reserved equally against every department of the Government, and as strongly against the judicial as against the other departments; and, of course, were left under the exclusive will of the States.

There still remained another misrepresentation of the conduct of the State, which had been made with the view of exciting odium. He alluded to the charge that South Carolina supported the tariff of 1816, and was therefore responsible for the protective system. To determine the truth of this charge, it becomes necessary to ascertain the real character of that law; whether it was a tariff for revenue or for protection; which presents the inquiry of what was the condition of the country at that period? The late war with Great Britain had just terminated, which, with the restrictive system that preceded it, had diverted a large amount of capital and industry from commerce to manufactures, particularly to the cotton and woollen branches. There was a debt, at the same time, of one hundred and thirty millions of dollars, hanging over the country; and the heavy war duties were still in existence. Under these circumstances, the question was presented, to what point the duties ought to be reduced? That question involved another—at what time the debt ought to be paid? which was a question of policy, involving in its consideration all the circumstances connected with the then condition of the country. Among the most prominent arguments in favor of an early discharge of the debt was, that the high duties which it would require to effect it would have at the same time the effect of sustaining the infant manufactures, which had been forced up under the circumstances to which he had adverted.

This view of the subject had a decided influence in determining in favor of an early payment of the debt. The sinking fund was accordingly raised from seven to ten millions of dollars, with the provision to apply the surplus which might remain in the treasury, as a contingent appropriation to that fund; and the duties were graduated to meet this increased expenditure. It was thus that the policy and justice of protecting the large amount of capital and industry, which had been diverted by the measures of the Government into new channels, as he had stated, was combined with the fiscal action of the Government; and which, while it secured a prompt payment of the debt, prevented the immense losses to the manufactures which would have followed a sudden and great reduction. Still, revenue was the main object, and protection but the incidental. The bill to reduce the duties was reported by the Committee of Ways and Means, and not of Manufactures; and it proposed a heavy reduction on the then existing rate of duties. But what, of itself, without other evidence, was decisive as to the character of the bill, is the fact that it fixed a much higher rate of duties on the unprotected than on the protected article. He would enumerate a few leading articles only: woollen and cotton, above the value of twenty-five cents on the square yard, though they were the leading objects of protection, were subject to a permanent duty of only twenty per centum. Iron, another leading article among the protected, had a protection of not more than nine per cent. as fixed by the act, and of but fifteen as reported in the bill. These rates were all below the average duties as fixed in the act, including the protected, the unprotected, and even the free articles. Mr. C. said he had entered into some calculations in order to ascertain the average rate of duties in the act. There was some uncertainty in the data, but he felt assured that it was not less than thirty per cent. ad valorem; showing an excess of the average duties, above that imposed on the protected articles enumerated, of more than ten per cent.; and thus clearly establishing the character of the measure, that it was for revenue and not protection.

Looking back, even at this distant period, with all our experience, he perceived but two errors in the act; the one in reference to iron, and the other the minimum duties on coarse cottons. As to the former, he conceived that the bill, as reported, proposed a duty relatively too low, which was still further reduced in its passage through Congress. The duty, at first, was fixed at seventy-five cents the hundredweight; but in the last stage of its passage, it was reduced; by a sort of caprice, occasioned by an unfortunate motion, to forty-five cents. This injustice was severely felt in Pennsylvania—the State, above all others, most productive of iron; and was the principal cause of that great re-action which has since thrown her so decidedly on the side of the protective policy. The other error was that as to coarse cottons, on which the duty was as much too high as that on iron was too low. It introduced, besides, the obnoxious minimum principle, which has since been so mischievously extended; and to that extent he was constrained, in candor, to acknowledge, as he wished to disguise nothing, the protective principle was recognised by the act of 1816. How this was overlooked at the time, it is not in his power to say. It escaped his observation, which he can account for only on the ground that the principle was then new, and that his attention was engaged by another important subject—the question of the currency, then so urgent, and with which, as chairman of the committee, he was particularly charged. With these exceptions, he again repeated, he saw nothing in the bill to condemn. Yet it was on the ground that the members from the State had voted for that bill, that the attempt is now made to hold up South Carolina as responsible for the whole system of protection which has since followed, though she has resisted its progress in every stage. Was there ever greater injustice? And how was it to be accounted for, but as forming a part of that systematic misrepresentation and calumny which has been directed for so many years, without interruption, against that gallant and generous State? And why has she thus been assailed? Merely because she abstained from taking any part in the Presidential canvass; believing that it had degenerated into a mere system of imposition on the people; controlled, almost exclusively, by those whose object it was to obtain the patronage of the Government, and that without regard to principle or policy. Standing apart from what she considered a contest in which the public had no interest, she has been assailed by both parties, with a fury altogether unparalleled; but which, pursuing the course which she believed liberty and duty required, she has met with a firmness equal to the fierceness of the assault. In the midst of this attack, he had not escaped.

With a view of inflicting a wound on the State, through him, he had been held up as the author of the protective system, and one of its most strenuous advocates. It was with pain that he alluded to himself on so deep and grave a subject as that now under discussion; and which, he sincerely believed, involved the liberty of the country. He now regretted, that under the sense of injustice, which the remarks of a Senator from Pennsylvania [Mr. WILKINS] excited for the moment, he had hastily given his pledge to defend himself against the charge which had been made in reference to his course in 1816; not that there would be any difficulty in repelling the charge, but because he felt a deep reluctance in turning the discussion, in any degree, from a subject of so much magnitude, to one of so little importance as the consistency or inconsistency of himself, or any other individual, particularly in connexion with an event so long since passed. But for this hasty pledge, he would have remained silent as to his own course on this occasion; and would have borne, with patience and calmness, this, with the many other misrepresentations with which he had been so incessantly assailed for many years.

The charge that he was the author of the protective system had no other foundation but that he, in common with the almost entire South, gave his support to the tariff of 1816. It is true that he advocated that measure, for which he might rest his defence, without taking any other, on the ground that it was a tariff for revenue, and not for protection; which he had established beyond the power of controversy. But his speech on the occasion had been brought in judgment against him, by the Senator from Pennsylvania. He had since cast his eyes over the speech; and he would surprise, he had no doubt, the Senator, by telling him that, with the exception of some hasty and unguarded expressions, he retracted nothing he had uttered on that occasion. He only asked that he might be judged in reference to it, in that spirit of fairness and justice which was due to the occasion; taking into consideration the circumstances under which it was delivered, and bearing in mind that the subject was a tariff for revenue and not for protection; for reducing and not raising the revenue. But, before he explained the then condition of the country, from which his main arguments in favor of the measure were drawn, it was nothing but an act of justice to himself, that he should state a fact in connexion with his speech, that was necessary to explain what he had called hasty and unguarded expressions. His speech was an impromptu; and, as such, he apologized to the House, as appears from the speech as printed, for offering his sentiments on the question, without having duly reflected on the subject. It was delivered at the request of a friend, when he had not previously the least intention of addressing the House; he alluded to Samuel D. Ingham, then, and now, as he was proud to say, a personal and political friend; a man of talents and integrity; with a clear head and firm and patriotic heart; then among the leading members of the House; in the palmy state of his political glory, though now for a moment depressed—depressed, did he say? no! it was his State which was depressed; Pennsylvania, and not Samuel D. Ingham! Pennsylvania, which had deserted him under circumstances, which, instead of depressing, ought to have elevated him in her estimation. He came to me, said Mr. C., when sitting at my desk, writing, and said that the House was falling into some confusion, accompanying it with a remark that I knew how difficult it was to rally so large a body when once broken on a tax bill, as had been experienced during the late war. Having a higher opinion of my influence than it deserved, he requested me to say something to prevent the confusion. I replied, said Mr. C., that I was at a loss what to say; that I had been busily engaged on the currency, which was then in great confusion, and which, as I had stated, had been placed particularly under my charge, as chairman of the committee on that subject. He repeated his request; and the speech which the Senator from Pennsylvania has complimented so highly was the result.

He (Mr. C.) would ask, whether the facts stated ought not, in justice, to be borne in mind by those who would hold him accountable, not only for the general scope of the speech, but for every word and sentence which it contained? But, said Mr. C., in asking this question, it was not his intention to repudiate the speech. All he asked was, that he might be judged by the rules which, in justice, belonged to the case. Let it be recollected that the bill was a revenue bill; and, of course, that it was constitutional. He need not remind the Senate, when the measure is constitutional, that all arguments calculated to show its beneficial operation may be legitimately pressed into service, without taking into consideration whether the subject to which the arguments refer be within the sphere of the constitution or not. If, for instance, a question were before the body to lay a duty on Bibles, and a motion be made to reduce the duty, or admit Bibles duty free; who could doubt that the argument in favor of the motion that the increased circulation of the Bibles would be in favor of the morality and religion of the country would be strictly proper? Or, who would suppose that he who had adduced it had committed himself, on the constitutionality of taxing the religion or morals of the country under the charge of the Federal Government? Again: Suppose the question to be to raise the duty on silk, or any other article of luxury, and that it should be supported on the ground that it was an article mainly consumed by the rich and extravagant; could it be fairly inferred that, in the opinion of the speaker, Congress had a right to pass sumptuary laws? He only asked that these plain rules be applied to his argument on the tariff of 1816. They turned almost entirely on the benefits which manufacturers conferred on the country in time of war, and which no one could doubt. The country had recently passed through such a state. The world was at that time deeply agitated by the effects of the great conflict which had so long raged in Europe, and which no one could tell how soon again might return. Bonaparte had but recently been overthrown; the whole southern part of this continent was in a state of revolution, and was threatened with the interference of the Holy Alliance, which, had it occurred, must almost necessarily have involved this country in a most dangerous conflict. It was under these circumstances that he had delivered the speech, in which he urged the House, that, in the adjustment of the tariff, reference ought to be had to a state of war as well as peace; and that its provisions ought to be fixed on the compound views of the two periods; making some sacrifice in peace, in order that the less might be made in war. Was this principle false? and, in urging it, did he commit himself to that system of oppression since grown up, and which has for its object the enriching of one portion of the country at the expense of the other?

Mr. C. said, the plain rule in all such cases was, that when a measure was proposed, the first thing was to ascertain its constitutionality: and, that being ascertained, the next was its expediency; which last opened the whole field of argument for and against. Every topic may be urged, calculated to prove it wise or unwise. So in a bill to raise imposts; it must first be ascertained that the bill is based on the principles of revenue, and that the money raised is necessary for the wants of the country. These being ascertained, every argument, direct and indirect, may be fairly offered, which may go to show that, under all the circumstances, the provisions of the bill are proper or improper. Had this plain and simple rule been adhered to, we should never have heard of the complaint of South Carolina. Her objection is not against the improper modification of a bill acknowledged to be for revenue; but that, under the name of imposts, a power, essentially different from the taxing power, is exercised; partaking much more of the character of a penalty than a tax. Nothing is more common than that things closely resembling in appearance should widely and essentially differ in their character. Arsenic, for instance, resembles flour; yet one is deadly poison, and the other that which constitutes the staff of life. So, duties imposed, whether for revenue or protection, may be called imposts; which, though nominally and apparently the same, yet differ essentially in their real character.

Mr. C. said he should now return to his speech on the tariff of 1816. To determine what his opinions really were on the subject of protection at that time, it would be proper to advert to his sentiments before and after that period. His sentiments preceding 1816, on this subject, are matter of record. He came into Congress in 1812, a devoted friend and supporter of the then administration; yet one of his first efforts was to brave the administration, by opposing its favorite measure, the restrictive system—embargo, non-intercourse, and all—and that upon the principle of free trade. The system remained in fashion for a time; but after the overthrow of Bonaparte, he (Mr. C.) had reported a bill, from the Committee on Foreign Relations, to repeal the whole system of restrictive measures.

While the bill was under consideration, a worthy man, then a member of the House, [Mr. McKim, of Baltimore,] moved to except the non-importation act, which he supported on the ground of encouragement to manufactures. He (Mr. C.) resisted the motion on the very grounds on which Mr. McKim supported it. He maintained that the manufactures were then receiving too much protection, and warned its friends that the withdrawal of the protection which the war and the high duties then afforded would cause great embarrassment; and that the true policy, in the mean time, was to admit foreign goods as freely as possible, in order to diminish the anticipated embarrassment on the return of peace; intimating, at the same time, his desire to see the tariff revised, with a view of affording a moderate and permanent protection.*

Such was his conduct before 1816. Shortly after that period he left Congress, and had no opportunity of making known his sentiments in reference to the protective system, which shortly after began to be agitated. But he had the most conclusive evidence that he considered the arrangement of the revenue in 1816 as growing out of the necessity of the case, and due to the consideration of justice; but that even at that early period he was not without his fears that even that arrangement would lead to abuse and future difficulties. He regretted that he had been compelled to dwell so long on himself; but trusted that whatever censure might be incurred would not be directed against him, but against those who had drawn his conduct into the controversy; and who might hope, by assailing his motives, to wound the cause with which he was proud to be identified.

He might add, that all the Southern States voted with South Carolina in support of the bill; not that they had any interest in manufactures, but on the ground that they had supported the war, and, of course, felt a corresponding obligation to sustain those establishments which had grown up under the encouragement it had incidentally afforded; while most of the New England members were opposed to the measure, principally, as he believed, on opposite principles.

He had now, he trusted, satisfactorily repelled the charge against the State and himself personally, in reference to the tariff of 1816. Whatever support the State had given the bill had originated in the most distinterested motives.

There was not, within the limits of the State, so far as his memory served him, a single cotton or woollen establisment. Her whole dependence was on agriculture, and the cultivation of

*See Mr. C.'s speech in the National Intelligencer, April, 1814.

two great staples, rice and cotton. Her obvious policy was to keep open the market of the world unchecked and unrestricted; to buy cheap and to sell high; but, from a feeling of kindness, combined with a sense of justice, she added her support to the bill. We had been told by the agents of the manufacturers, that the protection which the measure afforded would be sufficient; to which we the more readily conceded, as it was considered as a final adjustment of the question.

Let us now, said Mr. C., turn our eyes forward, and see what has been the conduct of the parties to this arrangement. Have Carolina and the South disturbed this adjustment? No, they have never raised their voice in a single instance against it; even though this measure, moderate comparatively as it is, was felt with no inconsiderable pressure on their interests. Was this example imitated on the opposite side? Far otherwise. Scarcely had the President signed his name, before application was made for an increase of duties, which was repeated with demands continually growing, till the passage of the act of 1828. What course now, he would ask, did it become Carolina to pursue in reference to these demands? Instead of acquiescing in them, because she had acted generously in adjusting the tariff of 1816, she saw, in her generosity on that occasion, additional motives for that firm and decided resistance which she has since made against the system of protection. She accordingly commenced a systematic opposition to all further encroachments, which continued from 1818 till 1828, by discussions and by resolutions, by remonstrances and by protests, through her Legislature. These all proved insufficient to stem the current of encroachment; but, notwithstanding the heavy pressure on her industry, she never despaired of relief till the passage of the act of 1828—that bill of abominations, engendered by avarice and political intrigue. Its adoption opened the eyes of the State, and gave a new character to the controversy. Till then the question had been whether the protective system was constitutional and expedient; but after that, she no longer considered the question whether the right of regulating the industry of the States was a reserved or delegated power, but what right a State possesses to defend her reserved powers against the encroachments of the Federal Government; a question, on the decision of which, the value of all the reserved powers depends. The passage of the act of 1828, with all its objectionable features, and with the odious circumstances under which it was adopted, had almost, if not entirely, closed the door of hope through the General Government. It afforded conclusive evidence that no reasonable prospect of relief from Congress could be entertained; yet the near approach of the period of the payment of the public debt, and the elevation of General Jackson to the Presidency, still afforded a ray of hope; not so strong, however, as to prevent the State from turning her eyes, for a final relief, to her reserved powers.

Under these circumstances commenced that inquiry into the nature and extent of the reserved powers of a State, and the means which they afforded of resistance against the encroachments of the General Government, which has been pursued with so much zeal and energy, and, he might add, intelligence. Never was there a political discussion carried on with greater activity, and which appealed more directly to the intelligence of a community. Throughout the whole, no address was made to the low and vulgar passions. But, on the contrary, the discussion turned upon the higher principles of political economy, connected with the operations of the tariff system, which are calculated to show its real bearing on the interests of the State, and on the structure of our political system; going to show the true character of the relations between the States and the General Government; and the means which the states possess of defending those powers which they reserved in forming the Federal Government.

In this great canvass, men of the most commanding talents and acquirements engaged with the greatest ardor; and the people were addressed through every channel, by essays in the public press, and by speeches in their public assemblies, until they had become thoroughly instructed on the nature of the oppression, and on the rights which they possess, under the constitution, to throw them off.

If gentlemen suppose that the stand taken by the people of Carolina rests on passion and delusion, they are wholly mistaken. The case was far otherwise. No community, from the legislator to the ploughman, were ever better instructed in their rights; and the resistance on which the State had resolved was the result of mature reflection, accompanied with a deep conviction that their rights had been violated, and the means of redress which they have adopted are consistent with the principles of the constitution.

But while this active canvass was carried on, which looked to the reserved powers as their final redress, if all others failed, the State at the same time cherished a hope, as I have already stated, that the election of General Jackson to the Presidency would prevent the necessity of a resort to extremities. He was identified with the interests of the staple States; and, having the same interest, it was believed that his great popularity—a popularity of the strongest character, as it rested on military services —would enable him, as they hoped, gradually to bring down the system of protection, without shock or injury to any interest. Under these views, the canvass in favor of General Jackson's election to the Presidency was carried on with great zeal, in conjunction with that active inquiry into the reserved powers of the States, on which final reliance was placed. But little did the people of Carolina dream that the man whom they were thus striving to elevate to the highest seat of power would prove so utterly false to all their hopes. Man is, indeed, ignorant of the future; nor was there ever a stronger illustration of the observation than is afforded by the result of that election! The very event on which they had built their hopes has been turned against them; and the very individual to whom they looked as a deliverer, and whom, under that impression, they strove for so many years to elevate to power, is now the most powerful instrument in the hands of his and their bitterest opponents to put down them and their cause!

Scarcely had he been elected, when it became apparent, from the organization of his cabinet, and other indications, that all their hopes of relief through him were blasted. The admission of a single individual into the cabinet, under the circumstances which accompanied that admission, threw all into confusion. The mischievous influence over the President, through which this individual was admitted into the cabinet, soon became apparent. Instead of turning his eyes forward to the period of the payment of the public debt, which was then near at hand, and to the present dangerous political crisis, which was inevitable, unless averted by a timely and wise system of measures, the attention of the President was absorbed by mere party arrangements, and circumstances too disreputable to be mentioned here, except by the most distant allusion.

Here, Mr. C. said, he must pause for a moment to repel a charge which has been so often made, and which even the President has reiterated in his proclamation—the charge that he had been actuated, in the part which he had taken, by feelings of disappointed ambition. Mr. C. again repeated, that he deeply regretted the necessity of noticing himself in so important a discussion, and that nothing could induce him to advert to his own course but the conviction that it was due to the cause, at which a blow was aimed, through him. It was only in this view that he noticed it.

Mr. C. said it ill became the Chief Magistrate to make this charge. The course which the State had taken, and which had led to the present controversy between her and the General Government, was taken as far back as 1828, in the very midst of that severe canvass which placed him in power; and in that very canvass Carolina had openly avowed and zealously maintained these very principles which he now officially pronounces to be treason and rebellion. That was the period at which he ought to have spoken. Having remained silent then, and having, under his approval, implied by that silence, received the support and the vote of the State, he, (Mr. C.,) if a sense of decorum did not prevent it, might recriminate, with the double charge of deception and ingratitude. His object, however, was not to assail the President, but to defend himself against a most unfounded charge. The time alone, when he pursued the course upon which this charge of disappointed ambition is founded, will, of itself, repel it in the eye of every unprejudiced and honest man. The doctrine which he now sustains, under the present difficulties, he openly avowed and maintained immediately after the act of 1828, that "bill of abominations," as it has been so often and properly termed. Was he at that period disappointed in any views of ambition which he might be supposed to entertain? He was Vice President of the United States, elected by an overwhelming majority. He was a candidate for re-election on the ticket with General Jackson himself, with a certain prospect of a triumphant success of that ticket, and with a fair prospect of the highest office to which an American citizen could aspire. What was his course under these prospects? Did he look to his own advancement, or to an honest and faithful discharge of his duty? Let facts speak for themselves. When the bill to which he had referred came from the other House to the Senate, the almost universal impression was, that its fate would depend upon his casting vote. It was known that, as the bill then stood, the Senate was nearly equally divided; and as it was a combined measure, originating with the politicians and manufacturers, and intended as much to bear upon the Presidential election as to protect manufacturers, it was believed that, as a stroke of political policy, its fate would be made to depend on his vote, in order to defeat General Jackson's election as well as his own. The friends of General Jackson were alarmed; and he (Mr. C.) was earnestly entreated to leave the chair, in order to avoid the responsibility, under the plausible argument that if the Senate should be equally divided, the bill would be lost without the aid of his casting vote. The reply to this entreaty was, that no consideration, personal to himself, could induce him to take such a course; that he considered the measure as of the most dangerous character, calculated to produce the most fearful crisis; that the payment of the public debt was just at hand, and that the great increase of revenue which it would pour into the treasury would accelerate the approach of that period; and that the country would be placed in the most trying of all situations, with an immense revenue, without the means of absorption upon any legitimate or constitutional object of appropriation, and would be compelled to submit to all the corrupting consequences of a large surplus, or to make a sudden reduction of the rates of duties, which would prove ruinous to the very interests which were then forcing the passage of the bill. Under these views he determined to remain in the chair, and, if the bill came to him, to give his casting vote against it; and, in doing so, to give his reasons, at large; but at the same time, he informed his friends that he would retire from the ticket, so that the election of General Jackson might not be embarrassed by any act of his. Sir, (said Mr. C.,) I was amazed at the folly and infatuation of that period. So completely absorbed was Congress in the game of ambition and avarice, from the double impulse of the manufacturers and politicians, that none but a few appeared to anticipate the present crisis at which now all are alarmed, but which is the inevitable result of what was then done. As to himself, he clearly foresaw what has since followed. The road of ambition lay open before him; he had but to follow the corrupt tendency of the times; but he chose to tread the rugged path of duty.

It was thus that the reasonable hope of relief through the election of General Jackson was blasted; but still, one other hope remained—that the final discharge of the public debt, an event near at hand, would remove our burden. That event would leave in the treasury a large surplus; a surplus that could not be expended under the most extravagant schemes of appropriation, having the least color of decency or constitutionality. That event at last arrived. At the last session of Congress, it was avowed on all sides, that the public debt, for all practical purposes, was in fact paid; the small surplus remaining being nearly covered by the money in the treasury and the bonds for duties which had already accrued; but with the arrival of this event, our last hope was doomed to be disappointed. After a long session of many months, and the most earnest effort on the part of South Carolina and the other Southern States to obtain relief, all that could be effected was a small reduction in the amount of the duties; but a reduction of such a character, that, while it diminished the amount of burden, distributed that burden more unequally than even the obnoxious act of 1828: reserving the principle adopted by the bill of 1816, of laying higher duties on the unprotected than the protected articles, by repealing almost entirely the duties laid upon the former, and imposing the burden almost entirely on the latter. It was thus, that instead of relief, instead of an equal distribution of the burdens and benefits of the Government, on the payment of the debt, as had been fondly anticipated, the duties were so arranged as to be, in fact, bounties on one side, and taxation on the other; and thus placing the two great sections of the country in direct conflict in reference to its fiscal action, and thereby letting in that flood of political corruption which threatens to sweep away our constitution and our liberty.

This unequal and unjust arrangement was pronounced, both by the administration, through its proper organ, the Secretary of the Treasury, and by the opposition, to be a permanent adjustment; and it was thus that all hope of relief through the action of the General Government terminated; and the crisis so long apprehended had at length arrived, at which the State was compelled to choose between absolute acquiescence in a ruinous system of oppression, or a resort to her reserved powers—powers of which she alone was the rightful judge, and which alone in this momentous juncture could save her. She determined on the latter.

The consent of two-thirds of her Legislature was necessary for the call of a convention, which was considered the only legitimate organ through which the people, in their sovereignty, could speak. After an arduous struggle, the State rights party succeeded; more than two-thirds of both branches of the Legislature favorable to a convention were elected; a convention was held, and the ordinance adopted. The convention was succeeded by a meeting of the Legislature, when the laws to carry the ordinance into execution were enacted; all of which had been communicated by the President, had been referred to the Committee on the Judiciary; and this bill is the result of their labor.

Having now, said Mr. C., corrected some of the prominent misrepresentations as to the nature of this controversy, and given a rapid sketch of the movement of the State in reference to it, he would next proceed to notice some objections connected with the ordinance, and the proceedings under it.

The first and most prominent of these is directed against what is called the test oath, which an effort has been made to render odious. So far from deserving the denunciation which had been levelled against it, he viewed this provision of the ordinance as but the natural result of the doctrines entertained by the State, and the position which she occupies. The people of that State believed that the Union is a union of States, and not of individuals; that it was formed by the States; and that the citizens of the several States were bound to it through the acts of their several States; that each State ratified the constitution for itself, and that it was only by such ratification of a State that any obligation was imposed upon the citizens. Thus believing, it was the opinion of the people of Carolina that it belonged to the State which had imposed the obligation to declare, in the last resort, the extent of that obligation, as far as her citizens were concerned; and this, upon the plain principles which exist in all analogous cases of compact between sovereign or political bodies. On this principle, the people of the State, acting in their sovereign capacity, in convention, precisely as they had adopted their own and the federal constitutions, had declared, by the ordinance, that the acts of Congress which had imposed duties under the authority to lay imposts, were acts, not for revenue, as intended by the constitution, but for protection, and therefore null and void. The ordinance, thus enacted by the people of the State themselves, acting as a sovereign community, was, to all intents and purposes, a part of the constitution of the State; and though of a peculiar character, was as obligatory on the citizens of that State as any portion of the constitution. In prescribing, then, the oath to obey the ordinance, no more was done than to prescribe an oath to obey the constitution. It was, in fact, but a particular oath of allegiance, and in every respect similar to that which is prescribed under the constitution of the United States to be administered to all officers of the State and Federal Governments; and was no more deserving the harsh and bitter epithets which had been heaped upon it, than that or any similar oath.

It ought to be borne in mind, that, according to the opinion which prevailed in Carolina, the right of resistance to the unconstitutional laws of Congress belongs to the State, and not to her individual citizens; and that, though the latter may, in a mere question of *meum* and *tuum*, resist, through the courts, an unconstitutional encroachment upon their rights, yet the final stand against usurpation rests not with them, but with the State of which they are members; and that such act of resistance by a State binds the conscience and allegiance of the citizen. But there appeared to be a general misapprehension as to the extent to which the State had acted under this part of the ordinance. Instead of sweeping every officer, by a general proscription of the minority, as has been represented in debate, as far as the knowledge of Mr. C. extends, not a single individual had been removed. The State had, in fact, acted with the greatest tenderness, all circumstances considered, towards citizens who differed from the majority; and, in that spirit, had directed the oath to be administered only in cases of some official act directed to be performed, in which obedience to the ordinance was involved.

It had been further objected that the State had acted precipitately. What! precipitately! after making a strenuous resistance for twelve years, by discussion here and in the other House of Congress; by essays in all forms; by resolutions, remonstrances, and protests on the part of her Legislature; and, finally, by attempting an appeal to the judicial power of the United States? He said attempting, for they had been prevented from bringing the question fairly before the court, and that by an act of that very majority in Congress which now upbraid them for not making that appeal; of that majority, who, on a motion of one of the members in the other House from South Carolina, refused to give to the act of 1828 its true title, that it was a protective, and not a revenue act. The State has never, it is true, relied upon that tribunal, the Supreme Court, to vindicate its reserved rights; yet they have always considered it as an auxiliary means of defence, of which they would gladly have availed themselves to test the constitutionality of protection, had they not been deprived of the means of doing so by the act of the majority.

Notwithstanding this long delay of more than ten years, under this continued encroachment of the Government, we now hear it on all sides, by friends and foes, gravely pronounced that the State has acted precipitately—that her conduct has been rash! That such should be the language of an interested majority, who, by means of this unconstitutional and oppressive system, are annually extorting millions from the South to be bestowed upon other sections, was not at all surprising. Whatever impedes the course of avarice and ambition will ever be denounced as rash and precipitate; and had South Carolina delayed her resistance fifty instead of twelve years, she would have heard from the same quarter the same language; but it was really surprising that those who were suffering in common with herself, and who have complained equally loud of their grievances, who had pronounced the very acts which she had asserted within her limits to be oppressive, unconstitutional, and ruinous, after so long a struggle—a struggle longer than that which preceded the separation of these States from the mother country—longer than the period of the Trojan war—should now complain of precipitancy! No, it is not Carolina which has acted precipitately, but her sister States, who have suffered in common with her, that have acted tardily. Had they acted as she has done, had they performed their duty with equal energy and promptness, our situation this day would be very different from what we now find it. Delays are said to be dangerous, and never was the maxim more true than in the present case—a case of monopoly. It is the very nature of monopolies to grow. If we take from one side a large portion of the proceeds of its labor, and give it to the other, the side from which we take must constantly decay, and that to which we give must prosper and increase. Such is the action of the protective system. It exacts from the South a large portion of the proceeds of its industry, which it bestows upon the other sections, in the shape of bounties to manufacturers and appropriations in a thousand forms—pensions, improvement of rivers and harbors, roads and canals, and in every shape that wit or ingenuity can devise. Can we, then, be surprised that the principle of monopoly grows, when it is so amply remunerated at the expense of those who support it? And this is the real reason of the fact which we witness: that all acts for protection pass with small minorities, but soon come to be sustained by great and overwhelming majorities. Those who seek the monopoly endeavor to obtain it in the most exclusive shape; and they take care, accordingly, to associate only a sufficient number of interests barely to pass it through the two Houses of Congress, on the plain principle that the greater the number from whom the monopoly takes, and the fewer on whom it bestows, the greater is the advantage to the monopolists. Acting in this spirit, we have often seen with what exact precision they count, adding wool to woollens, associating lead and iron, feeling their way until a bare majority is obtained, when the bill passes, connecting just as many interests as are sufficient to insure its success, and no more. In a short time, however, we have invariably found that this lean becomes a decided majority, under the certain operation which compels individuals to desert the pursuits which the monopoly has rendered unprofitable, that they may participate in those pursuits which it has rendered profitable. It is against this dangerous and growing disease that South Carolina has acted—a disease whose cancerous action would soon spread to every part of the system, had it not been speedily arrested.

There was another powerful reason why the action of the State could not be safely delayed. The public debt, as he had already stated, for all practical purposes, had already been paid; and, under the existing duties, a large annual surplus of many millions must come into the treasury. It was impossible to look at this state of things without seeing the most mischievous consequences; and, among others, if not speedily corrected, it would interpose powerful and almost insuperable obstacles to throwing off the burdens under which the South had been so long laboring. The disposition of the surplus would become a subject of a violent and corrupt struggle, and could not fail to rear up new and powerful interests in support of the existing system, not only in those sections which have been heretofore benefited by it, but even in the South itself. He could not but trace to the anticipation of this state of the treasury the sudden and extraordinary movements which had taken place at the last session in the Virginia Legislature, in which the whole South was vitally interested. It was impossible for any rational man to believe that that State could seriously have thought of effecting the scheme to which he alluded by her own resources, without powerful aid from the General Government.

It was next objected that the enforcing acts have legislated the United States out of South Carolina. He had already replied to this objection on another occasion, and would now but repeat what he then said—that they had been legislated out only to the extent that they had no right to enter. The constitution had admitted the jurisdiction of the United States within the limits of the several States only so far as the delegated powers authorized; beyond that they were intruders, and might rightfully be expelled; and that they had been efficiently expelled by the legislation of the State, through her civil process, as has been acknowledged on all sides in the debate, is only a confirmation of the truth of the doctrine for which the majority in Carolina had contended.

The very point at issue between the two parties there was, whether nullification was a peacful and an efficient remedy against an unconstitutional act of the General Government, and which might be asserted as such through the State tribunals? Both parties agree that the acts against which it was directed are unconstitutional and oppressive. The controversy was only as to the means by which our citizens might be protected against the acknowledged encroachments on their rights. This being the point at issue between the parties, and the very object of the majority being an efficient protection of the citizens through the State tribunals, the measures adopted to enforce the ordinance of course received the most decisive character. We were not children, to act by halves. Yet, for acting thus efficiently, the State is denounced and this bill reported, to overrule, by military force, the civil tribunals and civil process of the State! Sir, said Mr. C., I consider this bill, and the arguments which have been urged on this floor in its support, as the most triumphant acknowledgment that nullification is peaceful and efficient, and so deeply entrenched in the principles of our system, that it cannot be assailed but by prostrating the constitution, and substituting the supremacy of military force in lieu of the supremacy of the laws. In fact, the advocates of this bill refute their own argument. They tell us that the ordinance is unconstitutional; that it infracts the constitution of South Carolina; although to him the objection appears absurd, as it was adopted by the very authority which adopted the constitution itself. They also tell us that the Supreme Court is the appointed arbiter of all controversies between a State and the General Government. Why, then, do they not leave this controversy to that tribunal? Why do they not confide to them the abrogation of the ordinance, and the laws made in pursuance of it, and the assertion of that supremacy which they claim for the laws of Congress? The State stands pledged to resist no process of the court. Why, then, confer on the President the extensive and unlimited powers provided in this bill? Why authorize him to use military force to arrest the civil process of the State? But one answer can be given. That, in a contest between the State and the General Government, if the resistance be limited on both sides to the civil process, the State, by its inherent sovereignty, standing upon its reserved powers, will prove too powerful in such a controversy, and must triumph over the Federal Government, sustained by its delegated and limited authority; and, in this answer, we have an acknowledgment of the truth of those great principles for which the State has so firmly and nobly contended.

Having made these remarks, the great question is now presented—has Congress the right to pass this bill?—which he would next proceed to consider. The decision of this question involves the inquiry into the provisions of the bill. What are they? It puts at the disposal of the President the army and navy, and the entire militia of the country. It enables him, at his pleasure, to subject every man in the United States, not exempt from militia duty, to martial law; to call him from his ordinary occupation to the field, and, under the penalty of fine and imprisonment inflicted by a court-martial, to imbrue his hand in his brothers' blood. There is no limitation on the power of the sword, and that over the purse is equally without restraint; for, among the extraordinary features of the bill, it contains no appropriation; which, under existing circumstances, is tantamount to an unlimited appropriation. The President may, under its authority, incur any expenditure, and pledge the national faith to meet it. He may create a new national debt, at the very moment of the termination of the former—a debt of millions, to be paid out of the proceeds of the labor of that section of the country whose dearest constitutional rights this bill prostrates! Thus exhibiting the extraordinary spectacle, that the very section of the country which is urging this measure, and carrying the sword of devastation against us, are at the same time incurring a new debt, to be paid by those whose rights are violated; while those who violate them are to receive the benefits, in the shape of bounties and expenditures.

And for what purpose is the unlimited control of the purse and of the sword thus placed at the disposition of the Executive? To make war against one of the free and sovereign members of this confederation, which the bill proposes to deal with, not as a State, but as a collection of banditti or outlaws. Thus exhibiting the impious spectacle of this Government, the creature of the States, making war against the power to which it owes its existence.

The bill violates the constitution, plainly and palpably, in many of its provisions, by authorizing the President, at his pleasure, to place the different ports of this Union on an unequal footing, contrary to that provision of the constitution which declares that no preference should be given to one port over another. It also violates the constitution by authorizing him, at his discretion, to impose cash duties in one port, while credit is allowed in others; by enabling the President to regulate commerce, a power vested in Congress alone; and by drawing within the jurisdiction of the United States courts powers never intended to be conferred on them. As great as these objections were, they became insignificant in the provisions of a bill which, by a single blow, by treating the States as a mere lawless mass of individuals, prostrates all the barriers of the constitution. He would pass over the minor considerations, and proceed directly to the great point. This bill proceeds on the ground that the entire sovereignty of this country belongs to the American people, as forming one great community; and regards the States as mere fractions or counties, and not as an integral part of the Union, having no more rights to resist the encroachments of the Government than a county has to resist the authority of a State; and treating such resistance as the lawless acts of so many individuals, without possessing sovereign or political rights. It has been said that the bill declares war against South Carolina. No; it decrees a massacre of her citizens! War has something ennobling about it, and, with all its horrors, brings into action the highest qualities, intellectual and moral. It was, perhaps, in the order of Providence that it should be permitted for that very purpose. But this bill declares no war, except, indeed, it be that which savages wage—a war, not against the community, but the citizens of whom that community is composed. But he regarded it as worse than savage warfare—as an attempt to take away life under the color of law, without the trial by jury, or any other safeguard which the constitution has thrown around the life of the citizen! It authorizes the President, or even his deputies, when they may suppose the law to be violated, without the intervention of a court or jury, to kill without mercy or discrimination!

It was said by the Senator from Tennessee [Mr. GRUNDY] to be a measure of peace! Yes, such peace as the wolf gives to the lamb; the kite to the dove. Such peace as Russia gives to Poland; or death to its victim! A peace, by extinguishing the political existence of the State; by awing her into an abandonment of the exercise of every power which constitutes her a sovereign community. It is to South Carolina a question of self-preservation; and I proclaim it, that, should this bill pass, and an attempt be made to enforce it, it will be resisted at every hazard, even that of death itself. Death is not the greatest calamity; there are others still more terrible to the free and brave; and among them may be placed the loss of liberty and honor. There are thousands of her brave sons who, if need be, are prepared cheerfully to lay down their lives in defense of the

State, and the great principles of constitutional liberty for which she is contending. God forbid that this should become necessary! It never can be, unless this Government is resolved to bring the question to extremity, when her gallant sons will stand prepared to perform their last duty—to die nobly.

I go (said Mr. C.) on the ground that this constitution was made by the States; that it is a federal union of the States, in which the several States still retain their sovereignty. If these views be correct, he had not characterized the bill too strongly, which presents the question, whether they be or be not. He would not enter into the discussion of that question now. He would rest it, for the present, on what he had said on the introduction of the resolutions now on the table, under a hope that another opportunity would be afforded for more ample discussion. He would for the present confine his remarks to the objections which had been raised to the views which he had presented when he introduced them. The authority of Luther Martin had been adduced by the Senator from Delaware, to prove that the citizens of a State, acting under the authority of a State, were liable to be punished as traitors by this Government. As eminent as Mr. Martin was as a lawyer, and as high as his authority might be considered on a legal point, he could not accept it in determining the point at issue. The attitude which he occupied, if taken into view, would lessen, if not destroy, the weight of his authority. He had been violently opposed, in convention, to the constitution; and the very letter from which the Senator has quoted was intended to dissuade Maryland from its adoption. With this view, it was to be expected that every consideration calculated to effect that object should be urged; that real objections should be exaggerated; and that those having no foundation, except mere plausible deductions, should be presented. It is to this spirit that he attributed the opinion of Mr. Martin, in reference to the point under consideration. But if his authority is good on one point, it must be admitted to be equally so on another. If his opinion be sufficient to prove that a citizen of the State may be punished as a traitor when acting under allegiance to the State, it is also sufficient to show that no authority was intended to be given, in the constitution, for the protection of manufactures by the General Government; and that the provision in the constitution, permitting a State to lay an impost duty with the consent of Congress, was intended to reserve the right of protection to the States themselves, and that each State should protect its own industry. Assuming his opinion to be of equal authority on both points, how embarrassing would be the attitude in which it would place the Senator from Delaware, and those with whom he is acting—that of using the sword and the bayonet to enforce the execution of an unconstitutional act of Congress. He must express his surprise that the slightest authority in favor of power should be received as the most conclusive evidence, while that which is at least equally strong in favor of right and liberty is wholly overlooked or rejected.

Notwithstanding all that has been said, he must say, that neither the Senator from Delaware, [Mr. CLAYTON,] nor any other who had spoken on the same side, had directly and fairly met the great questions at issue. Is this a federal union? a union of States, as distinct from that of individuals? Is the sovereignty in the several States, or in the American people in the aggregate? The very language which we are compelled to use, when speaking of our political institutions, affords proof conclusive as to its real character. The terms union, federal, united, all imply a combination of sovereignties, a confederation of States. They are never applied to an association of individuals. Who ever heard of the United State of New York, of Massachusetts, or of Virginia? Who ever heard the term federal, or union, applied to the aggregation of individuals into one community? Nor is the other point less clear, that the sovereignty is in the several States, and that our system is a union of twenty-four sovereign powers, under a constitutional compact, and not of a divided sovereignty between the States severally and the United States. In spite of all that has been said, he maintained that sovereignty is in its nature indivisible. It is the supreme power in a State; and we might just as well speak of half a square, or half of a triangle, as of half a sovereignty. It is a gross error to confound the exercise of sovereign powers with sovereignty itself; or the delegation of such powers with a surrender of them. A sovereign may delegate his powers to be exercised by as many agents as he may think proper, under such conditions and with such limitations as he may impose; but to surrender any portion of his sovereignty to another is to annihilate the whole. The

Senator from Delaware [Mr. CLAYTON] calls this metaphysical reasoning, which he says he cannot comprehend. If by metaphysics he means that scholastic refinement which makes distinctions without difference, no one can hold it in more utter contempt than he, (Mr. C.;) but if, on the contrary, he means the power of analysis and combination, that power which reduces the most complex idea into its elements, which traces causes to their first principle, and, by the power of generalization and combination, unites the whole into one harmonious system—then, so far from deserving contempt, it is the highest attribute of the human mind. It is the power which raises man above the brute; which distinguishes his faculties from mere sagacity, which he holds in common with inferior animals. It is this power which has raised the astronomer from being a mere gazer at the stars to the high intellectual eminence of a Newton or a La Place; and astronomy itself, from a mere observation of insulated facts, into that noble science which displays to our admiration the system of the universe. And shall this high power of the mind, which has effected such wonders when directed to the laws which control the material world, be forever prohibited, under a senseless cry of metaphysics, from being applied to the high purpose of political science and legislation? He held them to be subject to laws as fixed as matter itself, and to be as fit a subject for the application of the highest intellectual power. Denunciation may indeed fall upon the philosophical inquirer into these first principles, as it did upon Galileo and Bacon, when they first unfolded the great discoveries which have immortalized their names; but the time will come when truth will prevail in spite of prejudice and denunciation, and when politics and legislation will be considered as much a science as astronomy and chemistry.

In connexion with this part of the subject, he understood the Senator from Virginia [Mr. RIVES] to say that sovereignty was divided; that a portion remained with the States severally, and that the residue was vested in the Union. By Union, he supposed that the Senator meant the United States. If such be his meaning—if he intended to affirm that the sovereignty was in the twenty-four States, in whatever light he might view them, their opinions would not disagree; but, according to his (Mr. C.'s) conception, the whole sovereignty was in the several States, while the exercise of sovereign powers was divided, a part being exercised under compact, through this General Government, and the residue through the seperate State Governments. But if the Senator from Virginia [Mr. Rives] meant to assert that the twenty-four States formed but one community, with a single sovereign power as to the objects of the Union, it would be but the revival of the old question, of whether the Union was a union between States, as distinct communities, or a mere aggregate of the American people, as a mass of individuals; and in this light his opinions would lead directly to consolidation.

But to return to the bill. It is said that the bill ought to pass, because the law must be enforced. The law must be enforced! The imperial edict must be executed. It is under such sophistry, couched in general terms, without looking to the limitations which must ever exist in the practical exercise of power, that the most cruel and despotic acts ever have been covered. It was such sophistry as this that cast Daniel into the lion's den, and the three innocents into the fiery furnace. Under the same sophistry, the bloody edicts of Nero and Caligula were executed. The law must be enforced! Yes, the "tea tax must be executed." This was the very argument which impelled Lord North and his administration in that mad career which forever separated us from the British crown. Under a similar sophistry, "that religion must be protected," how many massacres have been perpetrated? and how many martyrs have been tied to the stake? What! acting on this vague abstraction, are you prepared to enforce a law, without considering whether it be just or unjust, constitutional or unconstitutional? Will you collect money when it is acknowledged that it is not wanted? He who earns the money, who digs it from the earth with the sweat of his brow, has a just title to it against the universe. No one has a right to touch it without his consent, except his Government, and it only to the extent of its legitimate wants. To take more is robbery; and you propose by this bill to enforce the robbery by murder. Yes, to this result you must come by this miserable sophistry, this vague abstraction, of enforcing the law without a regard to the fact whether the law be just or unjust, constitutional or unconstitutional.

In the same spirit we are told that the Union must be preserved, without regard to the means. And how is it proposed to preserve the Union? By force! Does any man in his senses believe that this beautiful structure, this harmonious aggregate of States, produced by the joint consent of all, can be preserved by force? Its very introduction will be certain destruction of this Federal Union. No, no; you cannot keep the States united in their constitutional and federal bonds by force. Force may, indeed, hold the parts together; but such union would be the bond between master and slave; a union of exaction on one side, and of unqualified obedience on the other. That obedience which, we are told by the Senator from Pennsylvania, [Mr. WILKINS,] is the Union! Yes, exaction on the side of the master; for this very bill is intended to collect what can be no longer called taxes, (the voluntary contribution of a free people,) but tribute, tribute to be collected under the mouths of the cannon! Your custom-house is already transferred to a garrison, and that garrison with its batteries turned, not against the enemy of your country, but on subjects, (I will not say citizens,) on whom you propose to levy contributions. Has reason fled from our borders? Have we ceased to reflect? It is madness to suppose that the Union can be preserved by force. I tell you plainly that the bill, should it pass, cannot be enforced. It will prove only a blot upon your statute book, a reproach to the year, and a disgrace to the American Senate. I repeat that it will not be executed; it will rouse the dormant spirit of the people, and open their eyes to the approach of despotism. The country has sunk into avarice and political corruption, from which nothing could arouse it but some measure, on the part of the Government, of folly and madness, such as that now under consideration.

Disguise it as you may, the controversy is one between power and liberty; and he would tell the gentlemen who are opposed to him, that, strong as might be the love of power on their side, the love of liberty is still stronger on ours. History furnishes many instances of similar struggles, where the love of liberty has prevailed against power, under every disadvantage; and, among them, few more striking than that of our own revolution; where, strong as was the parent country, and feeble as were the colonies, yet, under the impulse of liberty and the blessing of God, they gloriously triumphed in the contest. There were, indeed, many and striking analogies between that and the present controversy; they both originated substantially in the same cause, with this difference, that, in the present case, the power of taxation is converted into that of regulating industry; in that, the power of regulating industry, by the regulation of commerce, was attempted to be converted into the power of taxation. Were he to trace the analogy further, we would find that the perversion of the taxing power, in one case, has given precisely the same control to the northern section over the industry of the southern section of the Union, which the power to regulate commerce gave to Great Britain over the industry of the colonies; and that the very articles in which the colonies were permitted to have a free trade, and those in which the mother country had a monopoly, are almost identically the same as those under which the Southern States are permitted to have a free trade by the act of 1832, and which the Northern States have, by the same act, secured a monopoly; the only difference is the means. In the former, the colonies were permitted to have a free trade with all countries south of Cape Finisterre, a cape in the northern part of Spain; while north of that the trade of the colonies was prohibited, except through the mother country, by means of her commercial regulations. If we compare the products of the country north and south of Cape Finisterre, we will find them almost identical with the list of the protected and unprotected articles contained in the act of last year. Nor does the analogy terminate here. The very arguments resorted to at the commencement of the American revolution, and the measures adopted, and the motives assigned to bring on that contest, (to enforce the law,) are almost identically the same.

But, said Mr. C., to return from this digression to the consideration of the bill. Whatever opinion may exist upon other points, there is one in which he would suppose there could be none: that this bill rests on principles which, if carried out, will ride over State sovereignties, and that it will be idle for any of its advocates hereafter to talk of State rights. The Senator from Virginia [Mr. RIVES] says that he is the advocate of State rights; but he must permit me to tell him that, although he may differ in premises from the other gentlemen with whom he acts on this occasion, yet in supporting this bill he obliterates every vestige of distinction between him and them, saving only that, professing the principles of '98, his example will be more pernicious than that of the most open and bitter opponents of the rights of the

States. He would also add, what he was compelled to say, that he must consider him [Mr. RIVES] as less consistent than our old opponents, whose conclusions were fairly drawn from their premises, whilst his premises ought to have led him to opposite conclusions. The gentleman has told us that the new-fangled doctrines, as he chose to call them, had brought State rights into disrepute. He must tell him, in reply, that what he called new-fangled are but the doctrines of '98; and that it is he, [Mr. RIVES,] and others with him, who, professing these doctrines, had degraded them by explaining away their meaning and efficacy. He [Mr. RIVES] had disclaimed, in behalf of Virginia, the authorship of nullification. Mr. C. would not dispute that point. If Virginia choose to throw away one of her brightest ornaments, she must not hereafter complain that it had become the property of another. But while, as a representative of Carolina, he had no right to complain of the disavowal of the Senator from Virginia, he must believe that he [Mr. RIVES] had done his native State great injustice by declaring on this floor that, when she gravely resolved, in '98, that "in cases of deliberate and dangerous infractions of the constitution, the States, as parties to the compact, have the right, and are in duty bound, to interpose to arrest the progress of the evil, and to maintain, within their respective limits, the authorities, rights, and liberties appertaining to them," she meant no more than to ordain the right to protest and remonstrate. To suppose that, in putting forth such a solemn declaration, which she afterwards sustained by so able and elaborate an argument, she meant no more than to assert what no one had ever denied, would be to suppose that the State had been guilty of the most egregious trifling that ever was exhibited on so solemn an occasion.

Mr. C. said that, in reviewing the ground over which he had passed, it would be apparent that the question in controversy involved that most deeply important of all political questions, whether ours was a federal or a consolidated Government—a question on the decision of which depends, as he solemnly believed, the liberty of the people, their happiness, and the place which we are destined to hold in the moral and intellectual scale of nations. Never was there a controversy in which more important consequences were involved, not excepting that between Persia and Greece, decided by the battles of Marathon,

Platea, and Salamis, which gave ascendancy to the genius of Europe over that of Asia, and which, in its consequences, has continued to affect the destiny of so large a portion of the world, even to this day. There is, said Mr. C., often close analogies between events apparently very remote, which is strikingly illustrated in this case. In the great contest between Greece and Persia, between European and Asiatic polity and civilization, the very question between the federal and consolidated form of government was involved. The Asiatic Governments, from the remotest time, with some exceptions on the eastern shore of the Mediterranean, have been based on the principle of consolidation, which considers the whole community as but a unit; and consolidates its powers in a central point. The opposite principle has prevailed in Europe; Greece, throughout all her States, was based on a federal system. All were united in one common but loose bond, and the Governments of the several States partook, for the most part, of a complex organization, which distributed political power among different members of the community. The same principles prevailed in ancient Italy; and, if we turn to the Teutonic race, our great ancestors, the race which occupies the first place in power, civilization, and science, and which possess the largest and the fairest part of Europe, we will find that their Governments were based on the federal organization, as has been clearly illustrated by a recent and able writer on the British constitution, (Mr. Palgrave,) from whose writings he introduced the following extract:

"In this manner the first establishment of the Teutonic States was effected. They were assemblages of sects, clans, and tribes; they were confederated hosts and armies, led on by princes, magistrates, and chieftains, each of whom was originally independent, and each of whom lost a portion of his pristine independence in proportion as he and his compeers became united under the supremacy of a sovereign, who was superinduced upon the State first as a military commander, and afterwards as a King. Yet, notwithstanding this political connexion, each member of the State continued to retain a considerable portion of the rights of sovereignty. Every ancient Teutonic monarchy must be considered as a federation; it is not a unit, of which the smaller bodies politic therein contained are the fractions, but they are the integers, and the State is the multiple which results from them. Dukedoms and counties, burghs and baronies, towns and townships, and shires, form the kingdom—all, in a certain degree, strangers to each other, and separate in jurisdiction, though all obedient to the supreme executive authority. This general description, though not always strictly applicable in terms, is always so substantially and in effect; and hence it becomes necessary to discard the language which has been very generally employed in treating on the English constitution. It has been supposed that the kingdom was reduced into a regular and gradual subordination of Government, and that the various legal districts of which it is composed arose from the divisions and subdivisions of the country. But this hypothesis, which tends greatly to perplex our history, cannot be supported by fact; and instead of viewing the constitution as a whole, and then proceeding to its parts, we must examine it synthetically, and assume that the supreme authorities of the State were created by the concentration of the powers originally belonging to the members and corporations of which it is composed." [Here Mr. C. gave way for a motion to adjourn.]

On the next day, Mr. C. proceeded by remarking that he had omitted at their proper place, in the course of his observations yesterday, two or three points to which he would now advert before he resumed the discussion where he had left off. He had stated that the ordinance and acts of South Carolina were directed, not against the revenue, but against the system of protection. But it might be asked, if such was her object, how happens it that she has declared the whole system void, revenue as well as protection, without discrimination? It is this question which he proposed to answer. Her justification would be found in the necessity of the case; and, if there be any blame, it could not attach to her. The two were so blended, throughout the whole, as to make the entire revenue system subordinate to the protection, so as constitute a complete system of protection, in which it was impossible to discriminate the two elements of which it is composed. South Carolina at least could not make the discrimination, and she was reduced to the alternative of acquiescing in a system which she believed to be unconstitutional, and which she felt to be oppressive and ruinous, or to consider the whole as one, equally contaminated through all its parts, by the unconstitutionality of the protective portion; and, as such, to be resisted by the act of the State. He maintained that the State had a right to regard it in the latter character, and that if a loss of revenue followed, the fault was not hers, but of this Government, which had improperly blended together, in a manner not to be separated by the State, two systems wholly dissimilar. If the sincerity of the State be doubted; if it be supposed that her action is against revenue as well as protection, let the two be separated; let so much of the duties as are intended for revenue be put in one bill, and the residue intended for protection be put in another; and he pledged himself that the ordinance and the acts of the State would cease as to the former, and be directed exclusively against the latter.

He had also stated, in the course of his remarks yesterday, and trusted he had conclusively shown, that the act of 1816, with the exception of a single item, to which he had alluded, was, in reality, a revenue measure, and that Carolina and the other States, in supporting it, had not incurred the slightest responsibility in relation to the system of protection which had since grown up, and which now so deeply distracts the country. Sir, said Mr. C., I am willing, as one of the representatives of Carolina, and I believe I speak the sentiment of the State, to take that act as the basis of a permanent adjustment of the tariff, simply reducing the duties, in an average proportion, on all the items, to the revenue point. I make that offer now to the advocates of the protective system; but I must, in candor, inform them, that such an adjustment would distribute the revenue between the protected and unprotected articles more favorably to the State, and to the South, and less so to the manufacturing interest, than an average uniform ad valorem; and, accordingly, more so than that now proposed by Carolina through her convention. After such an offer, no man who valued his candor will dare to acuse the State, or those who have represented her here, with inconsistency in reference to the point under consideration.

He omitted, also, on yesterday, to notice a remark of the Senator from Virginia, [Mr. RIVES,] that the only difficulty in adjusting the tariff grew out of the ordinance and the acts of South Carolina. He must attribute an assertion, so inconsistent with the facts, to an ignorance of the occurrences of the last few years, in reference to this subject, occasioned by the absence of the gentleman from the United States, to which he himself has alluded in his remarks. If the Senator will take pains to inform himself, he will find that this protective system advanced with a continued and rapid step, in spite of petitions, remonstrances, and protests, of not only Carolina, but also of Virginia and of all the Southern States, until 1828; when Carolina, for the first time, changed the character of her resistance, by holding up her reserved rights as the shield of her defense against further encroachment. This attitude alone, unaided by a single State, arrested the further progress of the system; so that the question from that period to this, on the part of the manufacturers, has been, not how to acquire more, but to retain that which they have acquired. He would inform the gentleman, that if this attitude had not been taken on the part of the State, the question would not now be, how duties ought to be repealed, but a question as to the protected articles, between prohibition on one side, and the duties established by the act of 1828 on the other. But a single remark will be sufficient in reply to what he must consider the invidious remark of the Senator from Virginia, [Mr. RIVES.] The act of 1832, which has not yet gone into operation, and which was passed but a few months since, was declared by the supporters of the system to be a permanent adjustment; and the bill proposed by the Treasury Department, not essentially different from the act itself, was in like manner declared to be intended, by the administration, as a permanent arrangement. What has occurred since, except this ordinance, and these abused acts of the calumniated State, to produce this mighty revolution in reference to this odious system? Unless the Senator from Virginia can assign some other cause, he is bound, upon every principle of fairness, to retract this unjust aspersion upon the acts of South Carolina.

After noticing another omission, Mr. C. said he would proceed with his remarks. The Senator from Delaware, [Mr. CLAYTON,] as well as others, had relied with great emphasis on the fact, that we are citizens of the United States. I, said Mr. C., do not object to the expression, nor shall I detract from the proud and elevated feelings with which it is associated; but he trusted that he might be permitted to raise the inquiry, in what manner we are citizens of the United States, without weakening the patriotic feeling with which he trusted it would ever be uttered. If, by citizen of the United States he meant a citizen at large, one whose citizenship extended to the entire geographical limits of the country, without having a local citizenship in some State or Territory, a sort of citizen of the world, all he had to say was, that such a citizen would be a perfect nondescript; that not a single individual of this description could be found in the entire mass of our population. Notwithstanding all the pomp and display of eloquence on the occasion, every citizen is a citizen of some State or Territory, and, as such, under an express provision of the constitution, is entitled to all privileges and immunities of citizens in the several States; and it is in this, and in no other sense, that we are citizens of the United States. The Senator from Pennsylvania, [Mr. DALLAS,] indeed, relies upon that provision in the constitution which gives Congress the power to establish a uniform rule of naturalization, and the operation of the rule actually established under this authority, to prove that naturalized citizens are citizens at large, without being citizens of any of the States. He did not deem it necessary to examine the law of Congress upon this subject, or to reply to the argument of the Senator, though he could not doubt that he [Mr. D.] had taken an entirely erroneous view on the subject. It was sufficient that the powers of Congress extended simply to the establishment of a uniform rule, by which foreigners might be naturalized in the several States or Territories, without infringing, in any other respect, in reference to naturalization, the rights of the States, as they existed before the adoption of the constitution.

Having supplied the omissions of yesterday, Mr. C. now resumed the subject at the point where his remarks then terminated. The Senate would remember that he stated, at their close, that the great question at issue was, whether ours is a federal or a consolidated system of government; a system in which the parts, to use the emphatic language of Mr. Palgrave, are the integers, and the whole the multiple, or in which the whole is a unit, and the parts the fractions; that he had stated that on the decision of this question, he believed, depends not only the liberty and prosperity of this country, but the place which we are destined to hold in the intellectual and moral scale of nations. He had stated, also, in his remarks on this point, that there was a striking analogy between this and the great struggle between Persia and Greece, which had been decided by the battles of Marathon, Platea, and Salamis, and which had immortalized the names of Miltiades and Themistocles. He had illustrated this analogy, by showing that centralism, or consolidation, with the exception of a few nations along the eastern border of the Mediterranean, had been the pervading principle in the Asiatic Governments; while the federal principle, or, what is the same in principle, that system which organizes a community in reference to its parts, had prevailed in Europe.

Among the few exceptions in the Asiatic nations, the Government of the twelve tribes of Israel, in its early period, was the most striking. Their Government, at first, was a mere confederation, without any central power, till a military chieftain, with the title of King, was placed at its head, without, however, merging the original organization of the twelve distinct tribes. This was the commencement of that central action among that peculiar people, which, in three generations, terminated in a permanent division of their tribes. It is impossible even for a careless reader to peruse the history of that event without being forcibly struck with the analogy in the causes which led to their separation, and those which now threaten us with a similar calamity. With the establishment of the central power in the King commenced a system of taxation, which, under King Solomon, was greatly increased, to defray the expense of rearing the temple, of enlarging and embellishing Jerusalem, the seat of the central Government, and the other profuse expenditures of his magnificent reign. Increased taxation was followed by its natural consequences—discontent and complaint, which before his death began to excite resistance. On the succession of his son, Rehoboam, the ten tribes, headed by Jeroboam, demanded a reduction of the taxes; the temple being finished, and the embellishment of Jerusalem completed, and the money which had been raised for that purpose being no longer required, or, in other words, the debt being paid, they demanded a reduction of the duties—a repeal of the tariff. The demand was taken under consideration, and, after consulting the old men, (the counsellors of '98,) who advised a reduction, he then took the opinion of the younger politicians, who had since grown up, and knew not the doctrines of their fathers. He hearkened unto their counsel, and refused to make the reduction; and the secession of the ten tribes, under Jeroboam, followed. The tribes of Judah and Benjamin, which had received the disbursements, alone remained to the house of David.

But to return to the point immediately under consideration. He knew that it was not only the opinion of a large majority of our country, but it might be said to be the opinion of the age, that the very *beau ideal* of a perfect Government was the Government of a majority, acting through a representative body, without check or limitation in its power; yet if we may test this theory by experience and reason, we will find that, so far from being perfect, the necessary tendency of all Governments, based upon the will of an absolute majority, without constitutional check or limitation of power, is to faction, corruption, anarchy, and despotism; and this, whether the will of the majority be expressed directly through an assembly of the people themselves, or by their representatives. I know (said Mr. C.) that in venturing this assertion I utter that which is unpopular, both within and without these walls; but, where truth and liberty are concerned, such considerations should not be regarded. He would place the decision of this point on the fact, that no Government of the kind, among the many attempts which had been made, had ever endured for a single generation; but, on the contrary, had invariably experienced the fate which he had assigned to them. Let a single instance be pointed out, and he would surrender his opinion. But, if we had not the aid of experience to direct our judgment, reason itself would be a certain guide. The view which considers the community as a unit, and all its parts as having a similar interest, is radically erroneous. However small the community may be, and however homogeneous its interests, the moment that Government is put into operation, as soon as it begins to collect taxes, and to make appropriations, the different portions of the community must, of necessity, bear different and opposing relations in reference to the action of the Government. There must inevitably spring up two interests—a direction and a stockholder interest; an interest profiting by the action of the Government, and interested in increasing its powers and action; and another at whose expense the political machine is kept in motion. He knew how difficult it was to communicate distinct ideas on such a subject, through the medium of general propositions, without particular illustration;

and, in order that he might be distinctly understood, though at the hazard of being tedious, he would illustrate the important principle which he had ventured to advance by examples.

Let us then suppose a small community of five persons, separated from the rest of the world; and, to make the example strong, let us suppose them all to be engaged in the same pursuit, and to be of equal wealth. Let us further suppose that they determine to govern the community by the will of a majority; and, to make the case as strong as possible, let us suppose that the majority, in order to meet the expenses of the Government, lay an equal tax, say of one hundred dollars, on each individual of this little community. Their treasury would contain five hundred dollars. Three are a majority; and they, by supposition, have contributed three hundred as their portion, and the other two, (the minority,) two hundred. The three have the right to make the appropriations as they may think proper. The question is, how would the principle of the absolute and unchecked majority operate, under these circumstances, in this little community? If the three be governed by a sense of justice; if they should appropriate the money to the objects for which it was raised, the common and equal benefit of the five, then the object of the association would be fairly and honestly effected, and each would have a common interest in the Government. But, should the majority pursue an opposite course; should they appropriate the money in a manner to benefit their own particular interest, without regard to the interest of the two; (and that they will so act, unless there be some efficient check, he who best knows human nature will least doubt,) who does not see that the three and the two would have directly opposite interests, in reference to the action of the Government? The three, who contribute to the common treasury but three hundred dollars, could, in fact, by appropriating the five hundred to their own use, convert the action of the Government into the means of making money; and, of consequence, would have a direct interest in increasing the taxes. They put in three hundred, and take out five; that is, they take back to themselves all that they had put in; and, in addition, that which was put in by their associates; or, in other words, taking taxation and appropriation together, they have gained, and their associates have lost, two hundred dollars by the fiscal action of the Government.

An opposite interest, in reference to the action of the Government, is thus created between them; the one having an interest in favor and the other against the taxes; the one to increase, and the other to decrease the taxes; the one to retain the taxes when the money is no longer wanted, and the other to repeal them when the objects for which they were levied have been executed.

Let us now suppose this community of five to be raised to twenty-four individuals, to be governed in like manner by the will of a majority; it is obvious that the same principle would divide them into two interests; into a majority and a minority, thirteen against eleven, or in some other proportion; and that all the consquences, which he had shown to be applicable to the small community of five, would be equally applicable to the greater; the cause not depending upon the number, but resulting necessarily from the action of the Government itself. Let us now suppose that, instead of governing themselves directly in an assembly of the whole, without the intervention of agents, they should adopt the representative principle; and that, instead of being governed by a majority of themselves, they should be governed by a majority of their representatives. It is obvious that the operation of the system would not be affected by the change; the representatives being responsible to those who choose them, would conform to the will of their constituents, and would act as they would do, were they present, and acting for themselves; and the same conflict of interest which we have shown would exist in one case, would equally exist in the other. In either case, the inevitable result would be a system of hostile legislation on the part of the majority, or the stronger interest, against the minority, or the weaker interest; the object of which, on the part of the former, would be to exact as much as possible from the latter, which would necessarily be resisted by all the means in their power. Warfare, by legislation, would thus be commenced between the parties, with the same objects, and not less hostile, than that which is carried on between distinct and rival nations; the only distinction would be in the instruments and the mode. Enactments, in the one case, would supply what could only be effected by arms in the other; and the inevitable operation would be to engender the most hostile feelings between the parties, which would immerge every feeling of patriotism—that feeling which embraces the whole—and substitute in its place the most violent party attachment; and, instead of having one common centre of attachment, around which the affections of the community might rally, there would, in fact, be two; the interests of the majority, to which those who constitute that majority would be more attached than they would be to the whole, and that of the minority, to which they in like manner would also be more attached than to the interests of the whole. Faction would thus take the place of patriotism; and, with the loss of patriotism, corruption must necessarily follow; and, in its train, anarchy; and, finally, despotism, or the establishment of absolute power in a single individual, as a means of arresting the conflict of hostile interests; on the principle that it is better to submit to the will of a single individual, who, by being made lord and master of the whole community, would have an equal interest in the protection of all the parts.

Let us next suppose that, in order to avert the calamitous train of consequences, this little community should adopt a written constitution, with limitations restricting the will of the majority, in order to protect the minority against the oppressions which he had shown would necessarily result without such restrictions. It is obvious that the case would not be in the slightest degree varied, if the majority be left in possession of the right of judging exclusively of the extent of its powers, without any right on the part of the minority to enforce the restrictions imposed by the constitution on the will of the majority. The point is almost too clear for illustration. Nothing can be more certain than that when a constitution grants power, and imposes limitations on the exercise of that power, whatever interests may obtain possession of the Government will be in favor of extending the power at the expense of the limitation; and that, unless those in whose behalf the limitations were imposed have, in some form or mode, the right of enforcing them, the power will ultimately supersede the limitation, and the Government must operate precisely in the same manner as if the will of the majority governed without constitution or limitation of power.

He had thus presented all possible modes in which a Government, bound upon the will of an absolute majority, would be modified; and had demonstrated that, in all its forms, whether in a majority of the people, as in a mere democracy, or in a majority of their representatives, without a constitution, or with a constitution, to be interpreted as the will of the majority, the result would be the same: two hostile interests would inevitably be created by the action of the Government, to be followed by hostile legislation, and that by faction, corruption, anarchy, and despotism.

The great and solemn question here presented itself: Is there any remedy for these evils? on the decision of which depends the question, whether the people can govern themselves? which has been so often asked, with so much scepticism and doubt. There is a remedy, and but one, the effects of which, whatever may be the form, is to organize society in reference to this conflict of interests, which springs out of the action of Government; and which can only be done by giving to each part the right of self-protection; which, in a word, instead of considering the community of twenty-four as a single community, having a common interest, and to be governed by the single will of an entire majority, shall, upon all questions tending to bring the parts into conflict, the thirteen against the eleven, take the will, not of the twenty-four as a unit, but that of the thirteen and that of the eleven separately, the majority of each governing the parts; and, where they concur, governing the whole; and where they disagree, arresting the action of the Government. This he would call the concurring, as distinct from the absolute majority. It would not be, as was generally supposed, a minority governing a majority. In either way, the number would be the same, whether taken as the absolute, or as the concurring majority. Thus, the majority of the thirteen is seven, and of the eleven six, and the two together make thirteen, which is the majority of twenty-four. But though the number is the same, the mode of counting is essentially different; the one representing the stronger interest, and the other the weaker interest of the community. The first mistake was, in supposing that the Government of the absolute majority is the Government of this people; that *beau ideal* of a perfect Government, which had been so enthusiastically entertained in every age, by the generous and patriotic, where civilization and liberty had made the smallest progress. There could be no greater error; the Government of the people is the Government of the whole community; of the twenty-four; the self-government of all the parts; too perfect to be reduced to practice in the present, or any past stage of human society. The Government of the absolute majority, instead of the Government of the people, is but the Government of the strongest interests; and when not efficiently checked, is the most tyrannical and oppressive that can be devised. Between this ideal perfection on one side, and despotism on the other, none other can be devised but that which considers society, in reference to its parts, as differently affected by the action of the Government, and which takes the sense of each part separately, and thereby the sense of the whole in the manner already illustrated.

These principles, as he had already stated, are not affected by the number of which a community may be composed, and are just as applicable to one of thirteen millions, the number which composes ours, as of the small community of twenty-four, which I have supposed, for the purpose of illustration; and are not less applicable to the twenty-four States united in one community, than to the case of the twenty-four individuals. There is, indeed, a distinction between a large and small community, not affecting the principle, but the violence of the action. In the former, the similarity of the interests of all the parts will limit the oppression from the hostile action of the parts, in a great degree, to the fiscal action of the Government merely; but in the large community, spreading over a country of great extent, and having a great diversity of interests, with different kinds of labor, capital, and production, the conflict and oppression will extend, not only to a monopoly of the appropriations, on the part of the stronger interests, but will end in unequal taxes, and a general conflict between the entire interests of conflicting sections, which, if not arrested by the most powerful checks, will terminate in the most oppressive tyranny that can be conceived, or in the destruction of the community itself.

If we turn our attention from these supposed cases, and direct it to our Government and its actual operation, we will find a practical confirmation of the truth of what has been stated, not only of the oppressive operation of the system of an absolute majority, but also a striking and beautiful illustration, in the formation of our system, of the principle of the concurring majority, as distinct from the absolute, which he had asserted to be the only means of efficiently checking the abuse of power, and, of course, the only solid foundation of constitutional liberty. That our Government, for many years, has been gradually verging to consolidation, that the constitution has gradually become a dead letter, and that all restrictions upon the power of Government have been virtually removed, so as practically to convert the General Government into a Government of an absolute majority, without check or limitation, cannot be denied by any one who has impartially observed its operation.

It is not necessary to trace the commencement and gradual progress of the causes which have produced this change in our system; it is sufficient to state that the change has taken place within the last few years. What has been the result? Precisely that which might have been anticipated—the growth of faction, corruption, anarchy, and, if not despotism itself, its near approach, as witnessed in the provisions of this bill. And from what have these consequences sprung? We have been involved in no war. We have been at peace with all the world. We have been visited with no national calamity. Our people have been advancing in general intelligence, and, I will add, great and alarming as has been the advance of political corruption, the morals and virtue of the community at large have been advancing in improvement. What, he would again repeat, is the cause? No other can be assigned but a departure from the fundamental principles of the constitution, which has converted the Government into the will of an absolute and irresponsible majority, and which, by the laws which must inevitably govern in all such majorities, have placed in conflict the great interests of the country, by a system of hostile legislation; by an oppressive and unequal imposition of taxes; by unequal and profuse appropriations; and by rendering the entire labor and capital of the weaker interest subordinate to the stronger.

This is the cause, and these the fruits, which have converted the Government into a mere instrument of taking money from one portion of the community to be given to another, and which has rallied around it a great, a powerful, and mercenary corps of office-holders, office-seekers, and expectants, destitute of principle and patriotism, and who have no standard of morals or politics but the will of the Executive—the will of him who has the distribution of the loaves and the fishes. He held it impossible for any one to look at the theoretical illustration of the principle of the absolute majority in the cases which he had supposed, and not be struck with the practical illustration in the actual operation of our Government. Under every circumstance, the majority will ever have its American system—(he meant nothing offensive to any Senator)—but the real meaning of the American system is, that system of plunder which the stronger interest ever waged, and will ever wage, against the weaker, where the latter is not armed with some efficient and constitutional check to arrest its action. Nothing but such check on the part of the weaker interest can arrest it; mere constitutional limitations are wholly inefficient. Whatever interest obtains possession of the Government will, from the nature of things, be in favor of the powers, and against the limitations imposed by the constitution, and will resort to every device that can be imagined to remove those restraints. On the contrary, the opposite interest, (that which he had designated as the stockholding interest) the tax payers, (those on whom the system operates,) will resist the abuse of powers, and contend for the limitations. And it is on that point, then, that the contest between the delegated and the reserved powers will be waged; but, in this contest, as the interests in possession of the Government are organized and armed by all its powers and patronage, the opposite interest, if not in like manner organized and possessed of a power to protect themselves under the provisions of the constitution, will be as inevitably crushed as would be a band of unorganized militia when opposed by a veteran and trained corps of regulars. Let it never be forgotten that power can only be opposed by power, organization by organization; and on this theory stands our beautiful federal system of government. No free system was ever farther removed from the principle that the absolute majority, without check or limitation, ought to govern. To understand what our Government is, we must look to the constitution, which is the basis of the system. He did not intend to enter into any minute examination of the origin and the source of its powers; it was sufficient for his purpose to state, what he did fearlessly, that it derived its power from the people of the separate States, each ratifying by itself, each binding itself by its own separate majority, through its separate convention, and the concurrence of the majorities of the several States forming the constitution; thus taking the sense of the whole by that of the several parts representing the various interests of the entire community. It was this concurring and perfect majority which formed the constitution, and not that majority which would consider the American people as a single community, and which, instead of representing fairly and fully the interests of the whole, would but represent, as has been stated, the interest of the stronger section. No candid man can dispute that he had given a correct description of the constitution-making power, that power which created and organized the Government; which delegated to it, as a common agent, certain powers, in trust for the common good of all the States; and which had imposed strict limitations and checks against abuses and usurpations. In administering the delegated powers, the constitution provides, very properly, in order to give promptitude and efficiency, that the Government should be organized upon the principle of the absolute majority, or rather of two absolute majorities combined; a majority of the States considered as bodies politic, which prevails in this body, and a majority of the people of the States, estimated in federal numbers, in the other House of Congress. A combination of the two prevails in the choice of the President; and, of course, in the appointment of judges; they being nominated by the President and confirmed by the Senate. It is thus that the concurring and the absolute majorities are combined in one complex system; the one in forming the constitution, and the other in making and executing the laws; thus beautifully blending the moderation, justice, and equity of the former and more perfect majority, with the promptness and energy of the latter, but less perfect.

To maintain the ascendancy of the constitution over the law-making majority is the great and essential point on which the success of the system must depend; unless that ascendancy can be preserved, the necessary consequence must be, that the laws will supersede the constitution; and, finally, the will of the Executive, by the influence of its patronage, will supersede the laws; indications of which are already perceptible. This ascendancy can only be preserved through the action of the States, as organized bodies, having their own separate Governments, and possessed of the rights, under the structure of our system, of judging of the extent of their separate powers, and of interposing their authority to arrest the enactments of the General

Government within their respective limits. He would not enter, at this time, into the discussion of this important point, as it had been ably and fully presented by the Senator from Kentucky, [Mr. Bibb,] and others who had preceded him in this debate, on the same side, whose arguments not only remained unanswered, but were unanswerable. It was only by this power of interpretation that the reserved rights of the States could be peacefully and efficiently protected against the encroachments of the General Government, that the limitations imposed upon its authority would be enforced, and its movements confined to the orbit allotted to it by the constitution.

It had, indeed, been said in debate, that this could be effected by the organization of the General Government itself, particularly by the action of this body, which represented the States; and that the States themselves must look to the General Government for the preservation of many of the most important of their reserved rights. Mr. C. said he did not underrate the value to be attached to the organic arrangement of the General Government, and the wise distribution of its powers between the several departments, and, in particular, the structure and the important functions of this body; but to suppose that the Senate, or any department of this Government, was intended to be the guardian of the reserved rights, was a great and fundamental mistake. The Government, through all its departments, represents the delegated and not the reserved powers; and it was a violation of the fundamental principle of free institutions, to suppose that any but the responsible representative of any interest could be its guardian. The distribution of the powers of the General Government, and its organization, were arranged to prevent the abuse of power, in fulfilling the important trusts confided to it; and not, as preposterously supposed, to protect the reserved powers, which are confided wholly to the guardianship of the several States.

Against the view of our system which he had presented, and the right of the State to interpose, it was objected, that it would lead to anarchy and dissolution. He considered the objection as without the slightest foundation; and that, so far from tending to weakness or disunion, it was the source of the highest power and of the strongest cement. Nor was its tendency in this respect difficult of explanation. The Government of an absolute majority, unchecked by efficient constitutional restraint, though apparently strong, was in reality an exceedingly feeble Government. That tendency to conflict between the parts, which he had shown to be inevitable in such Governments, wasted the powers of the State in the hostile action of contending factions, which left very little more power than the excess of the strength of the majority over the minority. But a Government based upon the principle of the concurring majority, where each great interest possessed within itself the means of self-protection, which ultimately requires the mutual consent of all the parts, necessarily causes that unanimity in counsel, and ardent attachment of all the parts to the whole, which gives an irresistable energy to a Government so constituted.

He might appeal to history for the truth of these remarks, of which the Roman furnished the most familiar and striking. It was a well known fact, that, from the expulsion of the Tarquins to the time of the establishment of the tribunarian power, the Government fell into a state of the greatest disorder and distraction, and, he might add, corruption. How did this happen? The explanation will throw important light on the subject under consideration. The community was divided into two parts, the patricians and the plebeians, with the powers of the State principally in the hands of the former, without adequate check to protect the rights of the latter. The result was as might be expected. The patricians converted the powers of the Government into the means of making money, to enrich themselves and their dependants. They, in a word, had their American system, growing out of the peculiar character of the Government and condition of the country. This requires explanation. At that period, according to the laws of nations, when one nation conquered another, the lands of the vanquished belonged to the victors; and, according to the Roman law, the lands thus acquired were divided into parts, one allotted to the poorer class of the people, and the other assigned to the use of the treasury, of which the patricians had the distribution and administration. The patricians abused their power, by withholding from the people that which ought to have been allotted to them, and by converting to their own use that which ought to have gone to the treasury. In a word, they took to themselves the entire spoils of victory, and they had thus the most powerful motive to keep the State perpetually involved in war, to the utter impoverishment and oppression of the people. After resisting the abuse of power by all peaceable means, and the oppression becoming intolerable, the people at last withdrew from the city; they, in a word, seceded; and, to induce them to reunite, the patricians conceded to the plebeians, as the means of protecting their separate interests, the very power which he contended is necessary to protect the rights of the States, but which is now represented as necessarily leading to disunion. They granted to the people the right of choosing three tribunes from among themselves, whose persons should be sacred, and who should have the right of interposing their veto, not only against the passage of laws, but even against their execution; a power which those who take a shallow insight into human nature would pronounce inconsistent with the strength and unity of the State, if not utterly impracticable. Yet, so far from that being the effect, from that day the genius of Rome became ascendant, and victory followed her steps till she had established an almost universal dominion.

How can a result so contrary to all anticipation be explained? The explanation appeared to him to be simple. No measure or movement could be adopted without the concurring consent of both the patricians and plebeians, and each thus became dependent on the other, and, of consequence, the desire and objects of neither could be effected without the concurrence of the other. To obtain this concurrence, each was compelled to consult the good will of the other, and to elevate to office not simply those who might have the confidence of the order to which he belonged, but also that of the other. The result was, that men possessing those qualities which would naturally command confidence, moderation, wisdom, justice, and patriotism, were elevated to office; and these, by the weight of their authority and the prudence of their counsel, together with that spirit of unanimity necessarily resulting from the concurring assent of the two orders, furnishes the real explanation of the power of the Roman State, and of that extraordinary wisdom, moderation, and firmness, which in so remarkable a degree characterized her public men. He might illustrate the truth of the position which he had laid down, by a reference to the history of all free States, ancient and modern, distinguished for their power and patriotism; and conclusively show not only that there was not one which had not some contrivance, under some form, by which the concurring assent of the different portions of the community was made necessary in the action of Government, but also that the virtue, patriotism, and strength of the State were in direct proportion to the strength of the means of securing such assent. In estimating the operation of this principle in our system, which depends, as he had stated, on the right of interposition on the part of the State, we must not omit to take into consideration the amending power, by which new powers may be granted, or any derangement of the system be corrected, by the concurring assent of three-fourths of the States; and thus, in the same degree, strengthening the power of repairing any derangement occasioned by the executive action of a State. In fact, the power of interposition, fairly understood, may be considered in the light of an appeal against the usurpations of the General Government, the joint agent of all the States, to the States themselves, to be decided, under the amending power, affirmatively, in favor of the Government, by the voice of three-fourths of the States, as the highest power known under the system.

Mr. C. said that he knew the difficulty, in our country, of establishing the truth of the principle for which he contended, though resting upon the clearest reason, and tested by the universal experience of free nations. He knew that the Governments of the several States would be cited as an argument against the conclusion to which he had arrived, and which, for the most part, were constructed on the principle of the absolute majority; but, in his opinion, a satisfactory answer could be given: that the objects of expenditure which fell within the sphere of a State Government were few and inconsiderable; so that, be their action ever so irregular, it could occasion but little derangement. If, instead of being members of this great confederacy, they formed distinct communities, and were compelled to raise armies, and incur other expenses necessary for their defense, the laws which he had laid down as necessarily controlling the action of a State, where the will of an absolute and unchecked majority prevailed, would speedily disclose themselves in faction, anarchy, and corruption. Even as the case is, the operation of the causes to which he had referred were perceptible in some of the larger and more populous members of the Union, whose Governments had a powerful central action, and which already showed a strong tendency to that moneyed action which is the invariable forerunner of corruption and convulsions.

But to return to the General Government; we have now sufficient experience to ascertain that the tendency to conflict in its action is between southern and other sections. The latter, having a decided majority, must habitually be possessed of the powers of the Government, both in this and in the other House; and, being governed by that instinctive love of power so natural to the human breast, they must become the advocates of the power of Government, and in the same degree opposed to the limitations; while the other and weaker section is as necessarily thrown on the side of the limitations. In one word, the one section is the natural guardian of the delegated powers, and the other of the reserved; and the struggle on the side of the former will be to enlarge the powers, while that on the opposite side will be to restrain them within their constitutional limits. The contest will, in fact, be a contest between power and liberty, and such he considered the present; a contest in which the weaker section, with its peculiar labor, productions, and situation, has at stake all that can be dear to freemen. Should they be able to maintain in their full vigor their reserved rights, liberty and prosperity will be their portion; but if they yield, and permit the stronger interest to consolidate within itself all the powers of the Government, then will its fate be more wretched than that of the aborigines whom they have expelled, or of their slaves. In this great struggle between the delegated and reserved powers, so far from repining that his lot and that of those whom he represented is cast on the side of the latter, he rejoiced that such is the fact; for though we participate in but few of the advantages of the Government, we are compensated, and more than compensated, in not being so much exposed to its corruption. Nor did he repine that the duty, so difficult to be discharged, as the defence of the reserved powers against, apparently, such fearful odds, had been assigned to them. To discharge successfully this high duty requires the highest qualities, moral and intellectual; and, should we perform it with a zeal and ability in proportion to its magnitude, instead of being mere planters, our section will become distinguished for its patriots and statesmen. But, on the other hand, if we prove unworthy of this high destiny, if we yield to the steady encroachment of power, the severest and most debasing calamity and corruption will overspread the land. Every Southern man, true to the interests of his section, and faithful to the duties which Providence has allotted him, will be forever excluded from the honors and emoluments of this Government, which will be reserved for those only who have qualified themselves, by political prostitution, for admission into the Magdalen Asylum.

5 ON THE BILL FOR THE ADMISSION OF MICHIGAN, JANUARY 5, 1837

This speech of Calhoun's on the admission of Michigan illustrates well three of the themes of his political thought in the context of practice: the federal nature of the government, the weakness of majority rule, as such, and the importance of a true conservatism. The circumstances giving rise to Calhoun's speech were the refusal of a duly constituted convention meeting at Ann Arbor, Michigan, to accept the boundaries established by the act of Congress admitting Michigan as a state and the acceptance of these boundaries by the spontaneously organized convention which followed. Calhoun objected to the recognition of this second convention by Congress. The second convention was recognized and Michigan admitted.

I have (said Mr. C.) been connected with this Government more than half its existence, in various capacities, and during that long period I have looked on its action with attention, and have endeavored to make myself acquainted with the principles and character of our political institutions, and I can truly say that within that time no measure has received the sanction of Congress which has appeared to me more unconstitutional and dangerous than the present. It assails our political system in its weakest point, and where, at this time, it most requires defence.

The great and leading objections to the bill rest mainly on the ground that Michigan is a State. They have been felt by its friends to have so much weight, that its advocates have been compelled to deny the fact, as the only way of meeting the objections. Here, then, is the main point at issue between the friends and the opponents of the bill. It turns on a fact, and that fact presents the question—is Michigan a State?

If (said Mr. C.) there ever was a party committed on a fact, if there ever was one estopped from denying it, that party is the present majority in the Senate, and that fact, that Michigan is a State. It is the very party who urged through this body, at the last session, a bill for the admission of the State of Michigan, which accepted her constitution, and declared in the most explicit and strongest terms that she was a State. I will not take up the time of the Senate by reading this solemn declaration. It has frequently been read during this debate, and is familiar to all who hear me, and has not been questioned or denied. But it has been said there is a condition annexed to the declaration, with which she must comply, before she can become a State. There is, indeed, a condition, but it has been shown by my colleague and others, from the plain wording of the act, that the condition is not attached to the acceptance of the constitution, nor the declaration that she is a State, but simply to her admission into the Union. I will not repeat the argument, but, in order to place the subject beyond controversy, I shall recall to memory the history of the last session, as connected with the admission of Michigan. The facts need but to be referred to, in order to revive their recollection.

There were two points proposed to be effected by the friends of the bill at the last session. The first was to settle the controversy, as to boundary, between Michigan and Ohio, and it was that object alone which imposed the condition that Michigan should assent to the boundary prescribed by the act, as the condition of her admission. But there was another object to be accomplished. Two respectable gentlemen, who had been elected by the State as Senators, were then waiting to take their seats on this floor; and the other object of the bill was to provide for their taking their seats as Senators on the admission of the State; and for this purpose it was necessary to make the positive and unconditional declaration that Michigan was a State, as a

State only could choose Senators, by an express provision of the constitution; and hence the admission was made conditional, and the declaration that she was a State was made absolute, in order to effect both objects. To show that I am correct, I will ask the Secretary to read the third section of the bill.

[The section was read accordingly, as follows:

"Sec. 3. *And be it further enacted*, That as a compliance with the fundamental condition of admission contained in the last preceding section of this act, the boundaries of the said State of Michigan, as in that section described, declared, and established, shall receive the assent of a convention of delegates elected by the people of said State, for the sole purpose of giving the assent herein required; and as soon as the assent herein required shall be given, the President of the United States shall announce the same by proclamation; and thereupon, and without any further proceeding on the part of Congress, the admission of the said State into the Union, as one of the United States of America, on an equal footing with the original States in all respects whatever, shall be considered as complete, and the Senators and Representative who have been elected by the said State, as its representatives in the Congress of the United States, shall be entitled to take their seats in the Senate and House of Representatives, respectively, without further delay."] *

Mr. CALHOUN then asked, Does not every Senator see the

---

*The first sections of the bill are:

A Bill to admit the State of Michigan into the Union upon an equal footing with the original States.

Whereas, in pursuance of the act of Congress of June the fifteenth, eighteen hundred and thirty-six, entitled "An Act to establish the northern boundary of the State of Ohio, and to provide for the admission of the State of Michigan into the Union, upon the conditions therein expressed" a convention of delegates, elected by the people of the said State of Michigan, for the sole purpose of giving their consent to the boundaries of the said State of Michigan as described, declared, and established, in and by the said act, did on the fifteenth of December, eighteen hundred and thirty-six, assent to the provisions of said act: therefore,

Be it enacted, &c. That the State of Michigan shall be one, and is hereby declared to be one, of the United States of America, and admitted into the Union on an equal footing with the original States in all respects whatever.

SEC. 2. *And be it further enacted*, That the Secretary of the Treasury, in carrying into effect the thirteenth and fourteenth sections of the twenty-third of June, eighteen hundred and thirty-six, entitled "An Act to regulate the deposits of the public money", shall consider the State of Michigan as being one of the United States.

two objects—the one to settle the boundary, and the other to admit her Senators to a seat in this body; and that the section is so worded as to effect both, in the manner I have stated? If this needed confirmation, it would find it in the debate on the passage of the bill, when the ground was openly taken by the present majority, that Michigan had a right to form her constitution, under the ordinance of 1787, without our consent; and that she was, of right, and in fact, a State, beyond our control.

I will (said Mr. C.) explain my own views on this point, in order that the consistency of my course at the last and present session may be clearly seen.

My opinion was, and still is, that the movement of the people of Michigan, in forming for themselves a State constitution, without waiting for the assent of Congress, was revolutionary, as it threw off the authority of the United States over the Territory; and that we were left at liberty to treat the proceedings as revolutionary, and to remand her to her territorial condition, or to waive the irregularity, and to recognise what was done as rightfully done, as our authority alone was concerned.

My impression was, that the former was the proper course; but I also thought that the act remanding her back should contain our assent in the usual manner for her to form a constitution, and thus to leave her free to become a State. This, however, was overruled. The opposite opinion prevailed, that she had a perfect right to do what she had done, and that she was, as I have stated, a State, both in fact and right, and that we had no control over her; and our act accordingly recognised her as a State, from the time she had adopted her constitution, and admitted her into the Union on the condition of her assenting to the prescribed boundaries. Having thus solemnly recognised her as a State, we cannot now undo what was then done. There were, in fact, many irregularities in the proceedings, all of which were urged in vain against its passage; but the presidential election was then pending, and the vote of Michigan was considered of sufficient weight to overrule all objections, and correct all irregularities. They were all accordingly overruled, and we cannot now go back.

Such was the course and such the acts of the majority at the last session. A few short months have since passed. Other objects are now to be effected, and all is forgotten as completely as if they had never existed. The very Senators who then forced the act through, on the ground that Michigan was a State, have wheeled completely round, to serve the present purpose, and taken directly the opposite ground! We live in strange and inconsistent times. Opinions are taken up and laid down, as suits the occasion, without hesitation, or the slightest regard to principles or consistency. It indicates an unsound state of the public mind, pregnant with future disasters.

I turn to the position now assumed by the majority, to suit the present occasion; and, if I mistake not, it will be found as false in fact, and as erroneous in principle, as it is inconsistent with that maintained at the last session. They now take the ground that Michigan is not a State, and cannot, in fact, be a State, till she is admitted into the Union; and this on the broad principle that a Territory cannot become a State till admitted. Such is the position distinctly taken by several of the friends of this bill, and implied in the arguments of nearly all who have spoken in its favor. In fact, its advocates had no choice. As untenable as it is, they were forced on this desperate position. They had no other which they could occupy.

I have shown that it is directly in the face of the law of the last session, and that it denies the recorded acts of those who now maintain the position. I now go further, and assert that it is in direct opposition to plain and unquestionable matter of fact. There is no fact more certain than that Michigan is a State. She is in the full exercise of sovereign authority, with a Legislature and a Chief Magistrate. She passes laws; she executes them; she regulates titles; and even takes away life—all on her own authority. Ours has entirely ceased over her; and yet there are those who can deny, with all these facts before them, that she is a State. They might as well deny the existence of this hall! We have long since assumed unlimited control over the constitution, to twist, and turn, and deny it, as it suited our purpose. And it would seem that we are presumptuously attempting to assume like supremacy over facts themselves, as if their existence or non-existence depended on our volition. I speak freely. The occasion demands that the truth should be boldly uttered.

But those who may not regard their own recorded acts, nor the plain facts of the case, may possibly feel the awkward condition in which coming events may shortly place them. The admission of Michigan is not the only point involved in the passage of this bill. A question will follow, which may be presented to the Senate in a very few days, as to the right of Mr. Norvell and Mr. Lyon, the two respectable gentlemen who have been elected Senators by Michigan, to take their seats in this hall. The decision of this question will require a more sudden facing about than has been yet witnessed. It required seven or eight months for the majority to wheel about from the position maintained at the last session, to that taken at this, but there may not be allowed them now as many days to wheel back to the old position. These gentlemen cannot be refused their seats after the admission of the State, by those gentlemen who passed the act of the last session. It provides for the case. I now put it to the friends of this bill, and I ask them to weigh the question deliberately—to bring it home to their bosom and conscience before they answer—can a Territory elect Senators to Congress? The constitution is express. States only can choose Senators. Were not these gentlemen chosen long before the admission of Michigan, before the Ann Arbor meeting, and while Michigan was, according to the doctrines of the friends of this bill, a Territory? Will they, in the face of the constitution, which they are sworn to support, admit as Senators on this floor those who, by their own statement, were elected by a Territory? These questions may soon be presented for decision. The majority, who are forcing this bill through, are already committed by the act of the last session, and I leave them to reconcile, as they can, the ground they now take with the vote they must give when the question of their right to take their seats is presented for decision.

A total disregard of all principle and consistency has so entangled this subject, that there is but one mode left of extricating ourselves without tramping the constitution in the dust; and that is, to return back to where we stood when the question was first presented; to acquiesce in the right of Michigan to form a constitution, and erect herself into a State, under the ordinance of 1787; and to repeal so much of the act of the last session as prescribed the condition on which she was to be admitted. This was the object of the amendment that I offered last evening, in order to relieve the Senate from its present dilemma. The amendment involved the merits of the whole case. It was too late in the day for discussion, and I asked for indulgence till to-day, that I might have an opportunity of presenting my views. Under the iron rule of the present majority, the indulgence was refused, and the bill ordered to its third reading; and I have been thus compelled to address the Senate when it is too late to amend the bill, and after a majority have committed themselves both as to its principles and details. New as such proceedings are in this body, I complain not. I, as one of the minority, ask no favors. All I ask is, that the constitution be not violated. Hold it sacred, and I shall be the last to complain.

I now return to the assumption that a Territory cannot become a State till admitted into the Union, which is now relied on with so much confidence to prove that Michigan is not a State. I reverse the position. I assert the opposite, that a Territory cannot be admitted till she becomes a State; and in this I stand on the authority of the constitution itself, which expressly limits the power of Congress to admitting new States into the Union. But if the constitution had been silent, he would indeed be ignorant of the character of our political system who did not see that States, sovereign and independent communities, and not Territories, can only be admitted. Ours is a Union of States, a federal republic. States, and not Territories, form its component parts, bound together by a solemn league, in the form of a constitutional compact. In coming into the Union, the State pledges its faith to this sacred compact; an act which none but a sovereign and independent community is competent to perform; and, of course, a Territory must first be raised to that condition before she can take her stand among the confederated States of our Union. How can a Territory pledge its faith to the constitution? It has no will of its own. You give it all its powers, and you can at pleasure overrule all her actions. If she enters as a Territory, the act is yours, not hers. Her consent is nothing without your authority and sanction. Can you, can Congress, become a party to the constitutional compact? How absurd.

But I am told, if this be so, if a Territory must become a State before is can be admitted, it would follow that she might refuse to enter the Union after she had acquired the right of acting for herself. Certainly she may. A State cannot be forced into the Union. She must come in by her own free assent, given in her highest sovereign capacity, through a convention of the people of the State. Such is the constitutional provision; and those who make the objection must overlook both the constitution and the elementary principles of our Government, of which the right of self-government is the first; the right of every people to form their own Government, and to determine their political condition. This is the doctrine on which our fathers acted in our glorious Revolution, which has done more for the cause of liberty throughout the world than any event within the record of history, and on which the Government has acted from the first, as regards all that portion of our extensive territory that lies beyond the limits of the original States. Read the ordinance of 1787, and the various acts for the admission of new States, and you will find the principle invariably recognised and acted on, to the present unhappy instance, without any departure from it, except in the case of Missouri. The admission of Michigan is destined, I fear, to mark a great change in the history of the admission of new States, a total departure from the old usage, and the noble principle of self-government on which that usage was founded. Every thing, thus far, has been irregular and monstrous connected with her admission. I trust it is not ominous. Surrounded by lakes within her natural limits, (which ought not to have been departed from,) possessed of fertile soil and genial climate, with every prospect of wealth, power, and influence, who but must regret that she should be ushered into the Union in a manner so irregular and unworthy of her future destiny.

But I will waive these objections, constitutional and all. I will suppose, with the advocates of the bill, that a Territory cannot become a State till admitted into the Union. Assuming all this, I ask them to explain to me how the mere act of admission can transmute a Territory into a State? By whose authority would she be made a State? By ours? How can we make a State? We can form a Territory; we can admit States into the Union; but, I repeat the question, how can we make a State? I had supposed this Government was the creature of the States—formed by their authority, and dependent on their will for their existence. Can the creature form the creator? If not by our authority, then by whose? Not by her own: that would be absurd. The very act of admission makes her a member of the confederacy, with no other or greater power than is possessed by all the others; all of whom, united, cannot create a State. By what process, then, by what authority, can a Territory become a State, if not one before admitted? Who can explain? How full of difficulties, compared to the long-established, simple, and noble process which has prevailed to the present instant. According to old usage, the General Government first withdraws its authority over a certain portion of its territory, as soon as it has a sufficient population to constitute a State. They are thus left to themselves freely to form a constitution, and to exercise the noble right of self-government. They then present their constitution to Congress, and ask the privilege (for one it is of the highest character) to become a member of this glorious confederacy of States. The constitution is examined, and, if republican, as required by the federal constitution, she is admitted, with no other condition except such as may be necessary to secure the authority of Congress over the public domain within her limits. This is the old, the established form, instituted by our ancestors of the Revolution, who so well understood the great principles of liberty and self-government. How simple; how sublime! What a contrast to the doctrines of the present day, and the precedent which, I fear, we are about to establish! And shall we fear, so long as these sound principles are observed, that a State will reject this high privilege—will refuse to enter this Union? No; she will rush into your embrace, so long as your institutions are worth preserving. When the advantages of the Union shall have become a matter of calculation and doubt, when new States shall pause to determine whether the Union is a curse or blessing, the question which now agitates us will cease to have any importance.

Having now, I trust, established, beyond all controversy, that Michigan in a State, I come to the great point at issue—to the decision of which all that has been said is but preparatory—had the self-created assembly which met at Ann Arbor the authority to speak in the name of the people of Michigan, to assent to the conditions contained in the act of the last session, to supersede a portion of the constitution of the State, and to overrule the dissent of the convention of the people, regularly called by the constituted authorities of the State, to the condition of admission? I shall not repeat what I said when I first addressed the Senate on this bill. We all, by this time, know the character of that assemblage; that it met without the sanction of the authorities of the State, and that it did not pretend to represent one third of the people. We all know that the State had regularly convened a convention of the people, expressly to take into consideration the condition on which it was proposed to admit her into the Union, and that the convention, after full deliberation, had declined to give its assent by a considerable majority. With a knowledge of all these facts, I put the question—had the assembly a right to act for the State? Was it a convention of the people of Michigan, in the true, legal, and constitutional sense of that term? Is there one, within the limits of my voice, that can lay his hand on his breast, and honestly say it was? Is there one that does not feel that it was neither more nor less than a mere caucus—nothing but a party caucus—of which we have the strongest evidence in the perfect unanimity of those who assembled? Not a vote was given against admission. Can there be stronger proof that it was a meeting got up by party machinery, for party purpose?

But I go further. It was not only a party caucus, for party purpose, but a criminal meeting—a meeting to subvert the authority of the State, and to assume its sovereignty. I know not whether Michigan has yet passed laws to guard her sovereignty. It may be that she has not had time to enact laws for this purpose, which no community is long without; but I do aver, if there be such an act, or if the common law be in force in the State, the actors in that meeting might be indicted, tried, and punished, for the very act on which it is now proposed to admit the State into the Union. If such a meeting as this were to undertake to speak in the name of South Carolina, we would speedily teach its authors what they owed to the authority and dignity of the State. The act was not only in contempt of the authority of the State of Michigan, but a direct insult on this Government. Here is a self-created meeting, convened for a criminal object, which has dared to present to this Government an act of theirs, and to expect that we are to receive this irregular and criminal act as a fulfilment of the condition which we had prescribed for the admission of the State! Yet, I fear, forgetting our own dignity and the rights of Michigan, that we are about to recognise the validity of the act, and quietly to submit to the insult.

The year 1836 (said Mr. C.) is destined to mark the most remarkable change in our political institutions, since the adoption of the constitution. The events of the year have made a deeper innovation on the principles of the constitution, and evinced a stronger tendency to revolution, than any which have occurred from its adoption to the present day. Sir, (said Mr. C., addressing the Vice President,) duty compels me to speak of facts intimately connected with yourself. In deference to your feelings as presiding officer of the body, I shall speak of them with all possible reserve, much more reserve than I should otherwise have done if you did not occupy that seat. Among the first of these events, which I shall notice, is the caucus of Baltimore; that too, like the Ann Arbor caucus, has been dignified with the name of the convention of the people. This caucus was got up under the countenance and express authority of the President himself; and its edict, appointing you his successor, has been sustained, not only by the whole patronage and power of the Government, but by his active personal influence and exertion. Through its instrumentality he has succeeded in controlling the voice of the people, and for the first time the President has appointed his successor; and thus the first great step of converting our Government into a monarchy has been achieved. These are solemn and ominous facts. No one who has examined the result of the last election can doubt their truth. It is now certain that you are not the free and unbiased choice of the people of these United States. If left to your own popularity, without the active and direct influence of the President, and the power and patronage of the Government, acting through a mock convention of the people, instead of the highest, you would in all probability have been the lowest of the candidates.

During the same year, the State in which this ill-omened caucus convened has been agitated by revolutionary movements of the most alarming character. Assuming the dangerous doctrines that they were not bound to obey the injunctions of the constitution, because it did not place the powers of the State in the hands of an unchecked numerical majority, the electors belonging to the party of the Baltimore caucus who had been chosen to appoint the State Senators refused, to perform the functions for which they had been elected, with the deliberate intention to subvert the Government of the State, and reduce her to the territorial condition, till a new Government could be formed. And now we have before us a measure not less revolutionary, but of an opposite character. In the case of Maryland, those who undertook, without the authority of law or constitution, to speak and act in the name of the people of the State, proposed to place her out of the Union by reducing her from a State to a Territory; but in this, those who in like manner undertook to act for Michigan have assumed the authority to bring her into the Union without her consent, on the very condition which she had rejected by a convention of the people convened under the authority of the State. If we shall sanction the authority of the Michigan caucus, to force a State into the Union without its assent, why might we not here sanction a similar caucus in Maryland, if one had been called, to place the State out of the Union?

These occurrences, which have distinguished the past year, mark the commencement of no ordinary change in our political system. They announce the ascendency of the caucus system over the regularly constituted authorities of the country. I have long anticipated this event. In early life my attention was attracted to the working of the caucus system. It was my fortune to spend five or six years of my youth in the Northern portion of the Union, where, unfortunately, the system has so long prevailed. Though young, I was old enough to take interest in public affairs, and to notice the working of this odious party machine; and after reflection, with the experience then acquired, has long satisfied me that, in the course of time, the edicts of the caucus would eventually supersede the authority of law and constitution. We have at last arrived at the commencement of this great change, which is destined to go on till it has consummated itself in the entire overthrow of all legal and constitutional authority, unless speedily and effectually resisted. The reason is obvious: for obedience and disobedience to the edicts of the caucus, where the system is firmly established, are more certainly and effectually rewarded and punished, than to the laws and constitution. Disobedience to the former is sure to be followed by complete political disfranchisement. It deprives the unfortunate individual who falls under its vengeance of all public honors and emoluments, and consigns him, if dependent on the Government, to poverty and obscurity; while he who bows down before its mandates, it matters not how monstrous, secures to himself the honors of the State—becomes rich, and distinguished, and powerful. Offices, jobs, and contracts, flow on him and his connexions. But to obey the law and respect the constitution, for the most part, brings little except the approbation of conscience—a reward indeed high and noble, and prized by the virtuous above all others, but unfortunately little valued by the mass of mankind. It is easy to see what must be the end, unless, indeed, an effective remedy be applied. Are we so blind as not to see in this why it is that the advocates of this bill—the friends of the system—are so tenacious on the point that Michigan should be admitted on the authority of the Ann Arbor caucus, and no other? Do we not see why the amendment proposed by myself to admit her by rescinding the condition imposed at the last session should be so strenuously opposed? Why, even the preamble would not be surrendered, though many of our friends were willing to vote for the bill on that slight concession, in their anxiety to admit the State.

And here let me say that I listened with attention to the speech of the Senator from Kentucky, [Mr. CRITTENDEN.] I know the clearness of his understanding, and the soundness of his heart, and I am persuaded, in declaring that his objection to the bill was confined to the preamble, that he has not investigated the subject with the attention it deserves. I feel the objections to the preamble are not without some weight; but the true and insuperable objections lie far deeper in the facts of the case, which would still exist were the preamble expunged. It is these which render it impossible to pass this bill without trampling under foot the rights of the States, and subverting the first principles of our Government. It would require but a few steps more to effect a complete revolution, and the Senator from North Carolina has taken the first. I will explain. If you wish to mark the first indications of a revolution, the commencement of those profound changes in the character of a people which are working beneath, before a ripple appears on the surface, look to the change of language; you will first notice it in the altered meaning of important words, and which, as it indicates a change in the feelings and principles of the people, become in turn a powerful instrument in accelerating the change, till an entire revolution is effected. The remarks of the Senator will illustrate what I have said. He told us that the terms "convention of the people" were of very uncertain meaning, and difficult to be defined; but that their true meaning was, any meeting of the people in their individual and primary character, for political purpose. I know it is difficult to define complex terms, that is, to enumerate all the ideas that belong to them, and exclude all that do not; but there is always, in the most complex, some prominent idea which marks the meaning of the term, and in relation to which there is usually no disagreement. Thus, according to the old meaning, (and which I had still supposed was its legal and constitutional meaning,) a convention of the people invariably implied a meeting of the people, either by themselves, or by delegates expressly chosen for the purpose, in their high sovereign authority, in express contradistinction to such assemblies of individuals in their private character, or having only derivative authority. It is, in a word, a meeting of the people in the majesty of their power—in that in which they may rightfully make or abolish constitutions, and put up or put down Governments at their pleasure. Such was the august conception which formerly entered the mind of every American when the terms "convention of the people" were used. But now, according to the ideas of the dominant party, as we are told on the authority of the Senator from North Carolina, it means any meeting of individuals for political purposes, and, of course, applies to the meeting at Ann Arbor, or any other party caucus for party purposes, which the leaders choose to designate as a convention of the people. It is thus the highest authority known to our laws and constitution is gradually sinking to the level of those meetings which regulate the operation of political parties, and through which the edicts of their leaders are announced, and their authority enforced; or, rather, to speak more correctly, the latter are gradually rising to the authority of the former. When they come to be completely confounded, when the distinction between a caucus and the convention of the people shall be completely obliterated, which the definition of the Senator, and the acts of this body on this bill, would lead us to believe is not far distant, this fair political fabric of ours, erected by the wisdom and patriotism of our ancestors, and once the gaze and admiration of the world, will topple to the ground in ruins.

It has, perhaps, been too much my habit to look more to the future, and less to the present, than is wise; but such is the constitution of mind, that when I see before me the indications of causes calculated to effect important changes in our political condition, I am led irresistibly to trace them to their sources, and follow them out in their consequences. Language has been held in this discussion which is clearly revolutionary in its character and tendency, and which warns us of the approach of the period when the struggle will be between the conservatives and the destructives. I understood the Senator from Pennsylvania [Mr. BUCHANAN] as holding language countenancing the principle that the will of a mere numerical majority is paramount to the authority of law and constitution. He did not indeed announce distinctly this principle, but it might fairly be inferred from what he said; for he told us the people of a State, where the constitution gives the same weight to a smaller as to a greater number, might take the remedy into their own hand; meaning, as I understood him, that a mere majority might at their pleasure subvert the constitution and Government of a State, which he seemed to think was the essence of democracy. Our little State has a constitution that could not stand a day against such doctrines, and yet we glory in it as the best in the Union. It is a constitution which respects all the great interests of the State, giving to each a separate and distinct voice in the management of its political affairs, by means of which the feebler interests are protected against the preponderance of the greater. We call our State a republic, a commonwealth, not a democracy; and let me tell the Senator it is a far more popular Government than if it had been based on the simple principle of the numerical majority. It takes more voices to put the machine of Government in motion, than in those that the Senator would consider more popular. It represents all the interests of the State, and is in fact the Government of the people, in the true sense of the term, and not that of the mere majority, or the dominant interests.

I am not familiar with the constitution of Maryland, to which the Senator alluded, and cannot, therefore, speak of its structure with confidence; but I believe it to be somewhat similar in its character to our own. That it is a Government not without its excellence, we need no better proof than the fact, that though within the shadow of executive influence, it has nobly and successfully resisted all the seductions by which a corrupt and artful administration, with almost boundless patronage, has tempted to seduce her into its ranks.

Looking, then, to the approaching struggle, I take my stand immoveably. I am a conservative in its broadest and fullest sense, and such I shall ever remain, unless, indeed, the Government shall become so corrupt and disordered that nothing short of revolution can reform it. I solemnly believe that our political system is in its purity not only the best that ever was formed, but the best possible that can be devised for us. It is the only one by which free States, so populous and wealthy, and occupying so vast an extent of territory, can preserve their liberty. Thus thinking, I cannot hope for a better. Having no hope of a better, I am a conservative; and because I am a conservative, I am a States rights man. I believe that in the rights of the States are to be found the only effectual means of checking the over-action of this Government; to resist its tendency to concentrate all power here, and to prevent a departure from the constitution; or, in case of one, to restore the Government to its original simplicity and purity. State interposition, or, to express it more fully, the right of a State to interpose her sovereign voice, as one of the parties to our constitutional compact, against the encroachments of this Government, is the only means of sufficient potency to effect all this; and I am, therefore, its advocate. I rejoiced to hear the Senators from North Carolina [Mr. BROWN] and from Pennsylvania [Mr. BUCHANAN] do us the justice to distinguish between nullification and the anarchical and revolutionary movements in Maryland and Pennsylvania. I know they did not intend it as a compliment; but I regard it as the highest. They are right. Day and night are not more different—more unlike in every thing. They are unlike in their principles, their objects, and their consequences.

I shall not stop to make good this assertion, as I might easily do. The occasion does not call for it. As a conservative, and a States rights man, or, if you will have it, a nullifier, I have and shall resist all encroachments on the constitution, whether it be the encroachment of this Government on the States, or the opposite; the Executive on Congress, or Congress on the Executive. My creed is to hold both Governments, and all the departments of each, to their proper sphere, and to maintain the authority of the laws and the constitution against all revolutionary movements. I believe the means which our system furnishes to preserve itself are ample, if fairly understood and applied; and I shall resort to them, however corrupt and disordered the times, so long as there is hope of reforming the Government. The result is in the hands of the Disposer of events. It is my part to do my duty. Yet, while I thus openly avow myself a conservative, God forbid I should ever deny the glorious right of rebellion and revolution. Should corruption and oppression become intolerable, and cannot otherwise be thrown off; if liberty must perish, or the Government be overthrown, I would not hesitate, at the hazard of life, to resort to revolution, and to tear down a corrupt Government that could neither be reformed nor borne by freemen; but I trust in God things will never come to that pass. I trust never to see such fearful times; for fearful, indeed, they would be, if they should ever befall us. It is the last experiment, and not to be thought of till common sense and the voice of mankind would justify the resort.

Before I resume my seat, I feel called on to make a few brief remarks on a doctrine of fearful import, which has been broached in the course of this debate—the right to repeal laws granting bank charters, and, of course, of railroads, turnpikes, and joint stock companies. It is a doctrine of fearful import, and calculated to do infinite mischief. There are countless millions vested in such stocks, and it is a description of property of the most delicate character. To touch it is almost to destroy it. But, while I enter my protest against all such doctrines, I have been greatly alarmed with the thoughtless precipitancy (not to use a stronger phrase) with which the most extensive and dangerous privileges have been granted of late. It can end in no good, and, I fear, may be the cause of convulsions hereafter. We already feel the effects on the currency, which no one competent of judging but must see is in an unsound condition. I must say (for truth compels me) I have ever distrusted the banking system, at least in its present form, both in this country and Great Britain. It will not stand the test of time; but I trust that all shocks, or sudden revolution, may be avoided, and that it may gradually give way before some sounder and better-regulated system of credit which the growing intelligence of the age may devise. That a better may be substituted I cannot doubt, but of what it shall consist, and how it shall finally supersede the present uncertain and fluctuating currency, time alone can determine. All I can see is, that the present must, one day or another, come to an end, or be greatly modified, if that, indeed, can save it from an entire overthrow. It has within itself the seeds of its own destruction.

6 ON THE AMENDMENT PROPOSED TO MR. WEBSTER'S BILL IN REGARD TO PUBLIC DEPOSITS, JUNE 28, 1838

Calhoun's defense of the South, explicitly developed after the Nullification Crisis of 1832, left him open to the charge of partisanship. He saw his own position, as this speech suggests, not as a deviation from the American political tradition but as an adherence to the principles which this order should exemplify. Because he spoke in the light of theoretical principle, Calhoun thought of himself as politically independent, devoted to consistency and truth, and acting, always as it was his duty to act.

I rise to notice some remarks of the Senator from Kentucky, [Mr. CLAY,] intended to represent me as a partisan of the Administration. I have no fear that they would have the least possible effect within the limits of these walls, where my course is well known and understood. I confidently appeal to every Senator present, whether my acts and votes, on all occasions, have not been in strict conformity to principles which I have been known long to entertain. Not an instance can be pointed out to the contrary. But though the Senator's declarations will be harmless here, they may not be so beyond these walls, where they were intended to have an effect, if I should remain silent; and it is only on that account I notice them. I am no partisan of any man, nor any Administration. I am free to act on all questions according to my unbiassed judgment, unembarrassed by party trammels. I concur with the Administration on the great question of the Constitutional Treasury, and have, and will continue to give them, so far as that is concerned, a sincere, decided, and hearty support; and shall stand prepared to support or oppose whatever other measure they may propose, just as it may, or may not, accord with my principles and views of policy. I hope they may give me many opportunities to support, and few to oppose, them. It is my fortune to stand here alone, looking to no other guide in the discharge of my duty but God and my conscience. I seek neither office nor popular favor.

The Senator asks me if I belong to that sectional party in the South, which he intimates has views not very friendly to the continuance of the Union. He was not very explicit in his reference. If he means the party there which has stood up for Southern rights and interests—the party opposed to the Tariff and his American System, to unequal and excessive duties and appropriations, the party opposed to Abolition, and in favor of the direct trade—I am proud to say that I do belong to that party; but, if he refers to any party entertaining views or feelings hostile to the Union, I have only to say I know of no such party there, nor do I belong to any such.

Providence (Mr. President) has pleased to cast my lot in the weakest and most exposed section of the Union; and I have, and shall continue to defend it, as far as my abilities go, against all oppression and unconstitutional acts, without regarding how it may affect my popularity and standing in other quarters. Nor, in doing this, am I in the least actuated by a feeling of hostility towards this Union, or any section of the country. I defy my most bitter enemy to point out any act of injustice or oppression towards any other portion of the Union, that I have ever countenanced, unless, indeed, resistance to injustice towards my own should be considered injustice towards other sections, which might be benefitted by it. So far from hostility, I have been governed by directly the opposite motives—by a deep and an abiding attachment to the Union, and the most anxious desire to preserve it and its integrity. Our Union rests on justice—on the equal distribution of its advantages and burthens. So long as that is preserved, there is no danger of the Union; while, on the other hand, if it be habitually and permanently disregarded, nothing can preserve it. He knows nothing of the human heart, or the working of a political system extended over so wide a country, who does not see that there must be a constant tendency on the part of the stronger portion to monopolise all the advantages for itself, and to transfer all its burthens to the weaker. Nor is he less ignorant, who does not see that such a tendency must, in the end, prove fatal to the Government, if not steadily and successfully resisted. It has been my fortune to see and act on these principles, and in doing so I have been governed not only by a sense of justice towards those whom I represent, and the portion of the country to which they belong, but by deep devotion to the interest of the whole Union. The Senator seems to take a different view. He would seem to regard resistance to wrong as hostility to the Union, and the support of aggression as the means of preserving it. He habitually confines his censure to those who oppose oppression, without ever raising his voice against the oppressor. I am, however, glad to see that he does not entirely deny the truth of the principles on which I act. He is at last compelled to admit, that Abolition is making greater progress than he had anticipated, and to acknowledge that the time may come when he shall be compelled to take a stand and lead against the fanatics. We may then oppose aggression, I suppose, without losing attachment to the Union, at least on the Abolition question; but if we may do it in that case, I would ask why we may not also against the Tariff and American System, and other oppressive measures to which the South has been opposed? Why shall it be justifiable in the one and not in the other case?

The Senator thinks I have been too stern and uncompromising in my opposition to the fanatics, and that its effect has been to increase their number. He would take a more compromising course. He would have opened the doors of this chamber to their admission, and reasoned the case with them, whether we had a title to our property or not. Without adding a word, I leave those interested to judge which of the two courses is the safest and best.

The Senator regards the defeat of the Constitutional Treasury bill in the other House, as a complete overthrow, and raises the shout of victory. He greatly mistakes. It is but a skirmish at the commencement of a conflict, which is destined to last for years. The cause of the struggle is too deep to terminate with the first onset; and so far from being discouraged by the slight defeat which some half a dozen of votes would have turned into a victory, I feel a renewed assurance of final and complete triumph, if we but stand fast. What I always dreaded, as I have said, was the first shock. I never doubted, if it could be resisted, a final and glorious triumph awaited the cause we advocated. We have now met the first shock; and, so far from being overwhelmed, we have been defeated by only a few votes. Time is now working for us. The discussion is gone to the community. Truth and reason are on our side. Our arguments neither have, nor can be, answered; and time and reflection only are wanting to give them their full effect. The people are roused; and their attention is intensely directed to the subject, which will not fail to tell hereafter.

In the mean time, the difficulties on the opposite side will soon begin to present themselves. They have thus far had the easy task of being the assailants, but the very victory, of which they boast so much, throws the responsibility on them, and will compel them to move; and let me tell the Senator, when he comes to bring forward his gigantic scheme of blending into one the General and State Governments, and uniting the two with the great capitalists of the country in his fifty million bank, with the view of controlling the currency and industry of the country. When, in a word, he comes *to rear up his bank monarchy* to govern the country with despotic sway; he will begin to find his trouble. He will find it no easy task to fix on the seat of its empire, and place the despot on his throne; and whenever he attempts it, let me tell him, instead of a slight defeat of a few votes, as we have experienced, he will be overwhelmed with a Waterloo overthrow, from which he and his cause will never recover.

7 *ON THE REPORT OF THE SECRETARY OF THE TREASURY, JUNE 21, 1841*

The political setting of Calhoun's speech was the Whig program in an extra session of Congress, led by Clay, to create a new bank, obtain revenue by a tariff bill, pass a distribution bill and in general to reap the fruits of the recent victory of Harrison's election. Calhoun led the democratic opposition which was successful in defeating the Whig program. As usual Calhoun argues practical political issues in terms of principle. Calhoun's realistic conception of the problem of establishing the ideal government centers around the problem of directing the use of power to the ends of political principle. In practice Calhoun was particularly concerned with the possibilities for the misdirection of power which the control of public moneys by a strong central government opened to special interests. His speech analyzes this problem.

Mr. CALHOUN said, that it was impossible for any one to read the report of the Secretary, without being struck with the solicitude apparent throughout, to make out a large deficit in the revenue of the year. So great was his solicitude, that it betrayed him into numerous errors, which have been so fully exposed by the two Senators who proceded me on the same side, that I do not feel called on to add a word to what they have said in that respect. What I propose, in connection with what may be called the financial part of the report, is to show, by a brief and condensed statement, what would be the deficit at the end of the year, according to the data furnished by the Secretary himself, collected from different portions of his report, but all from himself, without adding an estimate or a figure of my own.

According, then, to his own data, the available means of the Treasury for the year, including the balance at the end of the last year, Treasury notes authorized to be issued during the year, and the revenue from all sources would be $24,942,935. This is made up, first, of the sum of $4,212,540, the actual receipts into the Treasury from the beginning of the year to the 4th March, including the issue of Treasury notes and the balance on hand at the commencement of the year, and in the next of the sum of $20,750,395, at which he estimates the receipts from the 4th March to the end of the year, including Treasury notes authorized to be issued. Both items are taken from the report, without the alteration of a figure. Cents are omitted, as they are throughout my statement. These together make the sum of $24,942,935, which, as I have stated, is the aggregate of the available means of the year, according to the data of the Secretary.

The actual demand on the Treasury for the year will be, on his data, $28,012,776. I have obtained the result, first, from his statement of the annual appropriations (he calls them definite appropriations) made during the last session, which he puts down at $17,937,981; next, from the permanent appropriations payable in the year, $1,781,115, followed by Treasury notes, which he estimates will fall due in the year, or come into the Treasury in payment of duties, making $5,283,831. These items are all taken from 12th page Treasury report, House document. In the table containing them, the item of Treasury notes is put down at $5,431,421; but there is a note appended, which gives the items that compose it, which, strange to tell, gives not that sum, but one I have stated, and is so footed, making a difference of nearly $150,000. I have taken the one I have, as I find the items that compose it, stated in another part of the report, according with those that give that sum. The next and last sum that composes the items, which makes up, according to the data of the Secretary, the demands on the Treasury for the year, is one of $3,009,849, the estimated difference between the outstanding appropriations at the end of this year, compared with those of the end of the last year. This sum I have obtained in the following manner. The Secretary estimates the demands on the Treasury, from the 4th of March to the end of the year, at $33,429,616, and that which will be required for the service of the year, from the 4th of March to the end, at $24,210,000. The difference between them ($9,-296,616) would, of course, be the amount of the outstanding appropriations, according to his estimate, at the end of this year. Take that from the sum of $12,306,265, which he states to be the amount of the outstanding appropriations, at the end of last year, (see 12th page of report,) and the difference will give the amount I have stated, as chargeable to the disbursements of the year; and all the items added, the aggregate amount of those disbursements, according to the Secretary's own data. Subtract the aggregate means of the year ($24,942,935) from the aggregate demands, ($28,012,776) and the deficit would be $3,069,841.

But from this, two items must be clearly deducted. First, the omission in stating, among the means of the year, the item of $215,151 of money in the mints belonging to the Treasury. Next, an overcharge in the disbursements of $1,110,611 of Treasury notes, issued under the act 1840, between the 31st December, 1840, and 4th of March, 1841, and which will not fall due till next year. Both the Senators who preceded me, have clearly shown this to be an overcharge. I will not attempt to add to their proof. These two items added make $1,325,762, and that sum substracted from $3,069,841 gives, for the deficit, according to the Secretary's own data, at the end of the year, the sum of $1,743,979. He estimates it at $16,088,215, making an over estimate on his own data of $14,039,036.

It is true that he makes out his deficit in part, by adding items that have not been, and a large part of them probably will not be, appropriated by Congress; but when we speak of deficits, we refer to the excess of the authorized demands on the Treasury over its available means, and not such demands as the Secretary, or any one else, may think ought to be authorized by law. In that sense there would be no limitation in the deficit.

Among items of this kind the Secretary has added one of four millions of dollars, to constitute a standing deposite in the

Treasury, that is, the projected Bank; and this he proposes to borrow, say at six per cent., which would make an annual charge of $240,000 on the people, that the Bank may have the use of it for nothing. I, for one, shall never agree to such a measure. If the Treasury is to be guarded against the contingency of an accidental deficit, a vote of credit authorizing the temporary use of Treasury notes, or, as called in England, exchequer bills, would be greatly preferable. There is another large item of nearly a million and a half, in addition to what has already been voted this year for fortifications, to which I shall not give my assent. The great changes that steam has made, and the still greater that it must make in the operations of war on the ocean, require that the whole subject of the defence of our maritime frontier should be reviewed by able and skillful officers, before we proceed any further in the present system of fortifications. Much that has been done, and what is proposed to be done, would prove, on such view, to be wholly useless—money thrown away. I say nothing of the other items of the kind; they are small. Nor will I undertake to show what will be the actual deficit, if any. It would be too hazardous. The Secretary can make it more or less, or nothing at all, at his pleasure. But if he should choose to leave the outstanding appropriations as they stood last year, there would be in the Treasury a considerable surplus, instead of a deficit. On the contrary, if he should undertake to spend the whole, he may increase the deficit by many millions. We know what his desire is, and it remains to be seen what he will do.

But, sir, another and more important question demands our attention. Why this deep and anxious solicitude to make out a large deficit? Does it originate in party feelings? Is the object to detract from his predecessors in office, by showing that they have left the finances in an embarrassed condition? It may be so in part, but it would be doing the Secretary great injustice to suppose that it was his sole or principle motive. No; it was much higher. It originated in the belief, that to make out a large and permanent deficit, for which no provision was made, was highly important, if not necessary, to carry out the measures which he and his party contemplated. Hence the solicitude—hence the zeal that has led to so many errors and discrepancies, and to so great an over-estimate.

What these measures are, for which such anxiety is felt, the Secretary has not left us to conjecture. He has told us plainly: they are, first and foremost, a funded debt, to be followed by a National Bank, and through it the restoration of the partnership of the Government with the banks, and that by a heavy addition to the taxes, by an increase of the tariff, and finally the distribution among the States of the revenue from the public lands.

The debt is to be funded in stocks, redeemable in eight years; and is to consist, in the first place, of his estimated deficit of upwards of sixteen millions, of which four millions is to be, in reality, a permanent loan to the Bank, without interest, as has been stated. In the next, of six millions to be subscribed by him as our share of the Bank stock, and then $9,367,214 of stock to be subscribed by him for the States. What right have we to authorize him to subscribe for the States? In virtue of what right can we give such authority?

The Secretary felt the difficulty; and to make out a show of right for such an extraordinary proposition, he has taken a liberty in using words unexampled in any public document that ever passed under my eyes. He has converted the fourth instalment under the deposite act of '36, proposed to be placed for safekeeping in the State Treasury for the use of the Government whenever called for, into a debt to the States! He speaks of it as *due* to the States in one place, and as *appropriated* to them in another. Where will he find the evidence of such debt, or the act making the appropriation? Will he point to the act of '36? that makes it, as plainly and strongly as words can, a mere deposite for safe keeping for our use, whenever called for; that is, a debt from the States to the Government, and not from it to them. And yet, the Secretary is so intent on carrying out his scheme, that he changes at pleasure the relations of the parties—makes the Government, and not the States, the debtor—proposes to subscribe their debt to the Government, as so much stock in the Bank to their credit, for which the Government is to pay them interest on the debt they owe it; and to cap the climax of perversion and absurdity, he provides that if any State should refuse to accept its share of the subscription, it shall go to the other States, thus taking from a State at his pleasure, what he says is due to it, and giving it to the other States, without leave or license! He deals with words, rights, and property, as if his will was the only standard of either; makes debts from the States, debts to them, and transfers what he asserts belongs to one, to others, just as it suits him! But I see that the committee has just reported a bill, which omits a provision founded on such monstrous perversion and abuse of language; and I shall omit the residue of the remarks I intended to make on this point. These items, which it is proposed should compose the projected debt, exceed thirty-one million of dollars; and exceed, by rather more than a million, the amount of the stock of the bank. Of this large funded debt, (nearly equal to half of that of Revolution,) upwards of nineteen millions is to go directly to the creation, or the benefit of the Bank, and the remaining twelve millions is no doubt intended to go into the hands of individuals, with the view, in part, of furnishing the means of meeting their subscription; that is, the Bank is to be manufactured out of the credit of the people. A mortgage, in the shape of public stocks, is to be laid on their industry and property, to the amount of thirty-one millions; that to be converted into cash, and thirty millions of it incorporated into a Bank, to be put under the control and management of seven directors, in this District! Add, that the Bank is to have the use of the public revenue, till wanted for disbursements, and that its notes are made equal to gold and silver everywhere, in its collections and disbursements, and you will have the project of the Secretary, that has been so much lauded by his party!

To meet this heavy incumbrance on the labor and property of the people, and to cover the deficit which would be caused by the distribution of the revenue from the lands, he next proposes to impose a heavy tax of 20 per cent on the importation of all articles now duty free, with the exception of those contained in the 5th section of the compromise act, and to raise the duty to 20 per cent., on all the articles which pay less than that; the effects of which would be double nearly the present duty or tax on imports.

To complete the list of these odious and oppressive measures, he proposes, finally, that unconstitutional, dangerous, and detestable measure—the distribution of the revenue from the public lands among the States; which must end in a final loss to the Government of this great and growing branch of revenue, and a permanent mortgage to stockholders, domestic and foreign, of the whole of the public domain, consisting of more than a thousand millions of acres; the noble inheritance bequeathed by our ancestors to us and our posterity.

Such are the measures proposed by the Secretary; and for the adoption of which he and the party in power display so much solicitude. A permanent funded debt lies at the bottom of the whole scheme, and hence the deep anxiety to make out a great deficiency in the revenue; in order to afford a plausible pretext to create such a debt. But I stop not here. I push my inquiry beyond the measures themselves to the motive of their authors, and ask why such solicitude to adopt them at this time? Why the zeal of the Secretary so strongly displayed in his report? Why the call of this extraordinary session at this sultry season, at such great inconvenience of the members, and heavy charge on the country? Why the universal and pressing demand through all the organs of the party for action, instant action? And why, finally, the decree of urgency here; the enactment of new rules to cut short inquiry and discussions, and the more rigid and despotic enforcement of the old ones, than has ever been known, to curtail debate? What is the motive for all this?

If we are to believe our opponents, it originates in the highest and purest motive of patriotism and humanity, that their object is to relieve the distress of the country. The distress of the country! *Who is meant by the country?* The great mass of the community, the people, who live on their own means and industry, and look not to Government for favors? Do they mean by the country the tax payers in contradistinction to tax consumers —those who support the Government, and not those who are supported by it? Are these measures intended to relieve them? Would it relieve them, to place on their industry and property a mortgage of more than thirty-one millions of dollars in the shape of a permanent funded debt, and which would annually extract from them nearly two millions of dollars to pay the interest only? Would it relieve them to impose an additional tax of at least twelve millions, by levying a duty on coffee, tea, and other articles, of 20 per cent.; that is, to take one pound in six of all they consume? Would it relieve them to surrender for ever the revenue from the public lands, which cannot be estimated at less than five millions of dollars annually, for the next ten years, with a prospect of a great increase in future, to be given away to speculators and dealers in State stocks, for which the Union is no way responsible, either in justice, equity, or honor? Would it relieve them to lay a permanent mortgage, virtually, on the whole of the public domain, in favor of stock-jobbers and speculators? You, gentlemen, (addressing the opposite side) promised relief and reform to the people. On this promise they have raised you to power. Is this the reform, this the relief you promised? Will you, can you, rise in your places here, and in derision, tell the deluded people that when you promised reform and relief, you meant debt, taxes, mortgages, and the giving away of their inheritance? You are silent, and will be silent; you dare not make such an avowal; and yet these are the only measures you propose.

But if it be not relief to *the people*, *to whom* can it be? To whom but those who are the tax consumers, and not the tax payers—who, in reality, support not the Government, but are supported by the Government? Who but the mercenary corps—no, I shall not use so strong a term—the dependent corps, who live, or expect to live, on the Government—the office holders and expectants, of whom so fearful a flight lit on this District on the 4th of March last? To this numerous body of not less than a hundred thousand actual dependants on Government, and more than twice that number of expectants, these measures would indeed be relief. The more that is extracted from the people by taxes, and by whatever other device it can be effected, the more goes to them. Their interests and that of the people are in direct conflict. That which oppresses the one pampers the other; that which takes from the one is gained to the other.

But these are not the only classes to whom these measures would bring relief. There are other and more powerful, who are looking on with the most intense anxiety, in the hope of gorging themselves by their means at the expense of the people. These look to debts, stocks, banks, distribution, and taxes, as the choicest of blessings. The greater the debt, the more abundantly the stock market is supplied, the more powerful and controlling the Bank, the greater the amount of the public revenue that is distributed, and the heavier the taxes, the better for them.

To all these, the measures so earnestly recommended in this report would bring great and substantial relief. They are in deep distress—hungry, famished, and howling for their prey. Well they may be. The system of measures by means of which they so long fed on the vitals of the people, has been utterly overthrown, and has left them in their present distressed and starved condition. The object now is to renew that system. Yes, sir, the very measures recommended by the Secretary, are the identical measures which divided the two great parties, the Republican and Federal, at the commencement of the Government, and which, after more than a half century of persevering and unyielding resistance, the former has succeeded in overthrowing. Will any one, can any one, venture to deny what I assert? Who is there so ignorant of our political history, as not to know that the first measure on which the great parties divided was the funded debt; the next the National Bank, and the partnership through it of the Government with the banks; and then the protective tariff, with all the unconstitutional and wasteful expenditures which have and must ever follow in its train? These are the measures which the illustrious leaders of the Republican party of former days so strenuously resisted, and which we have, after so long and severe a contest, overthrown. And these are the measures, which the party now in power propose to revive. With them they have associated another, of the same stamp, but, if possible, more obnoxious and dangerous than any; the corrupt and corrupting scheme of distribution. And yet, strange to tell, there are thousands and tens of thousands, who have ever called themselves Republicans—who have stood in the front rank, when the battle waxed the hottest, and the onset was most fierce, against this system—who still call themselves Republicans, and honestly believe themselves to be so, now found, making battle on the opposite side, to restore the measures, which they have done so much to overthrow! How wonderful the delusion! Time, it is to be hoped, may expel it, and restore them to their true position.

If this attempt to revive the now prostrate system of federalism should succeed, and it should be once firmly reinstated, with all its exaggerated features, I shall not say that it would lay the foundation of a revolution in the Government; no, that would be too weak; it would, of itself, be a revolution. The seat of Government and power would change, and pass from the people into the hands of one of the most corrupt and exacting moneyed oligarchies, of which history has left any record. The immortal framers of our Constitution intended to place the Government in the hands of the people—to establish a Federal Republic—a constitutional Democracy, in which the Government should be controlled by the people, and be administered for their good, and not for the profit and advantages of those in power and their dependants and partisans. Adopt these measures, and this would be reversed; the power would depart from the people—from the tax paying people—the honest and industrious, who support the Government, without looking for favors, and would pass into the hands of the master spirits, who would, for the time, control the Government by their herds of dependants and partisans, united with the powerful combination of interests which these measures are intended to associate with them. They would be too strong for the people. Yes, I proclaim it, pass these measures, let this system of universal plunder be once firmly fixed on the country, and the Government will be revolutionized.

Pause and reflect on his portentous concentration of power. Behold the numerous and powerful corps of dependants—the household troops, office holders, contractors, jobbers, and pensioners, counting, in their well formed and compact ranks, not less than one hundred thousand. These are to be placed under the most exact and severe party drill. None are to be recruited but those of tried fidelity, and none retained whose zeal is questionable. Cast your eyes next on the interest proposed to be associated with this corps; a formidable central Bank, through which the most foul and corrupt and dangerous of partnerships is to be restored with the banking system, with its countless host of officers, stockholders, and dependants. Then turn to the scheme of distribution, intended to enlist entire States, and draw into this vortex the dominant influence for the time of the Legislatures of every State in the Union, and thus combine both General and State Governments in favor of high taxes, wasteful expenditures, debts and stocks, and in support of profligate leaders, whose talents and influence may be necessary to uphold this scheme of plunder. Now, when we reflect that just in the same proportion that these measures subtract from the means of the people, in the same proportion must their voice be made more feeble and insignificant, while, in the same proportion, the voice of those to whom what is subtracted from them goes, must be made more potent and influential, can you regard the assertion as too bold, that should these measures succeed, the Government would be revolutionized—would pass from the hands of the people into that of the powerful moneyed oligarchy, which, whether intended or not, they must create? The heads of the oligarchy, with their dependants, and the dependants of their dependants, united with daring political leaders, would be more powerful than the people, weakened and dispirited as they must become in upholding and supporting this mighty mass of oppressive taxes and exactions, direct and indirect.

We are in the midst of a most powerful struggle. If our Government is ever destined to fall, it must fall by measures such as are recommended in this report. It can by no other. Of all measures, those connected with the fiscal action of the Government and the paper system, (I include banks, paper currency, and a funded debt,) require to be watched with the greatest jealousy by all people desirous of preserving their freedom. They are the passes through which revolution secretly enters, and consummates the overthrow of liberty, before the danger is perceived. If the voice of one could be heard, who has never raised it but in behalf of the people, I would say to them, watch with ceaseless vigilance these dangerous passes, and, especially, the fiscal action of the Government. There emphatically lies the danger which has overthrown so many free States, and is destined to overthrow ours, unless promptly met. The foundation of our system is equality—equal burthens and equal benefits to all, but it ought to be known—it is a truth with which all ought to be deeply impressed, *that the fiscal action of the Government can by no ingenuity or contrivance be made equal, and that its unequal action of itself, without other cause, must, in the end, destroy liberty, if not checked and moderated.* To check and moderate it is all that can be done. The right understanding of this momentous truth is indispensable to the preservation of our free and happy institutions. I pause for a moment to explain.

The fiscal action of the Government consists of two branches, taxation and expenditures, or, in other words, revenue and disbursements. Taxation, disconnected from expenditure and considered by itself, may be made substantially equal, though, even that, in so large a country as ours, and so different in its pursuits and production, is no easy matter; but, if they be taken together, and be regarded in their joint effects as part of one process, as they really are, it is impossible to make that process equal; unless, indeed, what may be taken from each individual by taxes, should be returned to him by disbursements, which would be absurd. It follows from this simple fact, that one portion of the community must necessarily put into the Treasury, in the form of taxes, more than they receive back in that of disbursements, and another portion receive back in disbursements more than they paid in taxes. To one portion, then, taxes are in reality taxes, while to another they are in truth bounties. The money collected in taxes is not lost, but transferred. What taxes take from one is passed by disbursements to another; and to him to whom more is returned in disbursements than what he paid in taxes, the difference is, as has been said, a bounty. Hence the inherent inequality of the fiscal action of the Government, and which, of itself, without other cause, must create two great conflicting parties; the one in favor of taxes and the other opposed. The higher the taxes the more profuse and wasteful the expenditures—the greater the gain to the one and the loss to the other. Hence the conflict, which extends not only to taxes and expenditures, but to all connected measures—the countless ways by which the proceeds of industry may be taken by law from one and transferred to another. It matters not what may be the form of the Government. It originates in the nature of the fiscal action, and is as true under popular Governments as others—under the Government of the many as that of the few or of one. It is the great disturbing cause—the primordeal disease of all Governments—that collect taxes and make disbursements. It may be moderated in its action by wise constitutional provisions, but can never be actually overcome.

In order to be more clearly understood, I will illustrate what I have stated in general terms, by tracing its operations in detail a suppositious case. For this purpose I shall select the two adjacent counties, lying on the other side of the Potomac—Fairfax, which is opposite to the District, and Loudon, above. Suppose, then, they formed a little Republic, governed by the will of a majority; suppose that they were equally wealthy, and that the income, annually, of their citizens, was $300,000 each.

Suppose, again, the majority to be so just as to impose an equal tax on each, say $100,000, making the annual receipts of the Treasury to be $200,000; and that Loudon, availing itself of its greater numbers, should appropriate the whole to herself, in the improvements of her roads and rivers, in granting pensions to her citizens, and the various other modes in which the public money may be spent. Is it not clear that her income would be increased, and that of Fairfax diminished, notwithstanding the equality of the taxes. The former would not only receive back in the shape of expenditures, what she had paid in that of taxes, but all that had been paid by the latter too, and her income annually would, in consequence, be increased by the addition of $100,000, while that of Fairfax would be diminished by the like sum, thus raising that of the former to $400,000 annually, and reducing the latter $200,000, making its income double the other, instead of being only equal. Thus far is clear, and is it not also obvious that just as the taxes are increased, just in the same proportion would Loudon gain and Fairfax lose, and that the latter, by increasing taxes, only, however, equally laid, might be utterly impoverished, simply by unequal disbursements, just as much so as by unequal taxes? Thus far there can be no doubt.

The case would not be varied, if the supposed Republic consisted of twenty counties, or only one. The only difference would be, that as you enlarged the extent, the inequality would tend more in a geographical direction, and as you contracted it, between classes, particularly between capital and labor; but each would finally end in a moneyed oligarchy if not checked. Indeed, it would the more rapidly reach that termination, if left to itself, in an extended country, than a small one, by concentrating the disbursements collected from all over a great extent of country in one part, and to the small portion of its citizens to whom the proceeds of the taxes would go in the first instance.

But to return to the case supposed. If to unequal disbursements, there should be added unequal taxation—if Fairfax should pay twice as much in taxes as Loudon, and the whole be expended in the latter; and if to this unequal taxation and disbursement, in favor of Loudon, she should add the advantages of the paper system, and a powerful Bank, based on public stock, that is a mortgage on the industry and property of the people, possessing the extraordinary privileges of having the use of the public revenue, and its notes received in the public dues, accompanied by the other measures proposed in this report, would not these combined, centralize a power there which would not only control Loudon, but, through it, Fairfax too? And must not the same causes, when applied on a large scale, to the Union itself, lead to the same result?

Such being the necessary tendency of the fiscal action of the Government, all real patriots—enlightened lovers of liberty—have ever been cautious in imposing taxes, and watchful in their disbursements. They never lay them but for indispensable objects, and then not if they can be avoided by the retrenchment of unnecessary expenditures, or strict economy in the collection and disbursement of the revenue. Such caution is the distinguishing characteristic of the real patriot, in popular Governments, while the opposite marks the character of him who is indifferent, or opposed to such Governments. Apply this principle to this report, and where does it place its author and the party with which he acts, and who have been so loud in its support? Instead of caution, has he not shown the greatest solicitude to make out a necessity for imposing taxes where it does not exist? Has he shown, or attempted to show, that his supposed deficit in the revenue may not be met by the retrenchment of useless expenditures, or economy in the collection or disbursement of the revenue? Has he even alluded to these resources, except in a single, vague, general, and unmeaning expression? Can he, or his party, say that there is no room for retrenchment, or economy? Will they turn round and confess that the charges of extravagant and wasteful expenditures against the late Administration and its predecessor are all false, and made for electioneering purposes? Do they intend to violate the solemn and oft-repeated pledges of reform, with as little compunction as the pledge to proscribe proscription? Is that too to furnish additional proof that we, in our infancy, have sunk to so degenerate a state that candidates may give the most solemn pledges before election, and violate them without a blush, and with perfect impunity, after they have attained power?

I fear that such will prove to be the fact, and that as much as reform and economy are really needed and deeply and solemnly as the party is pledged to carry it out, we are to hear no more about it. Indeed, a talented and influential member of the party, [Mr. EVANS,] openly told us in debate the other day, not only that there was no room for reduction of expenses, but spoke with something of scorn of retrenchment and economy. He told us, on the same occasion, that he was for action—action—and that he detested abstractions.

I do not, Mr. President, wonder that the Senator, with his sentiments, should detest abstractions. They stand between him and his desires. He wants debts, taxes, banks, tariffs, and distributions, and but for the hateful interposition of the Constitution, of justice, and of the right of free discussion—those odious abstractions—would reach his object without delay or impediment. The Senator stands not alone in his hatred of abstractions. He has high examples for his strong dislike. Bonaparte detested and denounced them, under the name of ideaology and Cromwell held them in as much abhorrence as the gentleman himself. They are, in fact, the object of detestation to every plunderer, and to none more so than the highwayman. He meets an honest traveller on the road. The one armed and the other unarmed. What stands between him and the purse of the traveller, but these detested abstractions—right, justice, and law? Would he pause and parley about them? No; he, too, is for action, action, action, meaning plunder, plunder, plunder.

But the Senator does not limit his dislike to abstractions. He has a mortal aversion to the interference of the Executive with the subject submitted by the Constitution to the action of Congress, and condemns, in strong language, the practice adopted by the Executive of recommending, in the annual message, the policy which, in his opinion, ought to be pursued by Congress. Does he forget that it is made his duty by the Constitution, not only to give information of the state of the Union, but *to recommend* such measures as he may deem necessary and expedient. But why should the Senator take such dislike to what he is pleased to call the interference of the Executive? Does he distrust the present incumbent? Does he fear that his influence or veto may also stand between him and the measures he is so impatient to adopt? I must say that I regard the constitutional powers of the Executive, properly understood, with feelings very different from the Senator. According to my opinion, when they are restricted within the limits assigned by the Constitution, they are highly salutary. They serve to moderate and check the overaction of Congress. This is eminently true of the veto power, which must, almost invariably, from its nature, interpose a shield between the weaker and stronger interests; and it is, perhaps, that circumstance which makes it so unacceptable to the Senator.

But there is another branch of Executive power which I regard in a very different light; I mean that which originates in the encroachments and overaction of Congress. The powers of the Executive of themselves are very little formidable; but when Congress stretches its powers—when it imposes oppressive taxes—enacts high protective tariff—branches out into lawless and wasteful expenditures—when it associates itself with the banks and paper systems—when, in a few words, it adopts the measures recommended in this report, it clothes the Executive with patronage and influence that may well be dreaded. It is that which makes the Executive truly formidable, and gives to the Presidential canvass such violence and corruption as to shake our system to its centre.

I shall now conclude my remarks with a hasty notice of what the Senator said in reference to myself. He undertook to remind me of the position I took in reference to the Sub-Treasury at the extraordinary session of 1837. I retain a vivid recollection of my course on that occasion, and especially as relates to what he would recall to my memory, and I assure him that time, so far from changing, has but confirmed the opinions I then expressed. I then, and still, object to a National Bank, because, among other reasons, it tends to centralize the business and currency of the country at the point where it is located; and to favor the Sub-Treasury, because it has no such tendency. I shall not undertake to repeat the reasons I then advanced in support of my opinion. It would be out of place; but I avail myself of the occasion to say, that I would not divest New York of a particle of her natural advantages, but, at the same time, I would resist any attempt to aggrandize her, or any other city, at the expense of the others. Our system is built on justice and equality, and I would be as rigid in observing it between one place and another as between individuals and individuals. Justice to all, and privileges to none, is my maxim.

8 ON THE VETO POWER, FEBRUARY 28, 1842

The political circumstances of this speech were Henry Clay's resolutions of February 1842 calling for a constitutional amendment to limit the veto power and in effect give the popular majority control of the government. The accession of Tyler to the presidency after Harrison's death robbed the Whigs of their election victory, for Tyler, as a Southerner and as a states' rights man vetoed the bank bill and opposed a high tariff. Calhoun's discussion was widely acclaimed at the time. The Congressional Globe speaks of it as "one of the ablest, most luminous, and unanswerable, ever delivered on the nature of this Government."[2] It served to restate in practical context his objections to majority rule, and it expressed his belief that the constitutional structure of American government was intended to express the concurrent voice. The speech is, in fact, a short essay on the nature of the American Government.

The Senator from Kentucky, in support of his amendment, maintained that the people of these States constitute a nation; that the nation has a will of its own; that the numerical majority of the whole was the appropriate organ of its voice; and that whatever derogated from it, to that extent departed from the genius of the Government, and set up the will of the minority against the majority. We have thus presented at the very threshold of the discussion, a question of the deepest import, not only as it regards the subject under consideration, but the nature and character of our Government; and that question is, are these propositions of the Senator true?* If they be, then he admitted the argument against the veto would be conclusive; not, however, for the reason assigned by him, that it would make the voice of a single functionary of the Government, (the President,) equivalent to that of some six Senators and forty members of the other House; but, for the far more decisive reason, according to his theory, that the President is not chosen by the voice of the numerical majority, and does not, therefore, according to his principle, represent truly the will of the nation.

It is a great mistake to suppose that he is elected simply on the principle of numbers. They constitute, it is true, the principal element in his election; but not the exclusive. Each State is, indeed, entitled to as many votes in his election, as it is to representatives in the other House; that is, to its Federal population; but to these, two others are added, having no regard to numbers for their representation in the Senate, which greatly increases the relative influence of the small States, compared to the large, in the Presidential election. What effect this latter element may have on the numbers necessary to elect a President, may be made apparent by a very short and simple calculation.

The population of the United States, in Federal numbers, by the late census, is 15,908,376. Assuming that sixty-eight thousand, the number reported by the committee of the other House, will be fixed on for the ratio of representation there, it will give, according to the calculation of the committee, two hundred and twenty-four members to the other House. Add fifty-two, the number of the Senators, and the electoral college will be found to consist of two hundred and seventy-six, of which one hundred and thirty-nine is a majority. If nineteen of the smaller States, excluding Maryland, be taken, beginning with Delaware and ending with Kentucky inclusive, they will be

---

*Mr. Clay here interrupted Mr. Calhoun, and said that he meant a majority according to the forms of the Constitution.

Mr. Calhoun, in return, said he had taken down the words of the Senator at the time, and would vouch for the correctness of his statement. The Senator not only laid down the propositions as stated, but he drew conclusions from them against the President's veto, which could only be sustained on the principal of the numerical majority. In fact, his course at the extra session, and the grounds assumed both by him and his colleague in this discussion, had their origin in the doctrines embraced in that proposition.

found to be entitled to one-hundred and forty votes, one more than a majority, with a federal population of only 7,227,869; while the seven other States, with a population of 8,680,507, would be entitled to but one hundred and thirty-six votes, three less than a majority, with a population of almost a million and a half greater than the others. Of the one hundred and forty electoral votes of the smaller States, thirty-eight would be on account of the addition of two to each State for their representation in this body, while of the larger there would be but fourteen on that account; making a difference of twenty-four votes on that account, being two more than the entire electoral votes of Ohio, the third State in point of numbers in the Union.

The Senator from Kentucky, with these facts, but acts in strict conformity to his theory of the Government, in proposing the limitation he has on the veto power; but as much cannot be said in favor of the substitute he has offered. The argument is as conclusive against the one, as the other, or any other modification of the veto that could possibly be devised. It goes farther, and is conclusive against the Executive department itself, as elected; for there can be no good reason offered why the will of the nation, if there be one, should not be as fully and perfectly represented in that department as in the Legislative.

But it does not stop there. It would be still more conclusive, if possible, against this branch of the Government. In constituting the Senate, numbers are totally disregarded. The smallest State stands on a perfect equality with the largest; Delaware, with her seventy-seven thousand, with New York with her two million and a half. Here a majority of States control, without regard to population; and fourteen of the smallest States, with a federal population of but 4,064,457, little less than a fourth of the whole, can, if they unite, overrule the twelve others, with a population of 11,844,919. Nay, more; they could virtually destroy the Government, and put a veto on the whole system, by refusing to elect Senators; and yet this equality among States, without regard to numbers, including the branch where it prevails, would seem to be the favorite with the Constitution. It cannot be altered without the consent of every State, and this branch of the Government where it prevails, is the only one that participates in the powers of all the others. As a part of the Legislative Department, it has full participation with the other, in all matters of legislation, except originating money bills, while it participates with the Executive in two of its highest functions, that of appointing to office and making treaties, and in that of the Judiciary, in being the high court before which all impeachments are tried.

But we have not yet got to the end of the consequences. The argument would be as conclusive against the Judiciary as against the Senate, or the Executive and his veto. The judges receive their appointments from the Executive and the Senate; the one nominating, and the other consenting to and advising the appointment; neither of which departments, as has been shown, is chosen by the numerical majority. In addition, they hold their office during good behavior, and can only be turned out by impeachment, and yet they have the power, in all cases in law and equity brought before them, in which an act of Congress is involved, to decide on its constitutionality—that is, in effect, to pronounce an absolute veto.

If, then, the Senator's theory be correct, its clear and certain result, if carried out in practice, would be to sweep away, not only the veto, but the Executive, the Senate, and the Judiciary, as now constituted, and to leave nothing standing in the midst of the ruins but the House of Representatives where only, in the whole range of the Government, numbers exclusively prevail. But as desolating as would be its sweep, in passing over the Government, it would be far more destructive in its whirl over the Constitution. There it would not leave a fragment standing admist the ruin in its rear.

In approaching this topic, let me premise, what all will readily admit, that if the voice of the people may be sought for any where with confidence it may be in the Constitution, which is conceded by all to be the fundamental and paramount law of the land. If, then, the people of these States do really constitute a nation, as the Senator supposes; if the nation has a will of its own, and if the numerical majority of the whole is the only appropriate and true organ of that will, we may fairly expect to find that will, pronounced through the absolute majority, pervading every part of that instrument, and stamping its authority on the whole. Is such the fact? The very reverse. Throughout the whole—from first to last—from beginning to the end—in its formation, adoption, and amendment, there is not the slightest evidence, trace, or vestige of the existence of the facts on which the Senator's theory rests; neither of the nation, nor its will, nor of the numerical majority of the whole, as its organ, as I shall next proceed to show.

The convention which formed it was called by a portion of the States; its members were all appointed by the States; received their authority from their separate States; voted by States in forming the Constitution; agreed to it, when formed, by States; transmitted it to Congress to be submitted to the States for their ratification; it was ratified by the people of each State in convention, each ratifying by itself, for itself, and bound exclusively by its own ratification, and by express provision it was not to go into operation, unless nine out of the twelve States should ratify, and then to be binding only between the States ratifying. It was thus put in the power of any four States, large or small, without regard to numbers, to defeat its adoption, which might have been done by a very small proportion of the whole, as will appear by reference to the first census. That census was taken very shortly after the adoption of the Constitution at which time the Federal population of the then twelve States was 3,462,279, of which the four smallest, Delaware, Rhode Island, Georgia, and New Hampshire, with a population of only 241,490, something more than the fourteenth part of the whole, could have defeated the ratification. Such was the total disregard of population in the adoption and formation of the Constitution.

It may, however, be said, it is true that the Constitution is the work of the States, and that there was no nation prior to its adoption; but that its adoption fused the people of the States into one so as to make a nation of what before constituted separate and independent sovereignties. Such as assertion would be directly in the teeth of the Constitution, which says that, when ratified, "it should be binding," (not over the States ratifying, for that would imply that it was imposed by some higher authority, nor between the individuals composing the States, for that would imply that they were all merged in one, but) "between the States ratifying the same;" and thus by the strongest implication, recognising them as the parties to the instrument, and as maintaining their separate and independent existence as States, after its adoption. But let that pass. I need it not to rebut the Senator's theory—to test the truth of the assertion, that the Constitution has formed a nation of the people of these States. I go back to the grounds already taken, that if such be the fact—if they really form a nation, since the adoption of the Constitution, and the nation has a will, and the numerical majority is its only proper organ, in that case, the mode prescribed for the amendment of the Constitution would furnish abundance and conclusive evidence of the fact. But here again, as in its formation and adoption, there is not the slightest trace or evidence, that such is the fact; on the contrary, most conclusive to sustain the very opposite opinion.

There are two modes in which amendments to the Constitution may be proposed. The one, such as that now proposed, by a resolution to be passed by two-thirds of both Houses; and the other by a call of a convention, by Congress, to propose amendments, on the application of two-thirds of the States; neither of which give the least countenance to the theory of the Senator. In both cases the mode of ratification, which is the material point, is the same, and requires the concurring assent of three-fourths of the States, regardless of population, to ratify an amendment. Let us now pause for a moment to trace the effects of this provision.

There are now twenty-six States, and the concurring assent, of course, of twenty States, is sufficient to ratify an amendment. It then results that twenty of the smaller States, of which Kentucky would be the largest, are sufficient for that purpose, with a population in federal numbers of only 7,652,097, less by several hundred thousand than the numerical majority of the whole, against the united voice of the other six, with a population of 8,216,279, exceeding the former by more than half a million. And yet this minority, under the amending power, may change, alter, modify or destroy every part of the Constitution, except that which provides for an equality of representation of the States in the Senate, while as if in mockery and derision of the Senator's theory, nineteen of the larger States, with a population, in federal numbers, of 14,526,073, cannot, even if united to a man, alter a letter in the Constitution, against the seven others, with a population of only 1,382,303; and this, too, under the existing Constitution, which is suposed to form the people of these States into a nation. Finally, Delaware, with a population of little more than 77,000, can put her veto on all the other States, on a proposition to destroy the equality of the States in the Senate. Can facts more clearly illustrate the total disregard of the numerical majority, as well in the process of amending, as in that of forming and adopting the Constitution?

All this must appear anomalous, strange and unaccountable, on the theory of the Senator, but harmonious and easily explained on the opposite; that ours is an union, not of individuals, united by what is called a social compact, for that would make it a nation; nor of Governments, for that would have formed a mere Confederacy, like the one superceded by the present Constitution; but an union of States, founded on a written, positive compact, forming a Federal Republic, with the same equality of rights among the States composing the Union, as among the citizens composing the States themselves. Instead of a nation, we are in reality an assemblage of nations, or peoples, (if the plural noun may be used where the language affords none,) united in their sovereign character immediately and directly by their own act, but without losing their separate and independent existence.

It results from all that has been stated, that either the theory of the Senator is wrong, or that our political system is throughout a profound and radical error. If the latter be the case, then that complex system of ours, consisting of so many parts, but blended, as was supposed, into one harmonious and sublime whole, raising its front on high and challenging the admiration of the world, is but a misshapen and disproportionate structure that ought to be demolished to the ground, with the single exception of the apartment allotted to the House of Representatives. Is the Senator prepared to commence the work of demolition? Does he believe that all other parts of this complex structure are irregular and deformed appendages; and that if they were taken down, and the Government erected exclusively on the will of the numerical majority, would effect as well, or better, the great objects for which it was instituted: "to establish justice; ensure domestic tranquillity; provide for the common defence; promote the general welfare; and secure the blessings of liberty to ourselves and our posterity." Will the Senator—will any one—can any one—venture to assert that? And if not, why not? There is the question, on the proper solution of which hangs not only the explanation of the veto, but that of the real nature and character of our complex, but beautiful and harmonious system of Government. To give a full and systematic solution, it would be necessary to descend to the elements of political science, and discuss principles little suited to a discussion in a deliberative assembly. I waive the attempt, and shall content myself with giving a much more matter of fact solution.

It is sufficient, for that purpose, to point to the actual operation of the Government, through all the stages of its existence, and the many and important measures which have agitated it from the beginning; the success of which one portion of the people regarded as essential to their prosperity and happiness, while other portions have viewed them as destructive of both. What does this imply, but a deep conflict of interests, real or supposed, between the different portions of the community, on subjects of the first magnitude—the currency, the finances, including taxation and disbursements; the Bank, the protective tariff, distribution, and many others; on all of which the most opposite and conflicting views have prevailed? And what would be the effect of placing the powers of the Government under the exclusive control of the numerical majority—of 8,000,000 over 7,900,000, of six States over all the rest—but to give the dominant interest, or combination of interests, an unlimited and despotic control over all others? What, but to vest it with the power to administer the Government for its exclusive benefit, regardless of all others, and indifferent to their oppression and wretchedness? And what, in a country of such vast extent and diversity of condition, institutions, industry, and productions, would that be, but to subject the rest to the most grinding despotism and oppression? But what is the remedy? It would be but to increase the evil, to transfer the power to a minority, to abolish the House of Representatives, and place the control exclusively in the hands of the Senate—in that of the four millions, instead of the eight. If one must be sacrificed to the other, it is better that the few should be to the many, than the many to the few.

What then is to be done, if neither the majority nor the minority, the greater nor the less part, can be safely trusted with the exclusive control? What but to vest the powers of the Government in the whole—the entire people—to make it in truth and reality the Government of the people, instead of the Government of a dominant over a subject part, be it the greater or less —of the whole people—self-government; and if this should prove impossible in practice, then to make the nearest approach to it, by requiring the concurrence in the action of the government, of the greatest possible number consistent with the great ends for which Government was instituted—justice and security, within and without. But how is that to be effected? Not certainly by considering the whole community as one, and taking its sense as a whole by a single process, which, instead of giving the voice of all, can but give that of a part. There is but one way by which it can possibly be accomplished; and that is by a judicious and wise division and organization of the Government and community, with reference to its different and conflicting interests, and by taking the sense of each part separately, and the concurrence of all as the voice of the whole. Each may be imperfect of itself, but if the construction be good and all the keys skilfully touched, there will be given out in one blended and harmonious whole, the true and perfect voice of the people.

But on what principle is such a division and organization to be made to effect this great object, without which it is impossible to preserve free and popular institutions? To this no general answer can be given. It is the work of the wise and experienced, having full and perfect knowledge of the country and the people in every particular for whom the Government is intended. It must be made to fit, and when it does, it will fit no other, and will be incapable of being imitated or borrowed. Without, then, attempting to do what cannot be done, I propose to point out, how that which I have stated has been accomplished in our system of Government, and the agency the veto is intended to have in effecting it.

I begin with the House of Representatives. There each State has a representation according to its federal numbers, and when met, a majority of the whole number of members controls its proceedings; thus giving to the numerical majority the exclusive control throughout. The effect is to place its proceedings in the power of eight millions of people over all the rest, and six of the largest States, if united, over the other twenty; and the consequence, if the House was the exclusive organ of the voice of the people, would be the domination of the stronger over the weaker interests of the community, and the establishment of an intolerable and oppressive despotism. To find the remedy against what would be so great an evil, we must turn to this body. Here an entirely different process is adopted to take the sense of the community. Population is entirely disregarded, and States, without reference to the number of people, are made the basis of representation; the effect of which is to place the control here in a majority of the States, which, had they the exclusive power, would exercise it as despotically and oppressively as would the House of Representatives.

Regarded, then, separately, neither truly represents the sense of the community, and each is imperfect of itself; but when united, and the concurring voice of each is made necessary to enact laws, the one corrects the defects of the other; and, instead of the less popular derogating from the more popular, as is supposed by the Senator, the two together give a more full and perfect utterance to the voice of the people than either would separately. Taken separately, six States might control the House, and a little upwards of four millions might control the Senate, by a combination of the fourteen smaller States; but by requiring the concurrent votes of the two, the six largest States must add eight others to have the control in both bodies. Suppose, for illustration, they should unite with the eight smallest, which would give the least number by which an act could pass both Houses, it will be found, by adding the population in federal numbers of the six largest to the eight smallest States, that the least number by which an act can pass both Houses, if the members should be true to those they represent, would be 9,788,570 against a minority of 6,119,797, instead of 8,000,000, against 7,900,000, if the assent of the most popular branch alone was required.

This more full and perfect expression of the voice of the people by the concurrence of the two, compared to either separately, is a great advance towards a full and perfect expression of their voice; but great as it is, it falls far short, and the framers of the Constitution were accordingly not satisfied with it. To render it still more perfect, their next step was to require the assent of the President, before an act of Congress could become a law, and, if he disapproved, to require two-thirds of both Houses to overrule his veto. We are thus brought to the point immediately under discussion, and which, on that account, claims a full and careful examination.

One of the leading motives for vesting the President with this high power, was, undoubtedly, to give him the means of protecting the portion of the powers allotted to him by the Constitution, against the encroachment of Congress. To make a division of power effectual, a veto in one form or another is indispensable. The right of each to judge for itself of the extent of the power alloted to its share, and to protect itself in its exercise, is what in reality is meant by a division of power. Without it, the allotment to each department would be a mere partition, and no division at all. Acting under this impression, the framers of the Constitution have carefully provided that his approval should be necessary, not only to the acts of Congress, but to every resolution, vote or order, requiring the consent of the two Houses, so as to render it impossible to elude it by any conceivable device. This of itself was an adequate motive for the provision, and were there no other, ought to be a sufficient reason for the rejection of this resolution. Without it, the division of power between the legislative and Executive departments, would have been merely nominal.

But it is not the only motive. There is another and deeper, to which the division itself of the Government into departments is subordinate; to enlarge the popular basis, by increasing the number of voices necessary to its action. As numerous as are the voices required to obtain the assent of the people through the Senate and the House to an act, it was not thought by the framers of the Constitution sufficient for the action of the Government in all cases. Nine thousand eight hundred, as large as is the number, were regarded as still too few, and six thousand one hundred too many to remove all motives for oppression; the latter being not too few to be plundered, and the former not too large to divide the spoils of plunder among. Till the increase of numbers on one side, and the decrease on the other reaches that point, there is no security for the weaker against the stronger, especially in so extensive a country as ours. Acting in the spirit of these remarks, the authors of the Constitution, although they deemed the concurrence of the Senate and the House as sufficient, with the approval of the President, to the enactment of laws in ordinary cases, yet, when he dissented, they deem it a sufficient presumption against the measure to require a still greater enlargement of the popular basis for its enactment. With this view, the assent of two-thirds of both Houses were required to overrule his veto, that is eighteen States in the Senate, and a constituency of ten millions six hundred thousand in the other House.

But it may be said that nothing is gained towards enlarging the popular basis of the Government by the veto powers; because the number necessary to elect a majority to the two Houses, without which the act could not pass, would be sufficient to elect him. That is true. But he may have been elected by a different portion of the people, or if not, great changes may take place during his four years, both in the Senate and the House, which may change the majority that brought him into power, and with it the measures and policy to be pursued. In either case he might find it necessary to interpose his veto to maintain his views of the Constitution, or the policy of the party of which he is the head, and which elevated him to power.

But a still stronger consideration for vesting him with the power may be found in the difference of the manner of his election, compared with that of the members of either House. The Senators are elected by the vote of the Legislatures of the respective States, and the members of the House by the people, who, in almost all the States, elect by districts. In neither is there the least responsibility of the members of any one State, to the Legislature or people of any other State. They are, as far as their responsibility may be concerned, solely and exclusively under the influence of the States and people, who respectively elect them. No so the President. The votes of the whole are counted in his election, which makes him more or less responsible to every part—to those who voted against him, as well as those to whom he owes his election, which he must feel sensibly. If he should be an aspirant for a re-election, he will desire to gain the favorable opinion of States that opposed him, as well as to retain that of those which voted for him. Even if he should not be a candidate for re-election, the desire of having a favorite elected, or maintaining the ascendency of his party, may have, to a considerable extent, the same influence over him. The effect, in either case, would be to make him look more to *the interest of the whole*—to soften sectional feelings and asperity—to be more of a patriot, than the partisan of any particular interest; and through the influence of these causes to give a more general character to the politics of the country, and thereby render the collision between sectional interests less fierce than it would be if legislation depended solely on the members of the two Houses, who owe no responsibility but to those who elected them. The same influence acts even on the aspirants for the Presidency, and is followed to a very considerable extent by the same softening and generalizing effects. In the case of the President, it may lead to the interposing of his veto against oppressive and dangerous sectional measures, even when supported by those to whom he owes his election. But, be the cause of interposing his veto what it may, its effect in all cases is to require a greater body of constituency, through the legislative organs, to put the Government in action against it—to require another key to be struck, and to bring out a more full and perfect response from the voice of the people.

There is still another impediment, if not to the enactment of laws, to their execution, to be found in the Judiciary Department. I refer to the right of the courts, in all cases coming before them in law or equity, where an act of Congress comes in question, to decide on its unconstitutionality, which, if decided against the law in the Supreme Court, is in effect a permanent veto. But here a difference must be made between a decision against the constitutionality of a law of Congress and that of States. The former acts as a restriction on the powers of this Government, but the later as an enlargement.

Such are the various processes of taking the sense of the people through the divisions and organization of the different departments of the Government, all of which, acting through their appropriate organs, are intended to widen its basis and render it more popular, instead of less, by increasing the number necessary to put it in action, and having for their object to prevent one portion of the community from aggrandizing or enriching itself at the expense of the other, and to restrict the whole to the sphere intended by the framers of the Constitution. Has it effected these objects? Has it prevented oppression and usurpation on the part of the Government? Has it accomplished the objects for which the Government was ordained, as enumerated in the preamble of the Constitution? Much, very much, certainly has been done, but not all. Many instances might be enumerated, in the history of the Government, of the violation of the Constitution—of the assumption of powers not delegated to it—of the perversion of those delegated to uses never intended—and of their being wielded by the dominant interest, for the time, for its aggrandizement, at the expense of the rest of the community—instances that may be found in every period of its existence, from the earliest to the latest, beginning with the Bank and bank connection at its outset, and ending with the Distribution act, at its late extraordinary session. How is this to be accounted for? What is the cause?

The explanation and cause will be found in the fact, that, as fully as the sense of the people is taken in the action of the Government, it is not taken fully enough. For, after all that has been accomplished in that respect, there are but two organs through which the voice of the community acts directly on the Government, and which, taken separately, or in combination, constitute the elements of which it is composed; the one is the majority of the States regarded in their corporate character as bodies politic, which in its simple form constitutes the Senate; and the other is the majority of the people of the States, of which, in its simple form, the House of Representatives is composed. These combined, in the proportions already stated, constitute the Executive Department, and that department and the Senate appoint the judges, who constitute the Judiciary. But it is only in their simple form in the Senate and the other House, that they have a steady and habitual control over the legislative acts of the Government. The veto of the Executive is rarely interposed; not more than about twenty times during the period of more than fifty years that the Government has existed. Their effects have been beneficially felt, but only casually, at long intervals, and without steady and habitual influence over the action of the Government. The same remarks are substantially applicable to what, for the sake of brevity, may be called the veto of the Judiciary; the right of negativing a law for the want of constitutionality, when it comes in question, in a case before the courts.

The Government, then, of the Union, being under no other habitual and steady control but these two majorities, acting through this and the other House, is, in fact, placed substantially under the control of the portion of the community, which the united majorities of the two Houses represent for the time, and which may consist of but fourteen States with a federal population of less than ten millions, against a little more than six, as has been already explained. But as large as is the former, and as small as is the latter, the one is not large enough, in proportion, to prevent it from plundering, under the forms of law, and the other small enough from being plundered; and hence the many instances of violation of the Constitution, of usurpation, of powers perverted, and wielded for selfish purposes, which the history of the Government affords. They furnish proof conclusive that the principle of plunder, so deeply implanted in all Governments, has not been eradicated in ours by all the precaution taken by its framers against it.

But in estimating the number of the constituency necessary to control the majority in the two Houses of Congress at something less than ten millions, I have estimated it altogether too high, regarding the practical operation of the Government. To form a correct conception of its practical operation in this respect, another element, which has in practice an important influence, must be taken into the estimate, and which I shall next proceed to explain.

Of the two majorities, which, acting either separately or in combination, control the Government, the numerical majority is by far the most influential. It has the exclusive control in the House of Representatives, and preponderates more than five to one in the choice of the President, assuming that the ratio of representation will be fixed at sixty-eight thousand, under the late census. It also greatly preponderates in appointment of the judges the right of nominating having much greater influence in making appointments than that of advising and consenting. From these facts, it must be apparent that the leaning of the President will be to that element of power to which he mainly owes his elevation, and on which he must principally rely, to secure his re-election, or maintain the ascendancy of the party and its policy, the head of which he usually is. This leaning of his must have a powerful effect on the inclination and tendency of the whole Government. In his hands are placed, substantially, all the honors and emoluments of the Government, and these, when greatly increased, as they are and ever must be when the powers of the Government are greatly stretched and increased, must give the President a corresponding influence over, not only the members of both Houses, but also public opinion, and through that, a still more powerful indirect influ ence over them; and thus they may be brought to sustain or oppose, through his influence measures which otherwise they would have opposed or sustained, and the whole Government be made to lean in the same direction with the Executive.

From these causes the Government, in all of its departments, gravitates steadily towards the numerical majority, and has been moving slowly towards it from the beginning; sometimes, indeed, retarded, or even stopped or thrown back, but, taking any considerable period of time, always advancing towards it. That it begins to make near approach to that fatal point, ample proof may be found in the oft-repeated declaration of the mover of this resolution and of many of his supporters at the extraordinary session, that the late Presidential election decided all the great measures which he so ardently pressed through the Senate. Yes, even here, in this chamber, in the Senate, which is composed of the opposing element, and on which the only effectual resistance to this fatal tendency exists that is to be found in the Government, we are told that the popular will as expressed in the presidential election is to decide not only the election, but every measure which may be agitated in the canvass in order to influence the result. When what was thus boldly insisted on comes to be an established principle of action, the end will be near.

As the Government approaches nearer and nearer to the one absolute and single power, the will of the greater number, its action will become more and more disturbed and irregular; faction, corruption, and anarchy, will more and more abound; patriotism will daily decay, and affection and reverence for the Government grow weaker and weaker, until the final shock occurs, when the system will rush to ruin; and the sword take the place of law and Constitution.

Let me not be misunderstood. I object not to that structure of the Government which makes the numerical majority the predominant element: it is, perhaps, necessary it should be so in all popular constitutional Governments like ours, which excludes classes. It is necessarily the exponent of the strongest interest, or combination of interests, in the community; and it would seem to be necessary to give it the preponderance, in order to infuse into the Government the necessary energy to accomplish the ends for which it was instituted. The great question is, How is due preponderance to be given to it, without subjecting the whole, in time, to its unlimited sway? which brings up the question, Is there anywhere, in our complex system of Government, a guard, check, or contrivance, sufficiently strong to arrest so fearful a tendency of the Government? Or, to express it in more direct and intelligible language, Is there anywhere in the system a more full and perfect expression of the voice of the people of the States calculated to counteract this tendency to the concentration of all the powers of the Government in the will of the numerical majority, resulting from the partial and imperfect expression of their voice through its organs?

Yes, fortunately, doubly fortunately, there is; not only a more full and perfect, but a full and perfect expression to be found in the Constitution, acknowledged by all to be the fundamental and supreme law of the land. It is full and perfect, because it is the expression of the voice of each State, adopted by the separate assent of each, by itself, and for itself, and is the voice of all by being that of each component part, united and blended into one harmonious whole. But it is not only full and perfect, but as just as it is full and perfect; for combining the sense of each, and therefore all, there is nothing left on which injustice, or oppression, or usurpation can operate. And, finally, it is as supreme as it is just, because, comprehending the will of all, by uniting that of each of the parts, there is nothing within or above to control it. It is indeed, the *vox populi vox Dei;* the creating voice that called the system into existence, and of which the Government itself is but a creature, clothed with delegated powers to execute its high behests.

We are thus brought to a question of the deepest import, and on which the fate of the system depends; How can this full, perfect, just, and supreme voice of the people, embodied in the Constitution, be brought to bear habitually and steadily in counteracting the fatal tendency of the Government to the absolute and despotic control of the numerical majority? Or, if I may be permitted to use so bold an expression, how is this, the Deity of our political system, to be successfully invoked, to interpose its all powerful creating voice to save from perdition the creature of its will and the work of its hand? If it cannot be done, ours, like all free Governments preceding it, must go the way of all flesh; but if it can be, its duration may be from generation to generation, to the latest posterity. To this all important question, I will not attempt a reply at this time. It would lead me far beyond the limits properly belonging to this discussion. I descend from the digression nearer to the subject immediately at issue, in order to reply to an objection to the veto power, taken by the Senator from Virginia, on this side the chamber, [Mr. ARCHER.] He rests his support of this resolution on the ground that the object intended to be effected by the veto has failed; that the framers of the Constitution regard the legislative department of the Government, as the one most to be dreaded, and that their motive for vesting the Executive with the veto, was to check its encroachments on the other departments; but that the Executive, and not the Legislature, had proved to be the most dangerous, and that the veto had become either useless or mischievous by being converted into a sword to attack, instead of a shield to defend as was originally intended.

I make no issue with the Senator, as to the correctness of his statement. I assume the facts to be as he supposes; not because I agree with him, but simply with the view of making my reply more brief.

Assuming, then, that the Executive Department has proved to be the more formidable, and that it requires to be checked, rather than to have the power of checking others, the first inquiry on that assumption, should be into the cause of its increase of power, in order to ascertain the seat and the nature of the danger; and the next, whether the measure proposed—that of divesting it of the veto, or modifying it as proposed—would guard against the danger apprehended.

I began with the first, and in entering on it, assert with confidence, that if the Executive has become formidable to the liberty or safety of the country or other departments of the Government, the cause is not in the Constitution, but in the acts and omissions of Congress itself.

According to my conception, the powers vested in the President by the Constitution, are few and effectually guarded, and are not of themselves at all formidable. In order to have a just conception of the extent of his powers, it must be borne in mind that there are but two classes of power known to the Constitution; and they are powers that are expressly granted, and those that are necessary to carry the granted powers into execution. Now, by a positive provision of the Constitution, all powers necessary to the execution of the granted powers, are expressly delegated to Congress, be they powers granted to the Legislative, Executive or Judical department, and can only be exercised by the authority of Congress, and in the manner prescribed by law. This provision will be found in what is called the residuary clause, which declares that Congress shall have power "to make all laws which shall be necessary and proper to carry into execution the foregoing powers," (those granted to Congress,) "and all other powers vested by this Constitution in the Government of the United States, or in any department or officer thereof." A more comprehensive provision cannot be imagined. It carries with it all powers necessary and proper to the execution of the granted powers, be they lodged where they may, and vests the whole, in terms not less explicit, in Congress; and here let me add, in passing, that the provision is as wise as it is comprehensive. It deposites the right of deciding what powers are necessary for the execution of the granted powers, where, and where only it can be lodged with safety, in the hands of the law-making power, and forbids any department or officer of the Government from exercising any power not expressly authorized by the Constitution or the laws, thus making ours emphatically a Government of *law and Constitution.*

Having now shown that the President is restricted by the Constitution to powers expressly granted to him, and that if any of his granted powers be such that they require other powers to execute them, he cannot exercise them without the authority of Congress, I shall now show that there is not one power vested in him that is any way dangerous, unless made so by the acts or permission of Congress. I shall take them in the order they stand in the Constitution.

He is, in the first place, made Commander-in-chief of the army and navy of the United States, and the militia, when called into actual service. Large and expensive military and naval establishments and numerous corps of militia, called into service, would no doubt increase very dangerously the power and patronage of the President; but neither can take place but by the action of Congress. Not a soldier can be enlisted, a ship of war built, nor a militiaman called into service, without its authority; and very fortunately our situation is such, that there is no necessity, and, probably, will be none, why his power and patronage should be dangerously increased by either of those means.

He is next vested with the power to make treaties and to appoint officers, with the advice and consent of the Senate; and here again his power can only be made dangerous by the action of one or both Houses of Congress. In the formation of treaties two-thirds of the Senate must concur; and it is difficult to conceive of a treaty that could materially enlarge his powers, that would not require an act of Congress to carry it into effect. The appointing power may, indeed, dangerously increase his patronage, if officers be uselessly multiplied and too highly paid; but if such should be the case, the fault would be in Congress, by whose authority exclusively they can be created or their compensation regulated.

But much is said in this connection, of the power of removal, justly accompanied by severe condemnation of the many and abusive instances of the use of the power, and the dangerous influence it gives the President, in all of which I fully concur. It is, indeed, a corrupting and dangerous power, when officers are greatly multiplied, and highly paid, and when it is perverted from its legitimate object, to the advancement of personal or party purposes. But I find no such power in the list of powers granted to the Executive, which is proof conclusive that it belongs to the class necessary and proper to execute some other power, if it exists at all, which none can doubt; and, for reasons already assigned, cannot be exercised without authority of law. If, then, it has been abused, it must be because Congress has not done its duty in permitting it to be exercised by the President without the sanction of law authorizing its exercise, and guarding against the abuses to which it is so liable.

The residue of the list are rather duties than rights; that of recommending to Congress such measures as he may deem expedient; of convening both Houses on extraordinary occasions; of adjourning them when they cannot agree on the time; of receiving ambassadors and other ministers; of taking care that the laws be faithfully executed, and commissioning the officers of the United States. Of all these, there is but one which claims particular notice, in connection with the point immediately under consideration; and that is his power as the administrator of the laws. But whatever power he may have in that capacity depends on the action of Congress. If Congress should limit its legislation to the few great subjects confided to it; so frame its laws as to leave as little as possible to discretion, and take care to see that they are duly and faithfully executed, the administrative powers of the President would be proportionally limited, and divested of all danger. But if, on the contrary, it should extend its legislation in every direction; draw within its action subjects never contemplated by the Constitution; multiply its acts, create numerous offices, and increase the revenue and expenditures proportionally, and, at the same time, frame its laws vaguely and loosely, and withdraw, in a great measure, its supervising care over their execution, his power would indeed become truly formidable and alarming. Now I appeal to the Senator and his friend, the author of this resolution, whether the growth of Executive power has not been the result of such a course on the part of Congress. I ask them whether his power has not in fact increased or decreased, just in proportion to the increase and decrease of the system of legislation, such as has been described? What was the period of its maximum increase, but the very period which they have so frequently and loudly denounced as the one most distinguished for the prevalence of Executive power and usurpation? Much of that power certainly depended on the remarkable man, then at the head of that Department, but much—far more, on the system of legislation, which the author of this resolution had built up with so much zeal and labor, and which carried the powers of the Government to a point beyond that to which it had ever before attained, drawing many and important powers into its vortex, of which the framers of the Constitution never dreamed. And here let me say to both of the Senators, and the party of which they are prominent members, that they labor in vain to bring down Executive power, while they support the system they so zealously advocate. The power they complain of is but its necessary fruit. Be assured that as certain as Congress transcends its assigned limits, and usurps powers never conferred, or streches those conferred beyond the proper limits, so surely will the fruits of its usurpation pass into the hands of the Executive. In seeking to become master, it but makes a master in the person of the President. It is only by confining itself to its alloted sphere, and a discreet use of its acknowledged powers, that it can retain that ascendency in the Government which the Constitution intended to confer on it.

Having now pointed out the cause of the great increase of the Executive power on which the Senator rested his objection to the veto power, and having satisfactorily shown, as I trust I have, that, if it has proved dangerous in fact, the fault is not in the Constitution, but in Congress, I would next ask him, in what possible way could the divesting the President of his veto, or modifying it as he proposes, limit his power? Is it not clear, that so far from the veto being the cause of the increase of his power, it would have acted as a limitation on it if it had been more freely and frequently used? If the President had vetoed the original Bank—the connection with the banking system—the tariffs of '24 and '28, and the numerous acts appropriating money for roads, canals, harbors, and a long list of other measures not less unconstitutional, would his power have been half as great as it now is? He has grown great and powerful, not because *he used* his veto, but because *he abstained* from using it. In fact, it is difficult to imagine a case in which its application can tend to enlarge his power, except it be the case of an act intended to repeal a law calculated to increase his power, or to restore the authority of one which, by an arbitrary construction of his power, he has set aside.

Now let me add, in conclusion, that this is a question, in its bearings, of vital importance to that wonderful and sublime system of Government which our patriotic ancestors established, not so much by their wisdom, as wise and experienced as they were, as by the guidance of a kind Providence, who, in his divine dispensation, so disposed events as to lead to the establishment of a system of government wiser than those who framed it. The veto, of itself, as important as it is, sinks into nothing compared to the principle involved. It is but one, and that by no means the most considerable, of those many wise devices which I have attempted to explain, and which were intended to strengthen the popular basis of our Government, and resist its tendency to fall under the control of the dominant interest, acting through the mere numerical majority. The introduction of this resolution may be regarded as one of the many symptoms of that fatal tendency, and of which we had such fearful indications in the bold attempt at the late extraordinary session, of forcing through a whole system of measures of the most threatening and alarming character, in the space of a few weeks, on the ground that they were all decided in the election of the late President; thus attempting to substitute the will of a majority of the people, in the choice of a Chief Magistrate, as the legislative authority of the Union, in lieu of the beautiful and profound system established by the Constitution.

9 *REMARKS AT THE MEETING OF CITIZENS OF CHARLESTON, MARCH 9, 1847*

Toward the end of his life, Calhoun became more and more aware that his defense of the Southern minority was to fail. In consequence, his search for political devices which might somehow protect the South and preserve national unity became more intense. In the following speech he proposed to an overflowing audience the formation of a Southern party. The meeting which Calhoun addressed had been called by citizens of Charleston when it became clear to the South that their success in defeating the Wilmot Proviso proposal to exclude slavery from the lands acquired from Mexico was not conclusive. They feared they would not be able to stem for long the growing Northern opposition to the extension of slavery in the territories. Later, in his "Discourse on the Constitution and Government of the United States", Calhoun was to propose a plural executive as a means for ensuring the South a place in The Union.

FELLOW-CITIZENS: In complying with the request of your committee to address you on the general state of our affairs, in connection with the Federal Government, I shall restrict my remarks to the subject of our peculiar domestic institution, not only because it is by far the most important to us, but also because I have fully expressed my views, in my place in the Senate, on the only other important subject—the Mexican war.

I fully concur in the address of your committee, and the resolutions accompanying it. The facts stated are unquestionable, and the conclusions irresistible.

Indeed, after all that has occurred during the last twelve months, it would be almost idiotic to doubt that a large majority of both parties in the non-slaveholding States have come to a fixed determination to appropriate all the territories of the United States now possessed, or hereafter to be acquired, to themselves, to the entire exclusion of the slaveholding States. Assuming, then, that to be beyond doubt, the grave, and, to us, vital question is presented for consideration: Have they the power to carry this determination into effect?

It will be proper to premise, before I undertake to answer this question, that it is my intention to place before you the danger with which we are threatened from this determination, plainly and fully, without exaggeration or extenuation,—and also the advantages we have for repelling it,—leaving it to you to determine what measures should be adopted for that purpose.

I now return to the question, and answer,—Yes, they have the power, as far as mere numbers can give it. They will have a majority in the next Congress in every department of the Federal Government. The admission of Iowa and Wisconsin will give them two additional States, and a majority of four in the Senate, which heretofore has been our shield against this and other dangers of the kind. We are already in a minority in the House of Representatives and the Electoral College; so that, with the loss of the Senate, we shall be in a minority in every department of the Federal Government, and ever must continue so if the non-slaveholding States should carry into effect their scheme of appropriating to their exclusive use all the territories of the United States. But, fortunately, under our system of government, mere numbers are not the only element of power. There are others, which would give us ample means of defending ourselves against the threatened danger, if we should be true to ourselves.

We have, in the first place, the advantage of having the constitution on our side, clearly and unquestionably, and in its entire fabric; so much so, that the whole body of the instrument stands opposed to their scheme of appropriating the territories to themselves. To make good this assertion, it is only necessary to remind you, that ours is a federal, and not a national or consolidated Government—a distinction essential to a correct understanding of the constitution, and our safety. It ought never to be forgotten or overlooked. As a federal Government, the States composing the Union are its constituents, and stand in the same relation to it, in that respect, as the individual citizens of a State do to its government. As constituent members of the Union, all the territories and other property of the Union belong to them as joint owners or partners, and not to the Government, as is erroneously supposed by some. The Government is but the agent intrusted with the management; and hence the constitution expressly declares the territory to be the property of the United States—that is, the States united, or the States of the Union, which are but synonymous expressions. And hence, also, Congress has no more right to appropriate the territories of the United States to the use of any portion of the States, to the exclusion of the others, than it has to appropriate in the same way, the forts, or other public buildings, or the navy, or any other property of the United States. That it has such a right, no one would venture to assert; and yet the one is placed exactly on the same ground with the other, by the constitution.

It was on this solid foundation that I placed the right of the slaveholding States to a full and equal participation in the territories of the United States, in opposition to the determination of the non-slaveholding States to appropriate them exclusively to themselves. It was my intention to urge them to a vote, but I was unable to do so in consequence of the great pressure of business during the last few days of the session. It was felt by those opposed to us, that if the foundation on which I placed my resolutions be admitted, the conclusion could not be successfully assailed: and hence the bold but unsuccessful attempt to assail the foundation itself, by contending that ours is a national or consolidated Government, in which the States would stand to the Union, as the counties do to the States, and be equally destitute of all political rights. Such a conclusion, if it could be established, would, indeed, place us and our peculiar domestic institutions, at the mercy of the non-slaveholding

States; but, fortunately, it cannot be maintained, without subverting the very foundation of our entire political system and denying the most incontrovertible facts connected with the formation and adoption of the constitution.

But, it may be asked, what do we gain by having the constitution ever so clearly on our side when a majority in the non-slaveholding States stand prepared to deny it? Possibly such may be the case; still we cannot fail to gain much by the advantage it gives us. I speak from long experience—I have never known truth, promptly advocated in the spirit of truth, fail to succeed in the end. Already there are many highly enlightened and patriotic citizens in those States, who agree with us on this great and vital point. The effects of the discussion will not improbably greatly increase their number; and, what is of no little importance, induce a still greater number to hesitate and abate somewhat in their confidence in former opinions, and thereby prepare the way to give full effect to another advantage which we possess. To understand what it is, it will be necessary to explain what is the motive and object of this crusade on the part of the non-slaveholding States against our peculiar domestic institution.

It is clear that it does not originate in any hostility of interests. The labor of our slaves does not conflict with the profit of their capitalists or the wages of their operatives; or in any way injuriously affect the prosperity of those States, either as it relates to their population or wealth. On the contrary, it greatly increases both. It is its products, which mainly stimulate and render their capital and labor profitable; while our slaves furnish, at the same time, an extensive and profitable market for what they make. Annihilate the products of their labor—strike from the list the three great articles which are, most exclusively, the products of their labor,—cotton, rice, and tobacco,—and what would become of the great shipping, navigating, commercial, and manufacturing interests of the non-slaveholding States? What of their Lowell and Waltham, their New-York and Boston, and other manufacturing and commercial cities? What, to enlarge the question, would become of the exports and imports of the Union itself; its shipping and tonnage; its immense revenue, on the disbursements of which, millions in those States, directly or indirectly, live and prosper? Fortunately, then, the crusade against our domestic institution does not originate in hostility of interests. If it did, the possibility of arresting the threatened danger, and saving ourselves, short of a disrupture of the Union, would be altogether hopeless; so predominant is the regard for interest in those States, over all other considerations.

Nor does it originate in any apprehension that the slaveholding States would acquire an undue preponderance in the Union, unless restricted to their present limits. If even a full share of the territories should fall to our lot, we could never hope to outweigh, by any increased number of slaveholding States the great preponderance which their population gives to the non-slaveholding States in the House of Representatives and the Electoral College. All we could hope for would be, to preserve an equality in the Senate, or, at most, to acquire a preponderance in that branch of the Government.

But, if it originates neither in the one nor the other of these, what are the real motives and objects of their crusade against our institution? To answer this, it will be necessary to explain what are the feelings and views of the people of the non-slaveholding States in reference to it, with their effects on their party operations, especially in relation to the Presidential election.

They may, in reference to the subject under consideration be divided into four classes. Of these, the abolitionists proper—the rabid fanatics, who regard slavery as a sin, and thus regarding it, deem it their highest duty to destroy it, even should it involve the destruction of the constitution and the Union—constitute one class. It is a small one, not probably exceeding five per cent. of the population of those States. They voted, if I recollect correctly, about 15,000, or at most 20,000 votes in the last test of their strength in the State of New-York, out of about 400,000 votes, which would give about five per cent. Their strength in that State, I would suppose, was fully equal to their average strength in the non-slaveholding States generally. Another class consists of the great body of the citizens of those States, constituting at least seven tenths of the whole, and who, while they regard slavery as an evil, and as such are disposed to aid in restricting and extirpating it, when it can be done consistently with the constitution, and without endangering the peace or prosperity of the country, do not regard it as a sin, to be put down by all and every means.

Of the other two, one is a small class perhaps not exceeding five per cent. of the whole, who view slavery as we do, more as an institution, and the only one, by which two races, so dissimilar as those inhabiting the slaveholding States, can live together nearly in equal numbers, in peace and prosperity, and that its abolition would end in the extirpation of one or the other race. If they regard it as an evil, it is in the abstract; just as government with all its toils, punishment with all its inflictions, and thousands of other things are evils, when viewed in the abstract; but far otherwise, when viewed in the concrete, because they prevent a greater amount of evil than they inflict, as is the case with slavery as it exists with us.

The remaining class is much larger, but still relatively a small one; less, perhaps, than twenty per cent. of the whole, but possessing great activity and political influence in proportion to its numbers. It consists of the political leaders of the respective parties, and their partizans and followers. They, for the most part, are perfectly indifferent about abolition, and are ready to take either side, for or against, according to the calculation of political chances; their great and leading object being to carry the elections, especially the Presidential, and thereby receive the honors and emoluments incident to power, both in the Federal and State Governments.

Such are the views and feelings of the several classes in the non-slaveholding States in reference to slavery, as it exists with us. It is manifest, on a survey of the whole, that the first class—that is, the abolition party proper—is the centre which has given the impulse that has put in motion this crusade against our domestic institution. It is the only one that has any decidedly hostile feelings in reference to it, and which, in opposing it, is actuated by any strong desire to restrict or destroy it.

But it may be asked how can so small a class rally a large majority of both parties in the non-slaveholding States to come to the determination they have, in reference to our domestic institution? To answer this question, it is necessary to go one step further and explain the habitual state of parties in those, and, in almost all the States of the Union.

There are few of the non-slaveholding States, perhaps not

more than two or three, in which the parties are not so nicely balanced, as to make the result of elections, both State and Federal, so doubtful as to put it in the power of a small party, firmly linked together, to turn the elections, by throwing their weight into the scale of the party which may most favor its views. Such is the abolition party. They have, from the first, made their views paramount to the party struggles of the day, and thrown their weight where their views could be best promoted. By pursuing this course, their influence was soon felt in the elections; and, in consequence, to gain them soon became the object of party courtship: first by the Whigs; but for the last twelve months, more eagerly by the Democrats, as if to make up for lost time. They are now openly courted by both; each striving by their zeal to win their favor by expressing their earnest desire to exclude what they call slavery from all the territories of the United States, acquired or to be acquired. No doubt the Mexican war, and the apprehension of large acquisition of territory to the slaveholding States, have done much to produce this state of things, but of itself it would have been feeble. The main cause or motive, then, of this crusade against our domestic institutions, is to be traced to the all-absorbing interest which both parties take, in carrying the elections, especially the Presidential. Indeed, when we reflect that the expenditure of the Federal Government, at all times great, is now swelled probably to the rate of seventy million of dollars annually, and that the influence of its patronage gives it great sway, not only over its own, but over the State elections,—which gives in addition a control over a vast amount of patronage,—and the control of the Federal patronage, with all its emoluments and honors, centres in the President of the United States,—it is not at all surprising, that both parties should take such absorbing interest in the Presidential election; acting, as both do, on the principle of turning opponents out of office, and bestowing honors and emoluments of Government on their followers, as the reward of partizan services. In such a state of things, it is not a matter for wonder, that a course of policy, so well calculated to conciliate a party like the abolitionists, as that of excluding slavery from the territories, should be eagerly embraced by both parties in the non-slaveholding States; when by securing their support, each calculates on winning the rich and glittering prize of the Presidency. In this is to be found the motive and object of the present crusade against our domestic institution, on the part of political leaders and their partizans in those States.

It would be a great mistake to suppose that it is the less dangerous, because it originates mainly in mere party considerations in connection with elections. It will be on that account but the more so, unless, indeed, it should be met by us with promptitude and unanimity. The absorbing, overriding interest, felt by both parties to carry the elections,—especially the Presidential,—would give such an impulse to their effort to conciliate the abolitionists, at our expense, if we should look on with apparent indifference, as would enlist in their favor the large portion of the non-slaveholding States, estimated at seven tenths of the whole, which are, as yet, well affected towards us, and utterly dishearten the small but intelligent class, which, as yet, is perfectly sound. The former would conclude, in that case, that we ourselves were ready to yield and surrender our domestic institution, as indefensible; and that the non-slaveholding States might carry their determination into full effect, without hazard to the constitution or the Union, or even disturbing the harmony and peace of the country. Indeed, such has already been our apparent indifference, that these opinions have been expressed, even on the floor of Congress. But, if we should act as we ought—if we, by our promptitude, energy, and unanimity, prove that we stand ready to defend our rights, and to maintain our perfect equality, as members of the Union, be the consequences what they may; and that the immediate and necessary effect of courting abolition votes, by either party, would be to lose ours, a very different result would certainly follow. That large portion of the non-slaveholding States, who, although they consider slavery as an evil, are not disposed to violate the constitution, and much less to endanger its overthrow, and with it the Union itself, would take sides with us against our assailants; while the sound portion, who are already with us, would rally to the rescue. The necessary effect would be, that the party leaders and their followers, who expect to secure the Presidential election, by the aid of the abolitionists, seeing their hopes blasted by the loss of our votes, would drop their courtship, and leave the party, reduced to insignificance, with scorn. The end would be, should we act in the manner indicated, the rally of a new party in the non-slaveholding States, more powerful than either of the old, who, on this great question, would be faithful to all of the compromises and obligations of the constitution; and who by uniting with us, would put a final stop to the further agitation of this dangerous question. Such would be the certain effect of meeting, with promptitude and unanimity, the determination of the non-slaveholding States to appropriate all the territories to their own use. That it has not yet been so met is certain; and the next question is—Why has it not been, and what is the cause of this apparent indifference in reference to a danger so menacing, if not promptly and unitedly met on our part?

In answering this important question, I am happy to say, that I have seen no reason to attribute this want of promptitude and unanimity to any division of sentiment, or real indifference, on the part of the people of the slaveholding States, or their delegates in Congress. On the contrary, as far as my observation extends, there is not one of their members of Congress who has given any certain indication of either. On the trying questions connected with the Wilmot Proviso, the votes of the members from the slaveholding States, at the last and present sessions, were unanimous.—To explain what is really the cause, I must again recur to what has already been stated; the absorbing interest felt in the elections,—especially the Presidential,—and the controlling influence which party leaders and their followers exercise over them. The great struggle between the parties is, which shall succeed in electing its candidate; in consequence of which the Presidential election has become the paramount question. All others are held subordinate to it by the leaders and their followers. It depends on them to determine whether it shall be admitted into the issue between the parties, in the Presidential contest, or whether it shall be partially or entirely excluded. Whether it shall be one or the other, is decided entirely in reference to its favorable or unfavorable bearing on the contest, without looking to the higher considerations of its effects on the prosperity, the institutions, or safety of the country. Nothing can more strongly illustrate the truth of what I have asserted, than the course of the parties in relation to the question which now claims your attention. Although none can be more intimately connected with the peace and safety of the Union, it is kept out of the issue between the parties, because it is seen that the Presidential vote of New-York, and many others of the non-slaveholding States, will, in all probability, depend on the votes of the abolitionists; and that the election of the President may, in like manner, depend on the votes of those States. And hence the leaders in them are tolerated by many of the leaders and their followers in the slaveholding States, in openly canvassing for the vote of the abolitionists, by acting in unison with them, in reference to a question, on the decision of which the safety of their own section, and that of the Union itself may depend. But while it is seen that the Presidential election may be secured by courting the abolition votes, it is at the same time seen, that it may be lost, if the consequence should be the loss of the vote of the slaveholding States; and hence the leaders are forced to attempt to secure the former without losing the latter. The game is a difficult one; but difficult as it is, they do not despair of success, with the powerful instruments which they have under their control. They have, in the first place, that of the party press, through which a mighty influence is exerted over public opinion. The line of policy adopted is for the party press to observe a profound silence on this great and vital question, or if they speak at all, so to speak as to give a false direction to public opinion. Acting in conformity to this policy, of the two leading organs at the seat of Government, one never alludes to the question; so that, as far as its remarks are concerned, no one could suppose that it was the cause of the least agitation or feeling in any portion of the Union. The other occasionally alludes to it, when it cannot well avoid doing so, but only to palliate the conduct of those who assail us, by confounding them with our defenders as agitators, and holding both up equally to the public censure. It is calculated by pursuing this course, that the people of the slaveholding States will be kept quiet, and in a state of indifference, until another and still more powerful instrument can be brought into play, by which it is hoped that slaveholders and abolitionists will be coerced to join in nominating and supporting the same candidate for the Presidency. I allude to what is called a National Convention, or Caucus, for nominating candidates for the Presidency and Vice-Presidency. Already the machinery has been put in motion, in order to coerce the oldest and most populous of the slaveholding States; and no doubt, will, in due season, be put in motion to effect the same object in all of them. Should it succeed—should the party machinery for President-making prove strong enough to force the slaveholding States to join in a convention to nominate and support a candidate who will be acceptable to the abolitionists, they will have committed the most suicidal act that a people ever perpetrated. I say acceptable; for it is clear that the non-slaveholding States will outnumber in convention the slaveholding, and that no one who is not acceptable to the abolitionists can receive their votes;—and of course, the votes of the States where they hold the balance; and that no other will be nominated, or, if nominated, be elected. And yet, there are not a few in the slaveholding States, men of standing and influence, so blinded by party feeling, or the prospect of personal gain or advancement by the success of their party, who advocate a step which must prove so fatal to their portion of the Union under existing circumstances. Can party folly, or rather madness, go further?

As to myself, I have ever been opposed to such conventions, because they are irresponsible bodies, not known to the constitution; and because they, in effect, set aside the constitution with its compromises, in reference to so important a subject as the election of the Chief Magistrate of the Union. I hold it far safer, and every way preferable, to leave the election where the constitution has placed it—to the Electoral College to choose; and if that fails to make a choice, to the House of Representatives, voting by States, to elect the President from the three candidates having the highest votes. But, if I had no objection to such conventions, under ordinary circumstances, I would regard the objection as fatal under the existing state of things, when all parties of the non-slaveholding States stand united against us on the most vital of all questions; and when to go into one would be, in effect, a surrender on our part. As both parties there have united to divest us of our just and equal rights in the public domain, it is time that both parties with us should unite in resistance to so great an outrage. Let us show at least as much spirit in defending our rights and honor, as they have evinced in assailing them. Let us, when our safety is concerned, show at least as firm a determination, and as much unanimity, as they do with no other interest on their part but the temporary one of succeeding in the Presidential contest. Henceforward, let all party distinction among us cease, so long as this aggression on our rights and honor shall continue, on the part of the non-slaveholding States. Let us profit by the example of the abolition party who, as small as they are, have acquired so much influence by the course they have pursued. As they make the destruction of our domestic institution the paramount question, so let us make, on our part, its safety the paramount question; let us regard every man as of our party, who stands up in its defence; and every one as against us, who does not, until aggression ceases. It is thus, and thus only, that we can defend our rights, maintain our honor, ensure our safety, and command respect. The opposite course, which would merge them in the temporary and mercenary party struggles of the day, would inevitably degrade and ruin us.

If we should prove true to ourselves and our peculiar domestic institution, we shall be great and prosperous, let what will occur. There is no portion of the globe more abundant in resources—agricultural, manufacturing and commercial—than that possessed by us. We count among our productions the great staples of cotton, rice, tobacco and sugar, with the most efficient, well fed, well clad, and well trained body of laborers for their cultivation. In addition to furnishing abundant means for domestic exchanges among ourselves, and with the rest of the world, and building up flourishing commercial cities, they would furnish ample resources for revenue. But far be it from us to desire to be forced on our own resources for protection. Our object is to preserve the Union of these States, if it can be done consistently with our rights, safety, and perfect equality with other members of the Union. On this we have a right to insist. Less we cannot take. Looking at the same time to our safety and the preservation of the Union, I regard it as fortunate that the promptitude and unanimity, on our part, necessary to secure the one, are equally so to preserve the other. Delay, indecision, and want of union among ourselves would in all probability, in the end, prove fatal to both. The danger is of a character—whether we regard our safety or the preservation of the Union—which cannot be safely tampered with. If not met promptly and decidedly, the two portions of the Union will gradually become thoroughly alienated, when no alternative will be left to us as the weaker of the two, but to sever all political ties, or sink down into abject submission. It is only by taking an early and decided stand, while the political ties are still strong, that a rally of the sound and patriotic of all portions of the Union can be successfully made to arrest so dire an alternative.

Having now pointed out the danger with which we are menaced, and the means by which it may be successfully met and resisted, it is for you and the people of the slaveholding States, to determine what shall be done, at a juncture so trying and eventful. In conclusion, it is my sincere prayer, that the Great Disposer of events may enlighten you and them to realize its full extent, and give the wisdom to adopt the best and most efficient course for our own security, and the peace and preservation of the Union.

10 ON THE OREGON BILL, JUNE 27, 1848

The Northern opposition to the extension of slavery in the territories, like the admission of "free" states into the Union, was a constant threat to the South. Calhoun dealt with the problem here by urging the minority rights of the Southern people to settlement in the territories. In the conflict between North and South he felt that time was running short. His sense of heightened crisis led him to argue that the core of the issue between North and South was the axiom that all men are created free and equal and to urge that freedom be limited in the intrests of unity. Calhoun's belief was that freedom from restriction could not be accorded to all men equally, but must be distributed unequally in such a way as to ensure the preservation of society. He points out in this speech that man's original condition is social and political and that his freedom is a reward to be earned by demonstrating capacity for responsible action.

There is a very striking difference between the position in which the slaveholding and non-slaveholding States stand in reference to the subject under consideration. The former desire no action of the Government; demand no law to give them any advantage in the Territory about to be established; are willing to leave it, and other Territories belonging to the United States, open to all their citizens, so long as they continue to be Territories, and when they cease to be so, to leave it to their inhabitants to form such governments as may suit them, without restriction or condition, except that imposed by the Constitution, as a prerequisite for admission into the Union. In short, they are willing to leave the whole subject where the Constitution and the great and fundamental principles of self-government place it. On the contrary, the non-slaveholding States, instead of being willing to leave it on this broad and equal foundation, demand the interposition of the Government, and the passage of an act to exclude the citizens of the slaveholding States from emigrating with their property into the Territory, in order to give their citizens and those they may permit, the exclusive right of settling it, while it remains in that condition, preparatory to subjecting it to like restrictions and conditions when it becomes a State. The 12th section of this bill is intended to assert and maintain this demand of the non-slaveholding States, while it remains a Territory, not openly or directly, but indirectly, by extending the provisions of the bill for the establishment of the Iowa Territory to this, and by ratifying the acts of the informal and self-constituted government of Oregon, which, among others, contains one prohibiting the introduction of slavery. It thus, in reality, adopts what is called the Wilmot proviso, not only for Oregon, but, as the bill now stands, for New Mexico and California. The amendment, on the contrary, moved by the Senator from Mississippi near me, [Mr. DAVIS,] is intended to assert and maintain the position of the slaveholding States. It leaves the Territory free and open to all the citizens of the United States, and would overrule, if adopted, the act of the self-constituted Territory of Oregon and the 12th section, as far as it relates to the subject under consideration. We have thus fairly presented the grounds taken by the non-slaveholding and the slaveholding States, or, as I shall call them for the sake of brevity, the northern and southern States, in their whole extent, for discussion.

The first question which offers itself for consideration is: Has the northern States the power which they claim, to exclude the southern from emigrating freely, with their property, into Territories belonging to the United States, and to monopolize them for their exclusive benefit?

It is, indeed a great question. I propose to discuss it calmly and dispassionately. I shall claim nothing which does not fairly and clearly belong to the southern States, either as members of this Federal Union, or appertaining to them in their separate and individual character; nor shall I yield any which belong to them in either capacity. I am influenced neither by sectional nor party considerations. If I know myself, I would repel as promptly and decidedly any aggression of the South on the North, as I would any on the part of the latter on the former. And let me add, I hold the obligation to repel aggression to be not much less solemn than that of abstaining from making aggression; and that the party which submits to it when it can be resisted, to be not much less guilty and responsible for consequences than that which makes it. Nor do I stand on party grounds. What I shall say in reference to this subject, I shall say entirely without reference to the Presidential election. I hold it to be infinitely higher than that and all other questions of the day. I shall direct my efforts to ascertain what is constitutional, right, and just, under a thorough conviction that the best and only way of putting an end to this, the most dangerous of all questions to our Union and institutions, is to adhere rigidly to the Constitution and the dictates of justice.

With these preliminary remarks, I recur to the question: Has the North the power which it claims under the 12th section of this bill? I ask at the outset, where is the power to be found? Not, certainly, in the relation in which the northern and southern States stand to each other. They are the constituent parts or members of a common Federal Union; and, as such, are equals in all respects, both in dignity and rights, as is declared by all writers on governments founded on such union, and as may be inferred from arguments deduced from their nature and character. Instead, then, of affording any countenance or authority in favor of the power, the relation in which they stand to each other furnishes a strong presumption against it. Nor can it be found in the fact that the South holds property in slaves. That, too, fairly considered, instead of affording any authority for the power, furnishes a strong presumption against it. Slavery existed in the South when the Constitution was framed, fully to the extent in proportion to their population as it does at this time. It is the only property recognized by it; the only one that entered into its formation as a political element, both in the adjustment of the relative weight of the States in the Government, and the apportionment of direct taxes; and the only one that is put under the express guarantee of the Constitution. It is well known to all conversant with the history of the formation and adoption of the Constitution, that the South was very jealous in reference to this property; that it constituted one of the difficulties, both to its formation and adoption, and that it would not have assented to either, had the Convention refused to allow to it its due weight in the Government, or to place it under the guarantee of the Constitution. Nor can it be found in the way that the territories have been acquired. I will not go into particulars in this respect at this stage of the discussion. Suffice it to say, the whole was acquired either by purchase out of the common funds of all the States, the South as well as the North, or by arms and mutual sacrifice of men and money, which, instead of giving any countenance in favor of the power claimed by the North, on every principle of right and justice, furnishes strong additional presumption against it.

But if it cannot be found in either, if it exists at all, the power must be looked for in the constitutional compact, which binds these States together in a Federal Union; and I now ask, can it be found there? Does that instrument contain any provision which gives the North the power to exclude the South from a free admission into the Territories of the United States with its peculiar property, and to monopolize them for its own exclusive use? If it in fact contains such power, expressed or implied, it must be found in a specific grant, or be inferred by irresistible deduction, from some clear and acknowledged power. Nothing short of the one or the other can overcome the strong presumption against it.

That there is no such specific grant, may be inferred beyond doubt from the fact that no one has ever attempted to designate it. Instead of that, it has been assumed—taken for granted without a particle of proof—that Congress has the absolute right to govern the Territories. Now, I concede, if it does in reality possess such power, it may exclude from the Territories who or what they please, and admit into them who or what they please; and of course may exercise the power claimed by the North to exclude the South from them. But I again repeat, where is this absolute power to be found? All admit that there is no such specific grant of power. If, then, it exists at all, it must be inferred from some such power. I ask, where is that to be found? The Senator from New York, behind me, [Mr. Dix,] points to the clause in the Constitution, which provides that "Congress shall have power to dispose of, and make all needful rules and regulations respecting, the territory or other property belonging to the United States." Now, I undertake to affirm and maintain, beyond the possibility of doubt, that so far from conferring absolute power to govern the Territories, it confers no governmental power whatever; no, not a particle. It refers exclusively to territory regarded simply as public lands. Every word relates to it in that character, and is wholly inapplicable to it considered in any other character but as property. Take the expression "dispose of," with which it begins. It is easily understood what it means when applied to lands, and is the proper and natural expression regarding the territory in that character, when the object is to confer the right to sell or make other disposition of it. But who ever heard the expression applied to government? And what possible meaning can it have when so applied? Take the next expression, "to make all needful rules and regulations." These regarded separately, might indeed be applicable to government in a loose sense; but they are never so applied in the Constitution. In every case where they are used in it, they refer to property, to things, or some process, such as the rules of court, or of the Houses of Congress for the government of their proceedings; but never to government, which always implies persons to be governed. But if there should be any doubt in this case, the words immediately following, which restricts them to making "rules and regulations respecting the territory or other property of the United States," must effectually expel it. They restrict their meaning, beyond the possibility of doubt, to territory regarded as property.

But if it were possible for doubt still to exist, another and conclusive argument still remains to show that the framers of the Constitution did not intend to confer by this clause governmental powers. I refer to the clause in the Constitution which delegates the power of exclusive legislation to Congress over this District, and "all places purchased by the consent of the Legislature of the State in which the same may be, for the erection of forts, magazines, arsenals, dock-yards, and other needful buildings." The places therein referred to are clearly embraced by the expression, "other property belonging to the United States," contained in the clause I have just considered.

But it is certain, that if it had been the intention of the framers of the Constitution to confer governmental powers over such places by that clause, they never would have delegated it by this. They were incapable of doing a thing so absurd. But it is equally certain, if they did not intend to confer such power over them, they could not have intended it over Territories. Whatever was conferred by the same words in reference to one, must have been intended to be conferred in reference to the other, and the reverse. The opposite supposition would be absurd. But, it may be asked, why the term territory was omitted in the delegation of exclusive legislation to Congress over the places enumerated? Very satisfactory reasons may, in my opinion, be assigned. The former were limited to places lying within the limits and jurisdiction of the States, and the latter to public land lying beyond both. The cession and purchase of the former, with the consent of the State within which they might be situated, did not oust the sovereignty or jurisdiction of the State. They still remained in the State, the United States acquiring only the title to the place. It therefore became necessary to confer on Congress, by express delegation, the exercise of exclusive power of legislation over this District, and such places, in order to carry out the object of the purchase and cession. It was simply intended to withdraw them from under the Legislatures of the respective States within which they might lie, and substitute that of Congress in its place, subject to the restrictions of the Constitution, and the objects for which the places were acquired, leaving, as I have said, the sovereignty still in the State in which they are situated, but in abeyance, as far as it extends to legislation. Thus, in the case of this District, since the retrocession to Virginia of the part beyond the Potomac, the sovereignty still continues in Maryland in the manner stated. But the case is very different in reference to Territories, lying, as they do, beyond the limits and jurisdiction of all the States. The United States possess not simply the right of ownership over them, but that of exclusive dominion and sovereignty; and hence it was not necessary to exclude the power of the States to legislate over them, by delegating the exercise of exclusive legislation to Congress. It would have been an act of supererogation. It may be proper to remark in this connection, that the power of exclusive legislation conferred in these cases must not be confounded with the power of absolute legislation. They are very different things. It is true, that absolute power of legislation is always exclusive, but it by no means follows that exclusive power of legislation or of government is likewise always absolute. Congress has the exclusive power of legislation as far as this Government is concerned, and the State Legislatures, as far as their respective Governments are concerned; but we all know that both are subject to many and important restrictions and conditions which the nature of absolute power excludes.

I have now made good the assertion I ventured to make, that the clause in the Constitution relied on by the Senator from New York, so far from conferring the absolute power of government over the territory claimed by him, and others who agree with him, confers not a particle of governmental power. Having conclusively established this, the long list of precedents cited by the Senator, to prop up the power which he sought in the clause, falls to the ground with the fabric which he raised; and I am thus exempted from the necessity of referring to them, and replying to them one by one.

But there is one precedent referred to by the Senator unconnected with the power, and on that account requires particular notice. I refer to the ordinance of 1787, which was adopted by the old Congress of the Confederation while the Convention that framed the Constitution was in session, and about one year before its adoption, and of course on the very eve of the expiration of the old Confederation. Against its introduction, I might object that the act of the Congress of the Confederation cannot rightfully form precedents for this Government; but I waive that. I waive also the objection that the act was consummated when that Government was *in extremis*, and could hardly be considered *compos mentis*. I waive also the fact that the ordinance assumed the form of a compact, and was adopted when only eight States were present, when the Articles of Confederation required nine to form compacts. I waive also the fact, that Mr. Madison declared that the act was without shadow of constitutional authority, and shall proceed to show, from the history of its adoption, that it cannot justly be considered of any binding force.

Virginia made the cession of the territory north of the Ohio, and lying between it and the Mississippi and the lakes, in 1784. It now contains the States of Ohio, Indiana, Illinois, Michigan, Wisconsin, and a very considerable extend of territory lying north of the latter. Shortly after the cession, a committee of three was raised, of whom Mr. Jefferson was one. They reported an ordinance for the establishment of the Territory, containing, among other provisions, one, of which Mr. Jefferson was the author, excluding slavery from the Territory after the year 1800. It was reported to Congress, but this provision was struck out. On the question of striking out, every southern State present voted in favor of it; and, what is more striking, every southern delegate voted the same way, Mr. Jefferson alone excepted. The ordinance was adopted without the provision. At the next session, Rufus King, then a member of the old Congress, moved a proposition, very much in the same shape of the sixth article (that which excludes slavery) in the ordinance as it now stands, with the exception of its proviso. It was referred to a committee, but there was no action on it. A committee was moved the next or the subsequent year, which reported without including or noticing Mr. King's proposition. Mr. Dane was a member of that committee, and proposed a provision the same as that in the ordinance as it passed, but the committee reported without including it. Finally, another committe was raised, at the head of which was Mr. Carrington, of Virginia, and of which Mr. Dane was also a member. That committee reported without including the amendment previously proposed by him. Mr. Dane moved his proposition, which was adopted, and the report of the committee thus amended became the ordinance of 1787.

It may be inferred from this brief historical sketch, that the ordinance was a compromise between the southern and northern States, of which the terms were, that slavery should be excluded from territory upon condition that fugitive slaves, who might take refuge in the Territory, should be delivered up to their owners, as stipulated in the proviso of the 6th article of the ordinance. It is manifest, from what has been stated, that the South was unitedly and obstinately opposed to the provision when first moved; that the proposition of Mr. King, without the proviso, was in like manner resisted by the South, as may be inferred from its entire want of success, and that it never could be brought to agree to it until the provision for the delivery up of fugitive slaves was incorporated in it. But it is well understood that a compromise involves not a surrender, but simply a waiver of the right or power; and hence, in the case of individuals, it is a well established legal principle, that an offer to settle by compromise a litigated claim, is no evidence against the justice of the claim on the side of the party making it. The South, to her honor, has observed with fidelity her engagements under this compromise; in proof of which, I appeal to the precedents cited by the Senator from New York, intended by him to establish the fact of her acquiescence in the ordinance. I admit that she has acquiesced in the several acts of Congress to carry it into effect; but the Senator is mistaken in supposing that it is proof of a surrender, on her part, of the power over the Territories which he claims for Congress. No, she never has, and I trust never will, make such a surrender. Instead of that, it is conclusive proof of her fidelity to her engagements. She has never attempted to set aside the ordinance, or to deprive the Territory, and the States erected within its limits, of any right or advantage it was intended to confer. But I regret that as much cannot be said in favor of the fidelity with which it has been observed on their part. With the single exception of the State of Illinois—be it said to her honor—every other State erected within its limits have pursued a course, and adopted measures, which have rendered the stipulations of the proviso to deliver up fugitive slaves nugatory. Wisconsin may also be an exception, as she has just entered the Union, and has hardly had time to act on the subject. They have gone further, and suffered individuals to form combinations, without an effort to suppress them, for the purpose of enticing and seducing the slaves to leave their masters, and to run them into Canada beyond the reach of our laws—in open violation, not only of the stipulations of the ordinance, but of the Constitution itself. If I express myself strongly, it is not for the purpose of producing excitement, but to draw the attention of the Senate forcibly to the subject. My object is to lay bare the subject under consideration just as a surgeon probes to the bottom and lays open a wound, not to cause pain to his patient, but for the purpose of healing it.

Mr. HANNEGAN. I am not aware that there is any such law in Indiana.

Mr. CALHOUN. I spoke on the authority of a report of one of the committees of this body.

Mr. BUTLER. In that report I alluded particularly to the northern and New England States; and Illinois, I believe, was the only exception.

Mr. CORWIN. Will the Senator allow me to inquire, what law on the statute-book of Ohio prevents the recapture of fugitive slaves?

Mr. CALHOUN. My colleague can doubtless refer to the law. I made the statement on the authority of his report.

Mr. CORWIN. There is no such law in Ohio.

Mr. CALHOUN. I am very happy to find that it is so; and I should be equally happy if the Senator will make it out that there are no organized bodies of individuals there for the purpose of pilfering our slaves.

Mr. CORWIN. Am I to understand the Senator, when he spoke of "incorporated individuals," as referring to the Legislature?

Mr. CALHOUN. No; merely organized individuals—a very different thing from corporations.

Mr. BUTLER. On that point I refer the Senator to the documents on the files of the Senate. If the gentleman desires to call out explanations of that kind, he can be gratified.

Mr. CALHOUN. I come now to another precedent of a similar character, but differing in this, that it took place under this Government, and not under that of the old Confederation; I refer to what is known as the Missouri compromise. It is more recent, and better known, and may be more readily despatched.

After an arduous struggle of more than a year, on the question whether Missouri should come into the Union, with or without restrictions prohibiting slavery, a compromise line was adopted between the North and the South; but it was done under circumstances which made it nowise obligatory on the latter. It is true, it was moved by one of her distinguished citizens, [Mr. Clay,] but it is equally so, that it was carried by the almost united vote of the North against the almost united vote of the South; and was thus imposed on the latter by superior numbers, in opposition to her strenuous efforts. The South has never given her sanction to it, or assented to the power it asserted. She was voted down, and has simply acquiesced in an arrangement which she has not had the power to reverse, and which she could not attempt to do without disturbing the peace and harmony of the Union—to which she has ever been adverse. Acting on this principle, she permitted the Territory of Iowa to be formed, and the State to be admitted into the Union, under the compromise, without objection; and that is now quoted by the Senator from New York to prove her surrender of the power he claims for Congress.

To add to the strength of this claim, the advocates of the power hold up the name of Jefferson in its favor, and go so far as to call him the author of the so-called Wilmot proviso, which is but a general expression of a power of which the Missouri compromise is a case of its application. If we may judge by his opinion of that case, what his opinion was of the principle, instead of being the author of the proviso, or being in its favor, no one could be more deadly hostile to it. In a letter addressed to the elder Adams, in 1819, in answer to one from him, he uses there remarkable expressions in reference to the Missouri question:

"The banks, bankrupt law, manufactures, Spanish treaty, are nothing. These are occurrences which, like waves in a storm, will pass under the ship. But the Missouri question is a breaker on which we lose the Missouri country by revolt, and what more, God only knows."

To understand the full force of these expressions, it must be borne in mind, that the questions enumerated were the great and exciting political questions of the day on which parties divided. The banks and bankrupt law had long been so. Manufactures (or what has since been called the protective tariff) was at the time a subject of great excitement, as was the Spanish treaty; that is, the treaty by which Florida was ceded to the Union, and by which the western boundary between Mexico and the United States was settled, from the Gulf of Mexico to the Pacific Ocean. All these exciting party questions of the day Mr. Jefferson regarded as nothing compared to the Missouri question. He looked on all of them as, in their nature, fugitive; and, to use his own forcible expression, "would pass off under the ship of state like waves in a storm." Not so that fatal question. It was a breaker on which it was destined to be stranded; and yet, his name is quoted by the incendiaries of the present day in support of, and as the author of, a proviso which would give indefinite and universal extenson of this fatal question to all the Territories. It was compromised the next year by the adoption of the line to which I have referred. Mr. Holmes, of Maine, long a member of this body, who voted for the measure, addressed a letter to Mr. Jefferson, enclosing a copy of his speech on the occasion. It drew out an answer from him which ought to be treasured up in the heart of every man who loves the country and its institutions. It is brief: I will send it to the Secretary to be read. The time of the Senate cannot be better occupied than in listening to it:

To John Holmes.

MONTICELLO, *April 22, 1820.*

I thank you, dear sir, for the copy you have been so kind as to send me of the letter to your constituents on the Missouri question. It is a perfect justification to them. I had for a long time ceased to read newspapers, or pay any attention to public affairs, confident they were in good hands, and content to be a passenger in our bark to the shore from which I am not distant. But this momentous question, like a fire bell in the night, awakened and filled me with terror. I considered it at once as the knell of the Union. It is hushed, indeed, for the moment; but this is a reprieve only, not a final sentence. A geographical line, coinciding with a marked principle, moral and political, once conceived and held up to the angry passions of men, will never be obliterated, and every new irritation will mark it deeper and deeper. I can say, with conscious truth, that there is not a man on earth who would sacrifice more than I would to relieve us from this heavy reproach, in any *practicable* way. The cession of that kind of property (for so it is misnamed) is a bagatelle, which would not cost me a second thought, if, in that way, a general emacipation and *expatriation* could be effected: and gradually, and with due sacrifices, I think it might be. But as it is, we have the wolf by the ears, and we can neither hold him, nor safely let him go. Justice is in one scale, and self-preservation in the other. Of one thing I am certain, that as the free passage of slaves from one State to another would not make a slave of a single human being who would not be so without it, so their diffusion over a greater surface would make them individually happier, and proportionally facilitate the accomplishment of their emancipation, by dividing the burden on a greater number of coadjutors. An abstinence, too, from this act of power, would remove the jealousy excited by the undertaking of Congress to regulate the condition of the different descriptions of men composing a State. This certainly is the exclusive right of every State, which nothing in the Constitution has taken from them, and given to the General Government. Could Congress, for example, say that the non-freemen of Connecticut shall be freemen, or that they shall not emigrate into any other State?

I regret that I am now to die in the belief, that the useless sacrifice of themselves by the generation of 1776, to acquire self-government and happiness to their country, is to be thrown away by the unwise and unworthy passions of their sons, and that my only consolation is to be, that I live not to weep over it. If they would but dispassionately weigh the blessings they will throw away, against an abstract principle, more likely to be effected by union than by scission, they would pause before they would perpetrate this act of suicide on themselves, and of treason against the hopes of the world. To yourself, as the faithful advocate of the Union, I tender the offering of my high esteem and respect.

THOMAS JEFFERSON.

Mark his prophetic words! Mark his profound reasoning!

"It [the question] is hushed *for the moment.* But this is a *reprieve only*, not a *final sentence.* A geographical line coinciding with a marked principle, moral and political, *once conceived and held up to the angry passions of men, will never be obliterated, and every new irritation will mark it deeper and deeper.*"

Twenty-eight years have passed since these remarkable words were penned, and there is not a thought which time has not thus far verified, and it is to be feared will continue to verify until the whole will be fulfilled. Certain it is, that he regarded the compromise line as utterly inadequate to arrest that fatal course of events which his keen sagacity anticipated from the question. It was but a "reprieve." Mark the deeply melancholy impression which it made on his mind:

"I regret that I am to die in the belief that the useless sacrifice of themselves by the generation of 1776, to acquire self-government and happiness for themselves, is to be thrown away by the unwise and unworthy passions of their sons, and that my only consolation is to be, that I shall live not to weep over it."

Can any one believe, after listening to this letter, that Jefferson is the author of the so-called Wilmot proviso, or ever favored it? And yet there are at this time strenuous efforts making in the North to form a purely sectional party on it, and that, too, under the sanction of those who profess the highest veneration for his character and principles! But I must speak the truth, while I vindicate the memory of Jefferson from so foul a charge. I hold he is not blameless in reference to this subject. He committed a great error in inserting the provision he did, in the plan he reported for the government of the Territory, as much modified as it was. It was the first blow—the first essay "to draw a geographical line coinciding with a marked principle, moral and political." It originated with him in philanthropic but mistaken views of the most dangerous character, as I shall show in the sequel. Others, with very different feelings and views, followed, and have given to it a direction and impetus, which, if not promptly and efficiently arrested, will end in the dissolution of the Union and the destruction of our political institutions.

I have, I trust, established beyond controversy, that neither the ordinance of 1787, nor the Missouri compromise, nor the precedents growing out of them, nor the authority of Mr. Jefferson, furnishes any evidence whatever to prove that Congress possesses the power over the Territory claimed by those who advocate the 12th section of this bill. But admit, for the sake of argument, that I am mistaken, and that the objections I have urged against them are groundless—give them all the force which can be claimed for precedents—and they would not have the weight of a feather against the strong presumption which I, at the outset of my remarks, showed to be opposed to the existence of the power. Precedents, even in a court of justice, can have but little weight, except where the law is doubtful, and should have little in a deliberative body in any case on a constitutional question, and none where the power to which it has been attempted to trace it does not exist, as I have shown, I trust, to be the case in this instance.

But while I deny that the clause relating to the territory and other property of the United States, confers any governmental, or that Congress possesses absolute, power over the Territories, I by no means deny that it has any power over them. Such a denial would be idle on any occasion, but much more so on this, when we are engaged in constituting a territorial government, without an objection being whispered from any quarter against our right to do so. If there be any Senator of that opinion, he ought at once to rise and move to lay the bill on the table, or to dispose of it in some other way, so as to prevent the waste of time on a subject upon which we have no right to act. Assuming, then, that we possess the power, the only questions that remain are, Whence is it derived? and, What is its extent?

As to its origin, I concur in the opinion expressed by Chief Justice Marshall, in one of the cases read by the Senator from New York, that it is derived from the right of acquiring territory, and I am the more thoroughly confirmed in it from the fact, that I entertained the opinion long before I knew it to be his. As to the right of acquiring territory, I agree with the Senator from New York, that it is embraced, without going further, both in the war and treaty powers. Admitting, then—what has never been denied, and what it would be idle to do so in a discussion which relates to territories acquired both by war and treaties—that the United States have the right to acquire territories, it would seem to follow, by necessary consequence, that they have the right to govern them. As they possess the entire right of soil, dominion, and sovereignty over them, they must necessarily carry with them the right to govern. But this Government, as the sole agent and representative of the United States—that is, the States of the Union in their Federal character—must, as such, possess the sole right, if it exists at all. But if there be any one disposed to take a different view of the origin of the power, I shall make no points with him, for whatever may be its origin, the conclusion would be the same, as I shall presently show.

But it would be a great error to conclude that Congress has the absolute power of governing the Territories, because it has the sole or exclusive power. The reverse is the case. It is subject to many and important restrictions and conditions, of which some are expressed and others implied. Among the former may be classed all the general and absolute prohibitions of the Constitution; that is, all those which prohibit the exercise of certain powers under any circumstance. In this class is included the prohibition of granting titles of nobility; passing *ex post facto* laws and bills of attainder; the suspension of the writ of *habeas corpus*, except in certain cases; making laws respecting the establishment of religion, or prohibiting its free exercise; and every other of like description, which conclusively shows that the power of Congress over the Territories is not absolute. Indeed, it is a great error to suppose, that either this or the State governments possess in any case absolute power. Such power can belong only to the supreme ultimate power called sovereignty, and that, in our system, resides in the people of the several States of the Union. With us, governments, both Federal and State, are but agents, or, more properly, trustees, and, as such, possess, not absolute, but subordinate and limited powers; for all powers possessed by such governments must, from their nature, be trust powers, and subject to all the restrictions to which that class of powers are.

Among them, they are restricted to the nature and the objects of the trust; and hence no government under our system, Federal or State, has the right to do anything inconsistent with the nature of the powers intrusted to it, or the objects for which it was intrusted, or, to express it in more usual language, for which it was delegated. To do either would be to pervert the power to purposes never intended, and would be a violation of the Constitution, and that in the most dangerous way it could be made, because more easily done and less easily detected. But there is another and important class of restrictions which more directly relate to the subject under discussion; I refer to those imposed on the trustees by the nature and character of the party who constituted the trustees, and invested them with the trust powers to be exercised for its benefit. In this case it is the United States, that is, the several States of the Union. It was they who constituted the Government as their representative or trustee, and intrusted it with powers to be exercised for their common and joint benefit. To them, in their united character, the territories belong, as is expressly declared by the Constitution. They are their joint and common owners, regarded as property or land; and in them, severally, reside the dominion and sovereignty over them. They are as much the territories of one State as another—of Virginia as of New York, of the southern as the Northern States. They are the territories of all, because they are the territories of each; and not of each, because they are the territories of the whole. Add to this the perfect equality of dignity, as well as rights, which appertain to them as members of a common Federal Union, which all writers on the subject admit to be a fundamental and essential relation between States so united; and it must be manifest that Congress, in governing the Territories, can give no preference or advantage to one State over another, or to one portion or section of the Union over another, without depriving the State or section over which the preference is given, or from which the advantage is withheld, of their clear and unquestionable right, and subverting the very foundation on which the Union and Government rest. It has no more power to do so than to subvert the Constitution itself. Indeed, the act itself would be its subversion. It would destroy the relation of equality on the part of the southern States, and sink them to mere dependents of the northern, to the total destruction of the Federal Union.

I have now shown, I trust, beyond controversy, that Congress has no power whatever to exclude the citizens of the southern States from emigrating with their property into the Territories of the United States, or to give an exclusive monopoly of them to the North. I now propose to go one step further, and show that neither the inhabitants of the Territories nor their Legislatures have any such right. A very few words will be sufficient for the purpose; for of all the positions ever taken, I hold that which claims the power for them to be the most absurd. If the Territories belong to the United States—if the ownership, dominion, and sovereignty over them be in the States of this Union, then neither the inhabitants of the Territories nor their Legislatures can exercise any power but what is subordinate to them; but if the contrary could be shown, which I hold to be impossible, it would be subject to all the restrictions to which I have shown the power of Congress is, and for the same reason, whatever power they might hold, would, in the case supposed, be subordinate to the Constitution, and controlled by the nature and character of our political institutions. But if the reverse be true—if the dominion and sovereignty over the Territories be in their inhabitants, instead of the United States, they would, indeed, in that case, have the exclusive and absolute power of governing them, and might exclude whom they pleased, or what they pleased. But, in that case, they would cease to be the Territories of the United States the moment we acquired them and permit them to be inhabited. The first half-dozen of squatters would become the sovereigns, with full dominion and sovereignty over them; and the conquered people of New Mexico and California would become the sovereigns of the country as soon as they become the Territories of the United States, vested with the full right of excluding even their conquerors. There is no escaping from the alternative, but by resorting to the greatest of all absurdities, that of a divided sovereignty—a sovereignty, a part of which would reside in the United States, and a part in the inhabitants of the Territory. How can sovereignty—the ultimate and supreme power of a State—be divided? The exercise of the powers of sovereignty may be divided, but how can there be two supreme powers?

We are next told the laws of Mexico preclude slavery; and assuming that they will remain in force until repealed, it is contended, that until Congress passes an act for their repeal, the citizens of the South cannot emigrate with their property into the territory acquired from her. I admit, the laws of Mexico prohibit, not slavery, but slavery in the form it exists with us. The Puros are as much slaves as our negroes, and are less intelligent and well treated. But I deny that the laws of Mexico can have the effect attributed to them. As soon as the treaty between the two countries is ratified, the sovereignty and authority of Mexico in the territory acquired by it becomes extinct, and that of the United States is substituted in its place, carrying with it the Constitution, with its overriding control over all the laws and institutions of Mexico inconsistent with it. It is true, the municipal laws of the territory not inconsistent with the condition and the nature of our political system would, according to the writers on the laws of nations, remain, until changed, not as a matter of right, but merely of sufferance, and as between the inhabitants of territory, in order to avoid a state of anarchy, before they can be brought under our laws. This is the utmost limits to which sufferance goes. Under it, the peon system would continue; but not to the exclusion of such of our citizens as may choose to emigrate with their slaves or other property that may be excluded by the laws of Mexico. The humane provisions of the laws of nations go no further than to protect the inhabitants in their property and civil rights, under their former laws, until others can be substituted. To extend them further and give them the force of excluding emigrants from the United States, because their property or religion are such as are prohibited from being introduced by the laws of Mexico, would not only exclude a great majority of the people of the United States from emigrating into the acquired territory, but would be to give a higher authority to the extinct authority of Mexico over the territory than to our actual authority over it. I say the great majority, for the laws of Mexico not only prohibit the introduction of slaves, but of many other descriptions of property, and also the Protestant religion, which Congress itself cannot prohibit. To such absurdity would the supposition lead.

I have now concluded the discussion, so far as it relates to the power; and have, I trust, established beyond controversy, that the Territories are free and open to all of the citizens of the United States, and that there is no power under any aspect the subject can be viewed in by which the citizens of the South can be excluded from emigrating with their property into any of them. I have advanced no argument which I do not believe to be true, nor pushed any one beyond what truth would strictly warrant. But, if mistaken; if my arguments, instead of being sound and true, as I hold them beyond controversy to be, should turn out to be a mere mass of sophisms, and if, in consequence, the barrier opposed by the want of power, should be surmounted, there is another still in the way, that cannot be. The mere possession of power is not of itself sufficient to justify its exercise. It must be in addition shown, that in the given case it can be rightfully and justly exercised. Under our system, the first inquiry is: Does the Constitution authorize the exercise of the power? If that be decided in the affirmative, the next is: Can it be rightfully and justly exercised under the circumstances? And it is not, until that, too, is decided in the affirmative, that the question of the expediency of exercising it is presented for consideration.

Now, I put the question solemnly to the Senators from the North: Can you rightly and justly exclude the South from territories of the United States, and monopolize them for yourselves, even if, in your opinion, you should have the power? It is this question I wish to press on your attention, with all due solemnity and decorum. The North and the South stand in the relation of partners in a common Union, with equal dignity and equal rights. We of the South have contributed our full share of funds, and shed our full share of blood for the acquisition of our territories. Can you, then, on any principle of equity and justice, deprive us of our full share in their benefit and advantages? Are you ready to affirm that a majority of the partners in a joint concern have the right to monopolize its benefits to the exclusion of the minority, even in cases where they have contributed their full share to the concern? But to present the case more strongly and vividly, I shall descend from generals to particulars, and shall begin with the Oregon Territory. Our title to it is founded, first, and in my opinion mainly, on our purchase of Louisiana; that was strengthened by the Florida treaty, which transferred to us the title also of Spain; and both by the discovery of the mouth of Columbia river by Captain Gray, and the exploration of the entire stream, from its source down to its mouth, by Lewis and Clark. The purchase of Louisiana cost fifteen millions of dollars; and we paid Spain five millions for the Florida treaty; making twenty in all. This large sum was advanced out of the common funds of the Union, the South, to say the least, contributing her full share. The discovery was made, it is true, by a citizen of Massachusetts; but he sailed under the flag and protection of the Union, and of course whatever title was derived from his discovery accrued to the benefit of the Union. The exploration of Lewis and Clark was at the expense of the Union. We are now about to form it into a Territory; the expense of governing which, while it remains so, must be met out of the common fund, and towards which the South must contribute her full share. The expense will not be small. Already there is an Indian war to be put down, and a regiment for that purpose and to protect the Territory has been ordered there. To what extent the expense may extend we know not, but will, not improbably, involve millions before the Territory becomes a State. I now ask, is it right, is it just, after having contributed our full share for the acquisition of the Territory, with the liability of contributing, in addition, our full share of the expense for its government, that we should be shut out of the Territory, and be excluded from participating in its benefits? What would be thought of such conduct in the case of individuals? And can that be right and just in Government which any right-minded man would cry out to be base and dishonest in private life? If it would be so pronounced in a partnership of thirty individuals, how can it be pronounced otherwise in one of thirty States?

The case of our recently acquired territory from Mexico, is, if possible, more marked. The events connected with the acquisition are too well known to require a long narrative. It was won by arms, and a great sacrifice of men and money. The South, in the contest, performed her full share of military duty, and earned a full share of military honor; has poured out her full share of blood freely, and has and will bear a full share of the expense; has evinced a full share of skill and bravery, and if I were to say even more than her full share of both, I would not go beyond the truth; to be attributed, however, to no superiority, in either respect, but to accidental circumstances, which gave both its officers and soldiers more favorable opportunities for their display. All have done their duty nobly, and high courage and gallantry are but common attributes of our people. Would it be right and just to close a territory thus won against the South, and leave it open exclusively to the North? Would it deserve the name of free soil, if one-half of the Union should be excluded, and the other half should monopolize it, when it was won by the joint expense and joint efforts of all? Is the great law to be reversed—that which is won by all should be equally enjoyed by all? These are questions which address themselves more to the heart than the head. Feeble must be the intellect which does not see what is right and just; and bad must be the heart, unless unconsciously under the control of deep and abiding prejudice, which hesitates in pronouncing on which side they are to be found. Now, I put the question to the Senators from the North, what are you prepared to do? Are you prepared to prostrate the barriers of the Constitution, and in open defiance of the dictates of equity and justice, to exclude the South from the territories, and monopolize them for the North? If so, vote against the amendment offered by the Senator from Mississippi, [Mr. DAVIS;] and if that should fail, vote against striking out the 12th section. We shall then know what to expect. If not, place us on some ground where we can stand as equals in rights and dignity, and where we shall not be excluded from what has been acquired at the common expense, and won by common skill and gallantry. All we demand is, to stand on the same level with yourselves, and to participate equally in what belongs to all. Less we cannot take.

I turn now to my friends of the South, and ask, what are you prepared to do? If neither the barriers of the Constitution nor the high sense of right and justice should prove sufficient to protect you, are you prepared to sink down into a state of acknowledged inferiority; to be stripped of your dignity of equals among equals, and be deprived of your equality of rights in this Federal partnership of States? If so, you are wofully degenerated from your sires, and will well deserve to change condition with your slaves; but if not, prepare to meet the issue. The time is at hand, if the question should not be speedily settled, when the South must rise up, and bravely defend herself, or sink down into base and acknowledged inferiority; and it is because I clearly perceive that this period is favorable for settling it, if it is ever to be settled, that I am in favor of pressing the question now to a decision—not because I have any desire whatever to embarrass either party in reference to the Presidential election. At no other period could the two great parties into which the country is divided be made to see and feel so clearly and intensely the embarrassment and danger caused by the question. Indeed, they must be blind not to perceive that there is a power in action that must burst asunder the ties that bind them together, strong as they are, unless it should be speedily settled. Now is the time, if ever. Cast your eyes to the North, and mark what is going on there: reflect on the tendency of events for the last three years in reference to this the most vital of all questions, and you must see that no time should be lost. I am thus brought to the question, How can the question be settled? It can, in my opinion, be finally and permanently adjusted but one way, and that is, on the high principles of justice and the Constitution. Fear not to leave it to them. The less you do the better. If the North and South cannot stand together on their broad and solid foundation, there is none other on which they can. If the obligations of the

Constitution and justice be too feeble to command the respect of the North, how can the South expect that she will regard the far more feeble obligations of an act of Congress? Nor should the North fear that by leaving it where justice and the Constitution leave it, she would be excluded from her full share of the territories. In my opinion, if it be left there, climate, soil, and other circumstances, would fix the line between the slaveholding and non-slaveholding States in about 36° 30′. It may zigzag a little, to accommodate itself to circumstances; sometimes passing to the north and at others passing to the south of it; but that would matter little, and would be more satisfactory to all, and tend less to alienation between the two great sections than a rigid, straight, artificial line, prescribed by an act of Congress.

And here let me say to Senators from the North, you make a great mistake in supposing that the portion which might fall to the South, of whatever line might be drawn, if left to soil, and climate, and circumstances to determine, would be closed to the white labor of the North, because it could not mingle with slave labor without degradation. The fact is not so. There is no part of the world where agricultural, mechanical, and other descriptions of labor are more respected than in the South, with the exception of two descriptions of employment, that of menial and body servants. No southern man—not the poorest or the lowest—will, under any circumstance, submit to perform either of them. He has too much pride for that, and I rejoice that he has. They are unsuited to the spirit of a freeman. But the man who would spurn them feels not the least degradation to work in the same field with his slave, or to be employed to work with them in the same field, or in any mechanical operation; and, when so employed, they claim the right, and are admitted, in the country portion of the South, of sitting at the table of their employers. Can as much, on the score of equality, be said for the North? With us, the two great divisions of society are not the rich and poor, but white and black; and all the former, the poor as well as the rich, belong to the upper class, and are respected and treated as equals, if honest and industrious, and hence have a position and pride of character of which neither poverty nor misfortune can deprive them.

But I go further, and hold that justice and the Constitution are the easiest and safest guard on which the question can be settled, regarded in reference to party. It may be settled on that ground simply by non-action—by leaving the Territories free and open to the emigration of all the world, so long as they continue so; and when they become States, to adopt whatever constitution they please, with the single restriction, to be republican, in order to their admission into the Union. If a party cannot safely take this broad and solid position, and successfully maintain it, what other can it take and maintain? If it cannot maintain itself by an appeal to the great principles of justice, the Constitution, and self-government, to what other, sufficiently strong to uphold them in public opinion, can they appeal? I greatly mistake the character of the people of this Union, if such an appeal would not prove successful, if either party should have the magnanimity to step forward and boldly make it. It would, in my opinion, be received with shouts of approbation by the patriotic and intelligent in every quarter. There is a deep feeling prevailing the country that the Union and our political institutions are in danger, which such a course would dispel.

Now is the time to take the step, and bring about a result so devoutly to be wished. I have believed from the beginning that this was the only question sufficiently potent to dissolve the Union and subvert our system of government, and that the sooner it was met and settled the safer and better for all. I have never doubted but that, if permitted to progress beyond a certain point, its settlement would become impossible, and am under deep conviction that it is now rapidly approaching it, and that if it is ever to be averted, it must be done speedily. In uttering these opinions, I look to the whole. If I speak earnestly, it is to save and protect all. As deep as is the stake of the South in the Union and our political institutions, it is not deeper than that of the North. We shall be as well prepared and as capable of meeting whatever may come as you.

Now, let me say, Senators, if our Union and system of government are doomed to perish, and we to share the fate of so many great people who have gone before us, the historian, who, in some future day, may record the events tending to so calamitous a result, will devote his first chapter to the ordinance of 1787, as lauded as it and its authors have been, as the first in that series which led to it. His next chapter will be devoted to the Missouri compromise, and the next to the present agitation. Whether there will be another beyond, I know not. It will depend on what we may do.

If he should possess a philosophical turn of mind, and be disposed to look to more remote and recondite causes, he will trace it to a proposition which originated in a hypothetical truism, but which, as now expressed and now understood, is the most false and dangerous of all political error. The proposition to which I allude has become an axiom in the minds of a vast majority on both sides of the Atlantic, and is repeated daily, from tongue to tongue, as an established and incontrovertible truth; it is, that "all men are born free and equal." I am not afraid to attack error, however deeply it may be intrenched, or however widely extended, whenever it becomes my duty to do so, as I believe it to be on this subject and occasion.

Taking the proposition literally, (it is in that sense it is understood,) there is not a word of truth in it. It begins with "all men are born," which is utterly untrue. Men are not born. Infants are born. They grow to be men. And concludes with asserting that they are born "free and equal," which is not less false. They are not born free. While infants they are incapable of freedom, being destitute alike of the capacity of thinking and acting, without which there can be no freedom. Besides, they are necessarily born subject to their parents, and remain so among all people, savage and civilized, until the development of their intellect and physical capacity enables them to take care of themselves. They grow to all the freedom, of which the condition in which they were born permits, by growing to be men. Nor is it less false that they are born "equal." They are not so in any sense in which it can be regarded; and thus, as I have asserted, there is not a word of truth in the whole proposition, as expressed and generally understood.

If we trace it back, we shall find the proposition differently expressed in the Declaration of Independence. That asserts that "all men are created equal." The form of expression, though less dangerous, is not less erroneous. All men are not created. According to the Bible, only two, a man and a woman, ever were, and of these one was pronounced subordinate to the other.

All others have come into the world by being born, and in no sense, as I have shown, either free or equal. But this form of expression being less striking and popular, has given way to the present, and under the authority of a document put forth on so great an occasion, and leading to such important consequences, has spread far and wide, and fixed itself deeply in the public mind. It was inserted in our Declaration of Independence without any necessity. It made no necessary part of our justification in separating from the parent country, and declaring ourselves independent. Breach of our chartered privileges, and lawless encroachment on our acknowledged and well-established rights by the parent country, were the real causes, and of themselves sufficient, without resorting to any other, to justify the step. Nor had it any weight in constructing the governments which were substituted in the place of the colonial. They were formed of the old materials and on practical and well-established principles, borrowed for the most part from our own experience and that of the country from which we sprang.

If the proposition be traced still further back, it will be found to have been adopted from certain writers on government who had attained much celebrity in the early settlement of these States, and with whose writings all the prominent actors in our Revolution were familiar. Among these, Locke and Sidney were prominent. But they expressed it very differently. According to their expression, "all men in the state of nature were free and equal." From this the others were derived; and it was this to which I referred when I called it a hypothetical truism. To understand why, will require some explanation.

Man, for the purpose of reasoning, may be regarded in three different states: in a state of individuality; that is, living by himself apart from the rest of his species. In the social; that is, living in society, associated with others of his species. And in the political; that is, being under government. We may reason as to what would be his rights and duties in either, without taking into consideration whether he could exist in it or not. It is certain, that in the first, the very supposition that he lived apart and separated from all others, would make him free and equal. No one in such a state could have the right to command or control another. Every man would be his own master, and might do just as he pleased. But it is equally clear, that man cannot exist in such a state; that he is by nature social, and that society is necessary, not only to the proper development of all his faculties, moral and intellectual, but to the very existence of his race. Such being the case, the state is a purely hypothetical one; and when we say all men are free and equal in it, we announce a mere hypothetical truism; that is, a truism resting on a mere supposition that cannot exist, and of course one of little or no practical value.

But to call it a state of nature was a great misnomer, and has led to dangerous errors; for that cannot justly be called a state of nature which is so opposed to the constitution of man as to be inconsistent with the existence of his race and the development of the high faculties, mental and moral, with which he is endowed by his Creator.

Nor is the social state of itself his natural state; for society can no more exist without government, in one form or another, than man without society. It is the political, then, which includes the social, that is his natural state. It is the one for which his Creator formed him, into which he is impelled irresistibly, and in which only his race can exist and all his faculties be fully developed.

Such being the case, it follows that any, the worst form of government, is better than anarchy; and that individual liberty, or freedom, must be subordinate to whatever power may be necessary to protect society against anarchy within or destruction from without; for the safety and well-being of society are as paramount to individual liberty as the safety and well-being of the race is to that of individuals; and in the same proportion, the power necessary for the safety of society is paramount to individual liberty. On the contrary, government has no right to control individual liberty beyond what is necessary to the safety and well-being of society. Such is the boundary which separates the power of government and the liberty of the citizen or subject in the political state, which, as I have shown, is the natural state of man—the only one in which his race can exist, and the one in which he is born, lives, and dies.

It follows from all this, that the quantum of power on the part of the government, and of liberty on that of individuals, instead of being equal in all cases, must necessarily be very unequal among different people, according to their different conditions. For just in proportion as a people are ignorant, stupid, debased, corrupt, exposed to violence within and danger from without, the power necessary for government to possess in order to preserve society against anarchy and destruction, becomes greater and greater, and individual liberty less and less, until the lowest condition is reached, when absolute and despotic power becomes necessary on the part of the government, and individual liberty extinct. So, on the contrary, just as a people rise in the scale of intelligence, virtue, and patriotism, and the more perfectly they become acquainted with the nature of government, the ends for which it was ordered, and how it ought to be administered, and the less the tendency to violence and disorder within, and danger from abroad, the power necessary for government becomes less and less, and individual liberty greater and greater. Instead, then, of all men having the same right to liberty and equality, as is claimed by those who hold that they are all born free and equal, liberty is the noble and highest reward bestowed on mental and moral development, combined with favorable circumstances. Instead, then, of liberty and equality being born with man; instead of all men and all classes and descriptions being equally entitled to them, they are high prizes to be won, and are in their most perfect state, not only the highest reward that can be bestowed on our race, but the most difficult to be won, and when won, the most difficult to be preserved.

They have been made vastly more so, by the dangerous error I have attempted to expose, that all men are born free and equal, as if those high qualities belonged to man without effort to acquire them, and to all equally alike, regardless of their intellectual and moral condition. The attempt to carry into practice this the most dangerous of all political error, and to bestow on all, without regard to their fitness either to acquire or maintain liberty, that unbounded and individual liberty supposed to belong to man in the hypothetical and misnamed state of nature, has done more to retard the cause of liberty and civilization, and is doing more at present, than all other causes combined. While it is powerful to pull down governments, it is still more powerful to prevent their construction on proper principles. It is the leading cause among those which have placed Europe in its present anarchical condition, and which mainly stands in the way of reconstructing good governments in the place of those which have been overthrown, threatening thereby the quarter of the globe most advanced in progress and civilization with hopeless anarchy, to be followed by military despotism. Nor are we exempt from its disorganizing effects. We now begin to experience the danger of admitting so great an error to have a place in the Declaration of our Independence. For a long time it lay dormant; but in the process of time it began to germinate, and produce its poisonous fruits. It had strong hold on the mind of Mr. Jefferson, the author of that document, which caused him to take an utterly false view of the subordinate relation of the black to the white race in the South, and to hold, in consequence, that the latter, though utterly unqualified to possess liberty, were as fully entitled to both liberty and equality as the former, and that to deprive them of it was unjust and immoral. To this error his proposition to exclude slavery from the territory northwest of the Ohio may be traced, and to that the ordinance of '87, and through it the deep and dangerous agitation which now threatens to ingulf, and will certainly ingulf, if not speedily settled, our political institutions, and involve the country in countless woes.

11 ON HENRY CLAY'S COMPROMISE RESOLUTIONS ON THE BILL TO ADMIT CALIFORNIA, MARCH 4, 1850

The admission of California would definitely place the South in the position of an impotent minority. On January 29, 1850 Henry Clay introduced a series of conciliatory resolutions proposing, among other points, that California should be admitted as a free state, but Congress should enact a fugitive slave law and that Congress should not decide concerning slavery in the rest of the Mexican cession. The debate which followed included both Webster and Calhoun once again, and extended in fact beyond the halls of Congress throughout the country. Calhoun, only partially recovered from pneumonia followed by a cold, unable to speak himself, had his last major speech read to the Senate. He was to live only a few weeks more. He asked that the North through the generous use of the power it possessed help avert disunion. He asked that the weakness of the South be recognized and that the foundations of an enduring political union be laid by restoring to the South on principle the power of self-protection which it had lost.

As much indisposed as I have been, Mr. President and Senators, I have felt it to be my duty to express to you my sentiments upon the great question which has agitated the country and occupied your attention. And I am under peculiar obligations to the Senate for the very courteous manner in which they have afforded me an opportunity of being heard to-day.

I had hoped that it would have been in my power during the last week to have delivered my views in relation to this all-engrossing subject, but I was prevented from doing so by being attacked by a cold which is at this time so prevalent, and which has retarded the recovery of my strength.

Acting under the advice of my friends, and apprehending that it might not be in my power to deliver my sentiments before the termination of the debate, I have reduced to writing what I intended to say. And, without further remark, I will ask the favor of my friend, the Senator behind me to read it.

Mr. MASON. It affords me great pleasure to comply with the request of the honorable Senator, and to read his remarks.

The honorable gentleman then read Mr. CALHOUN'S remarks as follows:

Mr. CALHOUN. I have, Senators, believed from the first that the agitation of the subject of slavery would, if not prevented by some timely and effective measure, end in disunion. Entertaining this opinion, I have, on all proper occasions, endeavored to call the attention of each of the two great parties which divide the country to adopt some measure to prevent so great a disaster, but without success. The agitation has been permitted to proceed, with almost no attempt to resist it, until it has reached a period when it can no longer be disguised or denied that the Union is in danger. You have thus had forced upon you the greatest and the gravest question that can ever come under your consideration: How can the Union be preserved?

To give a satisfactory answer to this mighty question, it is indispensable to have an accurate and thorough knowledge of the nature and the character of the cause by which the Union is endangered. Without such knowledge it is impossible to pronounce, with any certainty, by what measure it can be saved; just as it would be impossible for a physican to pronounce, in the case of some dangerous disease, with any certainty, by what remedy the patient could be saved, without familiar knowledge of the nature and character of the cause of the disease. The first question, then, presented for consideration, in the investigation I propose to make, in order to obtain such knowledge, is: What is it that has endangered the Union?

To this question there can be but one answer: that the immediate cause is the almost universal discontent which pervades all the States composing the southern section of the Union. This widely-extended discontent is not of recent origin. It commenced with the agitation of the slavery question, and has been increasing ever since. The next question, going one step further back, is: What has caused this widely-diffused and almost universal discontent?

It is a great mistake to suppose, as is by some, that it originated with demagogues, who excited the discontent with the intention of aiding their personal advancement, or with the disappointed ambition of certain politicians, who resorted to it as the means of retrieving their fortunes. On the contrary, all the great political influences of the section were arrayed against excitement, and exerted to the utmost to keep the people quiet. The great mass of the people of the South were divided, as in the other section, into Whigs and Democrats. The leaders and the presses of both parties in the South were very solicitous to prevent excitement and to preserve quiet; because it was seen that the effects of the former would necessarily tend to weaken, if not destroy, the political ties which united them with their respective parties in the other section. Those who know the strength of party ties will readily appreciate the immense force which this cause exerted against agitation and in favor of preserving quiet. But, as great as it was, it was not sufficiently so to prevent the wide-spread discontent which now pervades the section. No; some cause, far deeper and more powerful than the one supposed, must exist, to account for discontent so wide and deep. The question, then, recurs: What is the cause of this discontent? It will be found in the belief of the people of the southern States, as prevalent as the discontent itself, that they cannot remain, as things now are, consistently with honor and safety, in the Union. The next question to be considered is: What has caused this belief?

One of the causes is, undoubtedly, to be traced to the long-continued agitation of the slave question on the part of the North, and the many aggressions which they have made on the rights of the South during the time. I will not enumerate them at present, as it will be done hereafter, in its proper place.

There is another, lying back of it, with which this is intimately connected, that may be regarded as the great and primary cause. That is to be found in the fact that the equilibrium between the two sections in the Government, as it stood when the constitution was ratified and the Government put in action, has been destroyed. At that time there was nearly a perfect equilibrium between the two, which afforded ample means to each to protect itself against the aggression of the other; but, as it now stands, one section has the exclusive power of controlling the Government, which leaves the other without any adequate means of protecting itself against its encroachment and oppression. To place this subject distinctly before you, I have, Senators, prepared a brief statistical statement, showing the relative weight of the two sections in the Government under the first census of 1790 and the last census of 1840.

According to the former, the population of the United States, including Vermont, Kentucky, and Tennessee, which then were in their incipient condition of becoming States, but were not actually admitted, amounted to 3,929,827. Of this number the northern States had 1,977,899, and the southern 1,952,072, making a difference of only 25,827 in favor of the former States. The number of States, including Vermont, Kentucky, and Tennessee, was sixteen; of which eight, including Vermont, belonged to the northern section, and eight, including Kentucky and Tennessee, to the southern; making an equal division of the States between the two sections under the first census. There was a small preponderance in the House of Representatives, and in the electoral college, in favor of the northern, owing to the fact, that, according to the provisions of the Constitution, in estimating Federal numbers, five slaves count but three; but it was too small to affect sensibly the perfect equilibrium which, with that exception, existed at the time. Such was the equality of the two sections when the States composing them agreed to enter into a Federal Union. Since then the equilibrium between them has been greatly disturbed.

According to the last census the aggregate population of the

United States amounted to 17,063,357, of which the northern section contained 9,728,920 and the southern 7,334,437, making a difference in round numbers, of 2,400,000. The number of States had increased from sixteen to twenty-six, making an addition of ten States. In the meantime the position of Delaware had become doubtful as to which section she properly belongs. Considering her as neutral, the northern States will have thirteen and the southern States twelve; making a difference in the Senate of two Senators in favor of the former. According to the apportionment under the census of 1840, there were 223 members of the House of Representatives, of which the northern States had 135 and the southern States (considering Delaware as neutral) 87; making a difference in favor of the former in the House of Representatives of 48. The difference in the Senate of two members, added to this, gives to the North in the electoral college a majority of 50. Since the census of 1840 four States have been added to the Union; Iowa, Wisconsin, Florida, and Texas. They leave the difference in the Senate as it stood when the census was taken; but add two to the side of the North in the House, making the present majority in the House in its favor 50, and in the electoral college 52.

The result of the whole is to give the northern section a predominance in every part of the Government, and thereby concentrate in it the two elements which constitute the Federal Government—a majority of States and a majority of their population, estimated in federal numbers. Whatever section concentrates the two in itself possesses the control of the entire Government.

But we are just at the close of the sixth decade, and the commencement of the seventh. The census is to be taken this year, which must add greatly to the decided preponderance of the North in the House of Representatives and in the electoral college. The prospect is, also, that a great increase will be added to its present preponderance in the Senate during the period of the decade, by the addition of new States. Two Territories, Oregon and Minnesota, are already in progress, and strenuous efforts are making to bring in three additional States from the territory recently conquered from Mexico; which, if successful, will add three other States in a short time to the northern section, making five States; and increasing the present number of its States from fifteen to twenty, and of its Senators from thirty to forty. On the contrary, there is not a single territory in progress in the southern section, and no certainty that any additional State will be added to it during the decade. The prospect then, is, that the two sections in the Senate, should the efforts now made to exclude the South from the newly-acquired territories succeed, will stand, before the end of the decade, twenty northern States to twelve southern, (considering Delaware as neutral,) and forty northern Senators to twenty-four southern. This great increase of Senators, added to the great increase of members of the House of Representatives and the electoral college on the part of the North, which must take place under the next decade, will effectually and irretrievably destroy the equilibrium which existed when the Government commenced.

Had this destruction been the operation of time, without the interference of Government, the South would have had no reason to complain; but such was not the fact. It was caused by the legislation of this Government, which was appointed as the common agent of all, and charged with the protection of the interests and security of all. The legislation by which it has been effected may be classed under three heads. The first is, that series of acts by which the South has been excluded from the common territory belonging to all of the States, as the members of the Federal Union, and which have had the effect of extending vastly the portion allotted to the Northern section, and restricting within narrow limits the portion left the South; the next consists in adopting a system of revenue and disbursements, by which an undue proportion of the burden of taxation has been imposed upon the South, and an undue proportion of its proceeds appropriated to the North; and the last is a system of political measures by which the original character of the Government has been radically changed. I propose to bestow upon each of these, in the order they stand, a few remarks, with the view of showing that it is owing to the action of this Government that the equilibrium between the two sections has been destroyed, and the whole powers of the system centered in a sectional majority.

The first of the series of acts by which the South was deprived of its due share of the territories, originated with the Confederacy, which preceded the existence of this Government. It is to be found in the provision of the ordinance of 1787. Its effect was to exclude the South entirely from that vast and fertile region which lies between the Ohio and the Mississippi rivers, now embracing five States and one Territory. The next of the series is the Missouri compromise, which excluded the South from that large portion of Louisiana which lies north of 36° 30′, excepting what is included in the State of Missouri. The last of the series excluded the South from the whole of the Oregon Territory. All these, in the slang of the day, were what are called slave territories, and not free soil; that is, territories belonging to slaveholding powers, and open to the emigration of masters with their slaves. By these several acts, the South was excluded from 1,238,025 square miles, an extent of country considerably exceeding the entire valley of the Mississippi. To the South was left the portion of the Territory of Louisiana lying south of 36° 30′, and the portion north of it included in the State of Missouri; the portion lying south of 36° 30′, including the States of Louisiana and Arkansas; and the territory lying west of the latter and south of 36° 30′, called the Indian country. These, with the Territory of Florida, now the State, makes in the whole 283,503 square miles. To this must be added the territory acquired with Texas. If the whole should be added to the southern section, it would make an increase of 325,520, which would make the whole left to the South 609,-023. But a large part of Texas is still in contest between the two sections, which leaves it uncertain what will be the real extent of the portion of territory that may be left to the South.

I have not included the territory recently acquired by the treaty with Mexico. The North is making the most strenuous efforts to appropriate the whole to herself, by excluding the South from every foot of it. If she should succeed, it will add to that from which the South has already been excluded 526,078 square miles, and would increase the whole which the North has appropriated to herself to 1,764,023, not including the portion that she may succeed in excluding us from in Texas. To sum up the whole, the United States, since they declared their independence, have acquired 2,373,046 square miles of territory, from which the North will have excluded the South, if she should succeed in monopolizing the newly acquired territories, from about three-fourths of the whole, leaving to the South but about one-fourth.

Such is the first and great cause that has destroyed the equilibrium between the two sections in the Government.

The next is the system of revenue and disbursements which has been adopted by the Government. It is well known that the Government has derived its revenue mainly from duties on imports. I shall not undertake to show that such duties must necessarily fall mainly on the exporting States, and that the South, as the great exporting portion of the Union, has in reality paid vastly more than her due proportion of the revenue; because I deem it unnecessary, as the subject has on so many occasions been fully discussed. Nor shall I, for the same reason, undertake to show that a far greater portion of the revenue has been disbursed at the North than its due share, and that the joint effect of these causes has been to transfer a vast amount from South to North, which, under an equal system of revenue and disbursements, would not have been lost to her. If to this be added, that many of the duties were imposed, not for revenue, but for protection; that is, intended to put money, not in the treasury but directly into the pockets of the manufacturers, some conception may be formed of the immense amount which, in the long course of sixty years, has been transferred from South to North. There are no data by which it can be estimated with any certainty; but it is safe to say that it amounts to hundreds of millions of dollars. Under the most moderate estimate, it would be sufficient to add greatly to the wealth of the North, and thus greatly increase her population by attracting emigration from all quarters to that section.

This, combined with the great primary cause, amply explains why the North has acquired a preponderance over every department of the Government by its disproportionate increase of population and States. The former, as has been shown, has increased in fifty years 2,400,000 over that of the South. This increase of population during so long a period, is satisfactorily accounted for by the number of emigrants, and the increase of their descendants, which have been attracted to the northern section from Europe and the South, in consequence of the advantages derived from the causes assigned. If they had not existed; if the South had retained all the capital which has been extracted from her by the fiscal action of the Government; and, if it had not been excluded by the ordinance of '87 and the Missouri compromise from the region lying between the Ohio and the Mississippi rivers, and between the Mississippi and the Rocky Mountains north of 36° 30′, it scarcely admits of a doubt that it would have divided the emigration with the North, and by retaining her own people, would have at least equalled the North in population under the census of 1840, and probably under that about to be taken. She would also, if she had retained her equal rights in those territories, have maintained an equality in the number of States with the North, and have preserved the equilibrium between the two sections that existed at the commencement of the Government. The loss then of the equilibrium is to be attributed to the action of this Government.

But while these measures were destroying the equilibrium between the two sections, the action of the Government was leading to a radical change in its character, by concentrating all the power of the system in itself. The occasion will not permit me to trace the measures by which this great change has been consummated. If it did, it would not be difficult to show that the process commenced at an early period of the Government; that it proceeded, almost without interruption, step by step, until it absorbed virtually its entire powers. But, without going through the whole process to establish the fact, it may be done satisfactorily by a very short statement.

That the Government claims, and practically maintains, the right to decide in the last resort as to the extent of its powers, will scarcely be denied by any one conversant with the political history of the country. That it also claims the right to resort to force to maintain whatever power she claims, against all opposition, is equally certain. Indeed it is apparent, from what we daily hear, that this has become the prevailing and fixed opinion of a great majority of the community. Now, I ask, what limitation can possibly be placed upon the powers of a Government claiming and exercising such rights? And, if none can be, how can the separate governments of the States maintain and protect the powers reserved to them by the Constitution, or the people of the several States maintain those which are reserved to them, and among others, the sovereign powers by which they ordained and established, not only their separate State constitutions and governments, but also the Constitution and Government of the United States? But, if they have no constitutional means of maintaining them against the right claimed by this Government, it necessarily follows that they hold them at its pleasure and discretion, and that all the powers of the system are in reality concentrated in it. It also follows that the character of the Government has been changed, in consequence, from a Federal Republic, as it originally came from the hands of its framers, and that it has been changed into a great national consolidated Democracy. It has indeed, at present, all the characteristics of the latter, and not one of the former, although it still retains its outward form.

The result of the whole of these causes combined is, that the North has acquired a decided ascendency over every department of this Government, and through it a control over all the powers of the system. A single section, governed by the will of the numerical majority, has now, in fact, the control of the Government and the entire powers of the system. What was once a constitutional Federal Republic is now converted, in reality, into one as absolute as that of the Autocrat of Russia, and as despotic in its tendency as any absolute Government that ever existed.

As, then, the North has the absolute control over the Government, it is manifest that on all questions between it and the South, where there is a diversity of interests, the interest of the latter will be sacrificed to the former, however oppressive the effects may be, as the South possesses no means by which it can resist through the action of the Government. But if there was no question of vital importance to the South, in reference to which there was a diversity of views between the two sections, this state of things might be endured without the hazard of destruction to the South. But such is not the fact. There is a question of vital importance to the southern section, in reference to which the views and feelings of the two sections are as opposite and hostile as they can possibly be.

I refer to the relation between the two races in the southern section, which constitutes a vital portion of her social organization. Every portion of the North entertains views and feelings more or less hostile to it. Those most opposed and hostile regard it as a sin, and consider themselves under the most sacred obligation to use every effort to destroy it. Indeed to the extent that they conceive they have power, they regard themselves as implicated in the sin, and responsible for suppressing it by the use of all and every means. Those less opposed and hostile, regard it as a crime—an offence against humanity, as they call it; and although not so fanatical, feel themselves bound to use all efforts to effect the same objects; while those who are least opposed and hostile, regard it as a blot and a stain on the character of what they call the nation, and feel themselves accordingly bound to give it no countenance or support. On the contrary, the southern section regards the relation as one which cannot be destroyed without subjecting the two races to the greatest calamity, and the section to poverty, desolation, and wretchedness; and accordingly they feel bound by every consideration of interest and safety, to defend it.

This hostile feeling on the part of the North towards the social organization of the South long lay dormant, but it only required some cause to act on those who felt most intensely that they were responsible for its continuance, to call it into action. The increasing power of this Government, and of the control of the northern section over all its departments, furnished the cause. It was this which made an impression on the minds of many that there was little or no restraint to prevent the Government from doing whatever it might choose to do. This was sufficient of itself to put the most fanatical portion of the North in action for the purpose of destroying the existing relation between the two races in the South.

The first organized movement towards it commenced in 1835. Then, for the first time, societies were organized, presses established, lecturers sent forth to excite the people of the North, and incendiary publications scattered over the whole South, through the mail. The South was thoroughly aroused. Meetings were held everywhere, and resolutions adopted, calling upon the North to apply a remedy to arrest the threatened evil, and pledging themselves to adopt measures for their own protection if it was not arrested. At the meeting of Congress, petitions poured in from the North, calling upon Congress to abolish slavery in the District of Columbia, and to prohibit what they called the internal slave trade between the States, announcing at the same time that their ultimate object was to abolish slavery, not only in the District, but in the States and throughout the Union. At this period the number engaged in the agitation was small, and possessed little or no personal influence.

Neither party in Congress had, at that time, any sympathy with them or their cause. The members of each party presented their petitions with great reluctance. Nevertheless, as small and contemptible as the party then was, both of the great parties at the North dreaded them. They felt that, though small, they were organized in reference to a subject which had a great and commanding influence over the northern mind. Each party, on that account, feared to oppose their petitions, lest the opposite party should take advantage of the one who might do so, by favoring their petitions. The effect was, that both united in insisting that the petitions should be received, and that Congress should take jurisdiction of the subject for which they prayed. To justify their course, they took the extraordinary ground that Congress was bound to receive petitions on every subject, however objectionable it might be, and whether they had or had not jurisdiction over the subject. These views prevailed in the House of Representatives, and partially in the Senate, and thus the party succeeded in their first movements in gaining what they proposed—a position in Congress from which agitation could be extended over the whole Union. This was the commencement of the agitation, which has ever since continued, and which, as is now acknowledged, has endangered the Union itself.

As for myself, I believed, at that early period, if the party who got up the petitions should succeed in getting Congress to take jurisdiction, that agitation would follow, and that it would, in the end, if not arrested, destroy the Union. I then so expressed myself in debate, and called upon both parties to take grounds against assuming jurisdiction, but in vain. Had my voice been heeded, and had Congress refused to take jurisdiction, by the united votes of all parties, the agitation which followed would have been prevented, and the fanatical zeal that gives impulse to the agitation, and which has brought us to our present perilous condition, would have become extinguished from the want of something to feed the flame. *That* was the time for the North to show her devotion to the Union; but unfortunately both of the great parties of that section were so intent on obtaining or retaining party ascendency, that all other considerations were overlooked or forgotten.

What has since followed are but the natural consequences. With the success of their first movement, this small fanatical party began to acquire strength; and with that to become an object of courtship to both the great parties. The necessary consequence was a further increase of power, and a gradual tainting of the opinions of both of the other parties with their doctrines until the infection has extended over both; and the great mass of the population of the North who, whatever may be their opinion of the original abolition party, which still preserves its distinct organization, hardly ever fail, when it comes to acting, to cooperate in carrying out their measures. With the increase of their influence, they extended the sphere of their action. In a short time after the commencement of their first movement, they had acquired sufficient influence to induce the Legislatures of most of the northern States to pass acts which in effect abrogated the provision of the Constitution that provides for the delivery up of fugitive slaves. Not long after, petitions followed to abolish slavery in forts, magazines, and dock-yards, and all other places where Congress had exclusive power of legislation. This was followed by petitions and resolutions of Legislatures of the northern States and popular meetings, to exclude the southern States from all territories acquired or to be acquired, and to prevent the admission of any State hereafter into the Union which, by its constitution, does not prohibit slavery. And Congress is invoked to do all this expressly with the view to the final abolition of slavery in the States. That has been avowed to be the ultimate object from the beginning of the agitation until the present time; and yet the great body of both parties of the North, with the full knowledge of the fact, although disavowing the abolitionists, have cooperated with them in almost all their measures.

Such is a brief history of the agitation, as far as it has yet advanced. Now, I ask Senators, what is there to prevent its further progress, until it fulfills the ultimate end proposed, unless some decisive measure should be adopted to prevent it? Has any one of the causes, which has added to its increase from its original small and contemptible beginning until it has attained its present magnitude, diminished in force? Is the original cause of the movement, that slavery is a sin, and ought to be suppressed, weaker now than at the commencement? Or is the Abolition party less numerous or influential, or have they less influence over, or control over the two great parties of the North in elections? Or has the South greater means of influencing or controlling the movements of this Government now than it had when the agitation commenced? To all these questions but one answer can be given: no, no, no! The very reverse is true. Instead of being weaker, all the elements in favor of agitation are stronger now than they were in 1835, when it first commenced, while all the elements of influence on the part of the South are weaker. Unless something decisive is done, I again ask what is to stop this agitation, before the great and final object at which it aims—the abolition of slavery in the States—is consummated? Is it, then, not certain that if something decisive is not now done to arrest it, the South will be forced to choose between abolition and secession? Indeed, as events are now moving, it will not require the South to secede to dissolve the Union. Agitation will of itself effect it, of which its past history furnishes abundant proof, as I shall next proceed to show.

It is a great mistake to suppose that disunion can be effected by a single blow. The cords which bind these States together in one common Union are far too numerous and powerful for that. Disunion must be the work of time. It is only through a long process, and successively, that the cords can be snapped, until the whole fabric falls asunder. Already the agitation of the slavery question has snapped some of the most important, and has greatly weakened all the others, as I shall proceed to show.

The cords that bind the States together are not only many, but various in character. Some are spiritual or ecclesiastical; some political; others social. Some appertain to the benefit conferred by the Union, and others to the feeling of duty and obligation.

The strongest of those of a spiritual and ecclesiastical nature consisted in the unity of the great religious denominations, all of which originally embraced the whole Union. All these denominations, with the exception, perhaps, of the Catholics, were organized very much upon the principle of our political institutions; beginning with smaller meetings corresponding with the political divisions of the country, their organization terminated in one great central assemblage, corresponding very much with the character of Congress. At these meetings the principle clergymen and lay members of the respective denominations from all parts of the Union met to transact business relating to their common concerns. It was not confined to what appertained to the doctrines and discipline of the respective denominations, but extended to plans for disseminating the Bible, establishing missionaries, distributing tracts, and of establishing presses for the publication of tracts, newspapers, and periodicals, with a view of diffusing religious information, and for the support of the doctrines and creeds of the denomination. All this combined, contributed greatly to strengthen the bonds of the Union. The strong ties which held each denomination together formed a strong cord to hold the whole Union together; but, as powerful as they were, they have not been able to resist the explosive effect of slavery agitation.

The first of these cords which snapped, under its explosive force, was that of the powerful Methodist Episcopal Church. The numerous and strong ties which held it together are all broke, and its unity gone. They now form separate churches, and, instead of that feeling of attachment and devotion to the interests of the whole church which was formerly felt, they are now arrayed into two hostile bodies, engaged in litigation about what was formerly their common property.

The next cord that snapped was that of the Baptists, one of the largest and most respectable of the denominations. That of the Presbyterian is not entirely snapped, but some of its strands have given away. That of the Episcopal Church is the only one of the four great Protestant denominations which remains unbroken and entire.

The strongest cord of a political character consists of the many and strong ties that have held together the two great parties, which have, with some modifications, existed from the beginning of the Government. They both extended to every portion of the Union, and strongly contributed to hold all its parts together. But this powerful cord has fared no better than the spiritual. It resisted for a long time the explosive tendency of the agitation, but has finally snapped under its force—

if not entirely, in a great measure. Nor is there one of the remaining cords which have not been greatly weakened. To this extent the Union has already been destroyed by agitation, in the only way it can be, by snapping asunder and weakening the cords which bind it together.

If the agitation goes on, the same force, acting with increased intensity, as has been shown, will finally snap every cord, when nothing will be left to hold the States together except force. But surely that can, with no propriety of language, be called a union, when the only means by which the weaker is held connected with the stronger portion is *force*. It may, indeed, keep them connected; but the connection will partake much more of the character of subjugation, on the part of the weaker to the stronger, than the union of free, independent, and sovereign States, in one confederation, as they stood in the early stages of the Government, and which only is worthy of the sacred name of union.

Having now, Senators, explained what it is that endangers the Union, and traced it to its cause, and explained its nature and character, the question again recurs, How can the Union be saved? To this I answer, there is but one way by which it can be, and that is, by adopting such measures as will satisfy the States belonging to the southern section that they can remain in the Union consistently with their honor and their safety. There is, again, only one way by which that can be effected, and that is, by removing the causes by which this belief has been produced. Do *that*, and discontent will cease, harmony and kind feelings between the sections be restored, and every apprehension of danger to the Union removed. The question then is, By what can this be done? But, before I undertake to answer this question, I propose to show by what the Union cannot be saved.

It cannot, then, be saved by eulogies on the Union, however splendid or numerous. The cry of "Union, Union, the glorious Union!" can no more prevent disunion than the cry of "Health, health, glorious health!" on the part of the physician can save a patient lying dangerously ill. So long as the Union, instead of being regarded as a protector, is regarded in the opposite character, by not much less than a majority of the States, it will be in vain to attempt to conciliate them by pronouncing eulogies on it.

Besides, this cry of Union comes commonly from those whom we cannot believe to be sincere. It usually comes from our assailants. But we cannot believe them to be sincere; for, if they loved the Union, they would necessarily be devoted to the Constitution. It made the Union, and to destroy the Constitution would be to destroy the Union. But the only reliable and certain evidence of devotion to the Constitution is to abstain, on the one hand, from violating it, and to repel, on the other, all attempts to violate it. It is only by faithfully performing these high duties that the Constitution can be preserved, and with it the Union.

But how stands the profession of devotion to the Union by our assailants, when brought to this test? Have they abstained from violating the Constitution? Let the many acts passed by the northern States to set aside and annul the clause of the Constitution providing for the delivery up of fugitive slaves answer. I cite this, not that it is the only instance, (for there are many others,) but because the violation in this particular is too notorious and palpable to be denied. Again, have they stood forth faithfully to repel violations of the Constitution? Let their course in reference to the agitation of the slavery question, which was commenced and has been carried on for fifteen years, avowedly for the purpose of abolishing slavery in the States—an object all acknowledged to be unconstitutional—answer. Let them show a single instance, during this long period, in which they have denounced the agitators or their attempts to effect what is admitted to be unconstitutional, or a single measure which they have brought forward for that purpose. How can we, with all these facts before us, believe that they are sincere in their profession of devotion to the Union, or avoid believing their profession is but intended to increase the vigor of their assault and to weaken the force of our resistance?

Nor can we regard the profession of devotion to the Union, on the part of those who are not our assailants, as sincere, when they pronounce eulogies upon the Union, evidently with the intent of charging us with disunion, without uttering one word of denunciation against our assailants. If friends of the Union, their course should be to unite with us in repelling these assaults, and denouncing the authors as enemies of the Union. Why they avoid this, and pursue the course they do, it is for them to explain.

Nor can the Union be saved by invoking the name of the illustrious Southerner whose mortal remains repose on the western bank of the Potomac. He was one of us—a slaveholder and a planter. We have studied his history, and find nothing in it to justify submission to wrong. On the contrary, his great fame rests on the solid foundation that, while he was careful to avoid doing wrong to others, he was prompt and decided in repelling wrong. I trust that, in this respect, we profited by his example.

Nor can we find anything in his history to deter us from seceding from the Union, should it fail to fulfill the objects for which it was instituted, by being permanently and hopelessly converted into the means of oppressing instead of protecting us. On the contrary, we find much in his example to encourage us, should we be forced to the extremity of deciding between submission and disunion.

There existed then, as well as now, a Union—that between parent country and her then colonies. It was a union that had much to endear it to the people of the colonies. Under its protecting and superintending care, the colonies were planted and grew up and prospered, through a long course of years, until they became populous and wealthy. Its benefits were not limited to them. Their extensive agricultural and other productions gave birth to a flourishing commerce, which richly rewarded the parent country for the trouble and expense of establishing and protecting them. Washington was born and grew up to manhood under that Union. He acquired his early distinction in its service, and there is every reason to believe that he was devotedly attached to it. But his devotion was a rational one. He was attached to it, not as an end, but as a means to an end. When it failed to fulfill its end, and, instead of affording protection, was converted into the means of oppressing the colonies, he did not hesitate to draw his sword, and head the great movement by which that union was forever severed, and the independence of these States established. This was the great and crowning glory of his life, which has spread his fame over the whole globe, and will transmit it to the latest posterity.

Nor can the plan proposed by the distinguished Senator from Kentucky, nor that of the Administration, save the Union. I shall pass by, without remark, the plan proposed by the Senator, and proceed directly to the consideration of that of the Administration. I, however, assure the distinguished and able Senator, that in taking this course, no disrespect whatever is intended to him or his plan. I have adopted it, because so many Senators of distinguished abilities, who were present when he delivered his speech, and explained his plan, and who were fully capable to do justice to the side they support, have replied to him.

The plan of the Administration cannot save the Union, because it can have no effect whatever towards satisfying the States composing the southern section of the Union that they can, consistently with safety and honor, remain in the Union. It is, in fact, but a modification of the Wilmot proviso. It proposes to effect the same object, to exclude the South from all territory acquired by the Mexican treaty. It is well known that the South is united against the Wilmot proviso, and has committed itself, by solemn resolutions, to resist, should it be adopted. Its opposition *is not to the name*, but that which it *proposes to effect.* That the southern States hold to be unconstitutional, unjust, inconsistent with their equality as members of the common Union, and calculated to destroy irretrievably the equilibrium between the two sections. These objections equally apply to what, for brevity, I will call the Executive proviso. There is no difference between it and the Wilmot, except in the mode of effecting the object, and in that respect I must say that the latter is much the least objectionable. It goes to its object openly, boldly, and distinctly. It claims for Congress unlimited power over the territories, and proposes to assert it over the territories acquired from Mexico, by a positive prohibition of slavery. Not so the Executive proviso. It takes an indirect course, and in order to elude the Wilmot proviso, and thereby avoid encountering the united and determined resistance of the South, it denies, by implication, the authority of Congress to legislate for the territories, and claims the right as belonging exclusively to the inhabitants of the territories. But to effect the object of excluding the South, it takes care, in the mean time, to let in emigrants freely from the northern States, and all other quarters, except from the South, which it takes special care to exclude, by holding up to them the danger of having their slaves liberated under the Mexican laws. The necessary consequence is to exclude the South from the territory, just as effectually as would the Wilmot proviso. The only difference in this respect is, that what one proposes to effect directly and openly, the other proposes to effect indirectly and covertly.

But the Executive proviso is more objectionable than the Wilmot, in another and more important particular. The latter, to effect its object, inflicts a dangerous wound upon the Constitution, by depriving the southern States, as joint partners and owners of the territories, of their rights in them; but it inflicts no greater wound than is absolutely necessary to effect its object. The former, on the contrary, while it inflicts the same wound, inflicts others equally great, and, if possible, greater, as I shall next proceed to explain.

In claiming the right for the inhabitant, instead of Congress, to legislate for the territories, in the Executive proviso, it assumes that the sovereignty over the territories is vested in the former; or, to express it in the language used in a resolution offered by one of the Senators from Texas, [General HOUSTON, now absent,] they have "the same inherent right of self-government as the people in the States." The assumption is utterly unfounded, unconstitutional, without example, and contrary to the entire practice of the Government, from its commencement to the present time, as I shall proceed to show.

The recent movement of individuals in California to form a constitution and a State Government, and to appoint Senators and Representatives, is the first fruit of this monstrous assumption. If the individuals who made this movement had gone into California as adventurers, and if, as such, they had conquered the territory and established their independence, the sovereignty of the country would have been vested in them, as a separate and independent community. In that case, they would have had the right to form a constitution, and to establish a government for themselves; and if, afterwards, they thought proper to apply to Congress for admission into the Union as a sovereign and independent State, all this would have been regular, and according to established principles. But such is not the case. It was the United States who conquered California, and finally acquired it by treaty. The sovereignty, of course, is vested in them, and not in the individuals who have attempted to form a constitution and a State, without their consent. All this is clear, beyond controversy, unless it can be shown that they have since lost or been divested of their sovereignty.

Nor is it less clear, that the power of legislating over the acquired territory is vested in Congress, and not, as is assumed, in the inhabitants of the territories. None can deny that the Government of the United States have the power to acquire territories, either by war or treaty; but if the power to acquire exists, it belongs to Congress to carry it into execution. On this point there can be no doubt, for the Constitution expressly provides that Congress shall have power "to make all laws which shall be necessary and proper to carry into execution the foregoing powers," (those vested in Congress,) "and all other powers vested by this Constitution in *the Government* of the United States, or in *any department* or *office* thereof." It matters not, then, where the power is vested; for, if vested at all in the Government of the United States, or any of its departments or officers, the power of carrying it into execution is clearly vested in Congress. But this important provision, while it gives to Congress the power of legislating over territories, imposes important restrictions on its exercise, by restricting Congress to passing laws necessary and proper for carrying the power into execution. The prohibition extends, not only to all laws not suitable or appropriate to the object of the power, but also to all that are unjust, unequal, or unfair; for all such laws would be unnecessary and improper, and, therefore, unconstitutional.

Having now established beyond controversy, that the sovereignty over the territories is vested in the United States—that is in the several States composing the Union—and that the power of legislating over them is expressly vested in Congress, it follows that the individuals in California who have undertaken to form a constitution and a State, and to exercise the power of legislating without the consent of Congress, have usurped the sovereignty of the State and the authority of Congress, and have acted in open defiance of them both. In other words, what they have done, is revolutionary and rebellious in its character, anarchical in its tendency, and calculated to lead to the most dangerous consequences. Had they acted from premeditation and design, it would have been, in fact, actual rebellion; but such is not the case. The blame lies much less upon them than upon those who have induced them to take a course so unconstitutional and dangerous. They have been led into it by language held here, and the course pursued by the Executive branch of the Government.

I have not seen the answer of the Executive to the calls made by the two Houses of Congress for information as to the course which it took, or the part which it acted, in reference to what was done in California. I understand the answers have not yet been printed. But there is enough known to justify the assertion that those who profess to represent and act under the authority of the Executive, have advised, aided, and encouraged the movement, which terminated in forming what they call a Constitution and a State. Gen. Riley, who professed to act as civil governor, called the convention, determined on the number and distribution of the delegates, appointed the time and place of its meeting, was present during the session, and gave its proceedings his approbation and sanction. If he acted without authority, he ought to have been tried, or at least reprimanded and disavowed. Neither having been done, the presumption is that his course has been approved. This of itself is sufficient to identify the Executive with his acts, and to make it responsible for them. I touch not the question whether Gen. Riley was appointed or received the instructions under which he professed to act from the present Executive or its predecessor. If from the former, it would implicate the preceding as well as the present Administration. If not, the responsibility rests exclusively on the present.

It is manifest from this statement that the Executive Department has undertaken to perform acts preparatory to the meeting of the individuals to form their so-called constitution and government, which appertain exclusively to Congress. Indeed, they are identical in many respects with the provisions adopted by Congress, when it gives permission to a territory to form a constitution and government in order to be admitted as a State into the Union.

Having now shown that the assumption upon which the

Executive and the individuals in California acted throughout this whole affair is unfounded, unconstitutional, and dangerous, it remains to make a few remarks, in order to show that what has been done is contrary to the entire practice of the government from its commencement to the present time.

From its commencement until the time that Michigan was admitted, the practice was uniform. Territorial Governments were first organized by Congress. The Government of the United States appointed the governors, judges, secretaries, marshals, and other officers, and the inhabitants of the territory were represented by legislative bodies, whose acts were subject to the revision of Congress. This state of things continued until the government of a territory applied to Congress to permit its inhabitants to form a constitution and government, preparatory to admission into the Union. The preliminary act to giving permission was, to ascertain whether the inhabitants were sufficiently numerous to authorize them to be formed into a State. This was done by taking a census. That being done, and the number proving sufficient, permission was granted. The act granting it fixed all the preliminaries—the time and place of holding the Convention; the qualification of the voters; establishment of its boundaries, and all other measures necessary to be settled previous to admission. The act giving permission necessarily withdraws the sovereignty of the United States, and leaves the inhabitants of the incipient State as free to form their constitution and government as were the original States of the Union after they had declared their independence. At this stage, the inhabitants of the territory became for the first time a people, in legal and constitutional language. Prior to this, they were, by the old acts of Congress, called inhabitants, and not people. All this is perfectly consistent with the sovereignty of the United States, with the powers of Congress, and with the right of a people to self-government.

Michigan was the first case in which there was any departure from the uniform rule of acting. Here was a very slight departure from established usage. The ordinance of 1787 secured to her the right of becoming a State when she should have 60,000 inhabitants. Owing to some neglect, Congress delayed taking the census. In the mean time her population increased until it clearly exceeded more than twice the number which entitled her to admission. At this stage she formed a constitution and government without the census being taken by the United States, and Congress waived the omission, as there was no doubt she had more than a sufficient number to entitle her to admission. She was not admitted at the first session she applied, owing to some difficulty respecting the boundary between her and Ohio. The great irregularity, as to her admission, took place at the next session, but on a point which can have no possible connection with the case of California.

The irregularities in all other cases that have since occurred are of a similar nature. In all there existed territorial governments established by Congress, with officers appointed by the United States. In all the territorial government took the lead in calling conventions and fixing the preliminaries preparatory to the formation of a constitution and admission into the Union. They all recognized the sovereignty of the United States and the authority of Congress over the territories; and wherever there was any departure from established usage, it was done on the presumed consent of Congress, and not in defiance of its authority, or the sovereignty of the United States over the territories. In this respect California stands alone, without usage, or a single example to cover her case.

It belongs now, Senators, for you to decide what part you will act in reference to this unprecedented transaction. The Executive has laid the paper purporting to be the Constitution of California before you, and asks you to admit her into the Union as a State; and the question is, will you or will you not admit her? It is a grave question, and there rests upon you a heavy responsibility. Much, very much will depend upon your decision. If you admit her, you endorse and give your sanction to all that has been done. Are you prepared to do so? Are you prepared to surrender your power of legislation for the territories—a power expressly vested in Congress by the Constitution, as has been fully established? Can you, consistently with your oath to suport the Constitution, surrender the power? Are you prepared to admit that the inhabitants of the territories possess the sovereignty over them, and that any number, more or less, may claim any extent of territory they please, may form a constitution and government, and erect it into a State, without asking your permission? Are you prepared to surrender the sovereignty of the United States over whatever territory may be hereafter acquired to the first adventurers who may rush into it? Are you prepared to surrender virtually to the Executive department all the powers which you have heretofore exercised over the territories? If not, how can you, consistently with your duty and your oaths to support the Constitution, give your assent to the admission of California as a State, under a pretended constitution and government? Again, can you believe that the project of a constitution which they have adopted has the least validity? Can you believe that there is such a State in reality as the State of California? No; there is no such State. It has no legal or constitutional existence. It has no validity, and can have none without your sanction. How, then, can you admit it as *a State*, when, according to the provision of the Constitution, your power is limited to admitting new *States?* To be admitted, it must be a State, an existing State, independent of your sanction, before you can admit it. When you give your permission to the inhabitants of a territory to form a constitution and a State, the constitution and State they form derive their authority from the people, and not from you. The State before admitted is actually a State, and does not become so by the *act of admission*, as would be the case with California, should you admit her contrary to constitutional provisions and established usage heretofore.

The Senators on the other side of the chamber must permit me to make a few remarks in this connection particularly applicable to them, with the exception of a few Senators from the South, sitting on that side of the chamber. When the Oregon question was before this body not two years since, you took (if I mistake not) universally the ground that congress had the sole and absolute power of legislating for the territories. How then can you now, after the short interval which has elapsed, abandon the ground which you took, and thereby virtually admit that the power of legislating, instead of being in Congress, is in the inhabitants of the territories? How can you justify and sanction by your votes the acts of the Executive, which are in direct derogation of what you then contended for? But to approach still nearer to the present time, how can you, after condemning, little more than a year since, the grounds taken by the party which you defeated at the last election, wheel round and support by your votes the grounds which, as explained recently on this floor by the candidate of the party in the last election, are identical with those on which the Executive has acted in reference to California? What are we to understand by all this? Must we conclude that there is no sincerity, no faith in the acts and declarations of public men, and that all is mere acting or hollow profession? Or are we to conclude that the exclusion of the South from the territory acquired from Mexico is an object of so paramount a character in your estimation that right, justice, constitution, and consistency must all yield when they stand in the way of our exclusion?

But, it may be asked, what is to be done with California should she not be admitted? I answer, remand her back to the territorial condition, as was done in the case of Tennessee, in the early stage of the Government. Congress, in her case, had established a territorial government in the usual form, with governor, judges, and other officers appointed by the United States. She was entitled under the deed of cession to be admitted into the Union as a State as soon as she had sixty thousand inhabitants. The territorial government, believing it had that number, took a census, by which it appeared it exceeded it. She then formed a constitution, and applied for admission. Congress refused to admit her, on the ground that the census should be taken by the United States, and that Congress had not determined whether the territory should be formed into one or two States, as it was authorized to do under the cession. She returned quietly to her territorial condition. An act was passed to take a census by the United States, containing a provision that the territory should form one State. All afterwards was regularly conducted, and the territory admitted as a State in due form. The irregularities in the case of California are immeasurably greater, and offer much stronger reasons for pursuing the same course. But, it may be said, California may not submit. That is not probable; but if she should not, when she refuses it will then be time for us to decide what is to be done.

Having now shown what cannot save the Union, I return to the question with which I commenced, How can the Union be saved? There is but one way by which it can with any certainty; and that is, by a full and final settlement, on the principle of justice, of all the questions at issue between the two sections.

The South asks for justice, simple justice, and less she ought not to take. She has no compromise to offer but the Constitution, and no concession or surrender to make. She has already surrendered so much that she has little left to surrender. Such a settlement would go to the root of the evil, and remove all cause of discontent, by satisfying the South she could remain honorably and safely in the Union, and thereby restore the harmony and fraternal feelings between the sections which existed anterior to the Missouri agitation. Nothing else can, with any certainty, finally and forever settle the questions at issue, terminate agitation, and save the Union.

But can this be done? Yes, easily; not by the weaker party, for it can of itself do nothing—not even protect itself—but by the stronger. The North has only to will it to accomplish it—to do justice by conceding to the South an equal right in the acquired territory, and to do her duty by causing the stipulations relative to fugitive slaves to be faithfully fulfilled—to cease the agitation of the slave question, and to provide for the insertion of a provision in the Constitution, by an amendment, which will restore to the South in substance the power she possessed of protecting herself, before the equilibrium between the sections was destroyed by the action of this Government. There will be no difficulty in devising such a provision—one that will protect the South, and which at the same time will improve and strengthen the Government, instead of impairing and weakening it.

But will the North agree to do this? It is for her to answer this question. But, I will say, she cannot refuse, if she has half the love of the Union which she professes to have, or without justly exposing herself to the charge that her love of power and aggrandizement is far greater than her love of the Union. At all events, the responsibilty of saving the Union rests on the North, and not the South. The South cannot save it by any act of hers, and the North may save it without any sacrifice whatever, unless to do justice, and to perform her duties under the Constitution, should be regarded by her as a sacrifice.

It is time, Senators, that there should be an open and manly avowal on all sides, as to what is intended to be done. If the question is not now settled, it is uncertain whether it ever can hereafter be; and we, as the representatives of the States of this Union, regarded as governments, should come to a distinct understanding as to our respective views, in order to ascertain whether the great questions at issue can be settled or not. If you, who represent the stronger portion, cannot agree to settle them on the broad principle of justice and duty, say so; and let the States we both represent agree to separate and part in peace. If you are unwilling we should part in peace, tell us so, and we shall know what to do, when you reduce the question to submission or resistence. If you remain silent, you will compel us to infer by your acts what you intend. In that case, California will become the test question. If you admit her, under all the difficulties that oppose her admission, you compel us to infer that you intend to exclude us from the whole of the acquired territories, with the intention of destroying irretrievably the equilibrium between the two sections. We would be blind not to perceive, in that case, that your real objects are power and aggrandizement, and infatuated not to act accordingly.

I have now, Senators, done my duty in expressing my opinions fully, freely, and candidly, on this solemn occasion. In doing so, I have been governed by the motives which have governed me in all the stages of the agitation of the slavery question since its commencement. I have exerted myself, during the whole period, to arrest it, with the intention of saving the Union, if it could be done; and, if it could not, to save the section where it has pleased Providence to cast my lot, and which I sincerely believe has justice and the Constitution on its side. Having faithfully done my duty to the best of my ability, both to the Union and my section, throughout this agitation, I shall have the consolation, let what will come, that I am free from all responsibility.

NOTES

NOTES FOR FOREWORD:

1. *The Works of John C. Calhoun*, Richard K. Cralle, ed., Charleston, S. C., 1851-56.

NOTES FOR INTRODUCTION:

1. John C. Calhoun: *Works*, Vol.I, p.49, "A Disquisition on Government."
2. John Quincy Adams: *Memoirs of John Quincy Adams*, C. F. Adams, ed., Philadelphia, 1874-77, vol.V, p.361.
3. See Richard Hofstadter: *The American Political Tradition*, Chapter IV, "John C. Calhoun—The Marx of the Master Class."
4. Excellent biographical studies of Calhoun are available. In particular see C. M. Wiltse: *John C. Calhoun*, Gamaliel Bradford: *As God Made Them*, Chapter III, "John Caldwell Calhoun" and Margaret L. Coit: *John C. Calhoun.*
5. John C. Calhoun: *Life of John C. Calhoun*, New York, 1843, p.5. This work was attributed to R. M. T. Hunter although evidence shows that Calhoun wrote it.
6. John C. Calhoun: *Life of John C. Calhoun*, New York, 1843.
7. John C. Calhoun: *Annual Report of the American Historical Association for the Year 1899*, Vol.II, ed., J. F. Jameson, p.110, "To Mrs. Floride Calhoun 6, April, 1809."
8. John C. Calhoun: *Annals of Congress, 12th Congress, Part I, 1811-1812*, p.482 "Speech on the Second Resolution of the Committee on Foreign Relations," December 12, 1811.

9. John C. Calhoun: *Annals of Congress, 18th Congress, 2nd Session*, 1816-17, pp.851-58.
10. Andrew Jackson: Letter of July 11, 1831 in the Van Buren Papers in the Library of Congress. Quoted in Meigs: *Life of John C. Calhoun*, Vol.I, p.409.
11. Harriet Martineau: *Retrospect of Western Travel*, New York, 1838, Vol.I, p.147.
12. Henry Clay: *Congressional Globe, 27th Congress, 1st Session*, "Appendix," p.344.
13. John C. Calhoun: *Congressional Globe, 25th Congress, 2nd Session*, "Appendix," pp.176-181.
14. John C. Calhoun: *Congressional Globe, 25th Congress, 2nd Session*, "Appendix" p.62.
15. John C. Calhoun: *Works*, Vol.I, p.25, "A Disquisition on Government."
16. John C. Calhoun: *Works*, Vol.IV, p.551.
17. John C. Calhoun: *Works*, Vol.I, p.38, "A Disquisition on Government."
18. John C. Calhoun: *Works*, Vol.I, p.7, "A Disquisition on Government."
19. See particularly Charles M. Wiltse: *John C. Calhoun*, Vol.III and August O. Spain: *The Political Theory of John C. Calhoun* for excellent presentations of Calhoun's doctrine of minority rights. Calhoun has also excited European comment. See, for example, Dietrich Zwicker: *Der Amerikanische Staatsman John C. Calhoun, ein kampfer gegen die ideen von 1789*, Berlin, 1935; the chapter on Calhoun in Christopher Hollis: *The American Heresy*, London, 1927; or "John Calhoun of Fort Hill, the American as Aristocrat" in Basso Hamilton: *Mainstream*, London 1943.
20. John C. Calhoun: *Works*, Vol.I, p.26, "A Disquisition on Government."
21. John C. Calhoun: From a note on a conversation with Calhoun by J. M. Mason. Virginia Mason: *The Life and Diplomatic Correspondence of James Murray Mason*, pp.72-73.

22. John C. Calhoun: *Congressional Globe*, *31st Congress, 1st Session*, p.455. "Speech on Henry Clay's Compromise Resolutions On the Bill to Admit California," March 4, 1850.
23. John C. Calhoun: *Works*, Vol.I, p.4, "A Disquisition on Government."
24. John C. Calhoun: *Works*, Vol.I, pp.9-10, "A Disquisition on Government."
25. John C. Calhoun: *Works*, Vol.I, p.2, "A Disquisition on Government."
26. John C. Calhoun: *Works*, Vol.I, p.8, "A Disquisition on Government."
27. John C. Calhoun: *Works*, Vol.I, p.8, "A Disquisition on Government."
28. Senator Dixon Lewis as quoted in William M. Meigs: *The Life of John Caldwell Calhoun*, New York, 1917, Vol.II, p.97.
29. John C. Calhoun: *Annual Report of The American Historical Association for the Year 1899*, ed., J. F. Jameson, Vol.II, p.302. "Letter to Armistead Burt" Sept. 1, 1831.
30. John C. Calhoun: *Congressional Debates*, *Vol.XII*, *Part I*, 1835-36, pp.765-78.
31. John C. Calhoun: *Works*, Vol.V, p.190.
32. John C. Calhoun: *Congressional Debates*, *Vol.XIII*, *Part I*, 1836-37, p.566.
33. John C. Calhoun: *Works*, Vol.I, p.4, "A Disquisition on Government."
34. John C. Calhoun: *Works*, Vol.I, p.55, "A Disquisition on Government."
35. See Calhoun's Speech "On the Oregon Bill," this volume, and C. M. Wiltse's *John C. Calhoun*, especially Vol.III.
36. John C. Calhoun: *Works*, Vol.I, p.52, "A Disquisition on Government."
37. John C. Calhoun: *Works*, Vol.I, p.55, "A Disquisition on Government."

38. John C. Calhoun: *Works*, Vol.I, p.55, "A Disquisition on Government."
39. Ralph Waldo Emerson: *Essays, 2nd Series*, Boston, 1892, "Politics," p.204.
40. Ralph Waldo Emerson: *Essays, 2nd Series*, Boston, 1892, "Politics," p.206.
41. Ralph Waldo Emerson: *Essays, 2nd Series*, Boston, 1892, "Politics," p.210.
42. John C. Calhoun: *Works*, Vol.I, p.8, "A Disquisition on Government."

NOTES FOR *A DISQUISITION ON GOVERNMENT:*

1. Calhoun's debt to Greek thought, in particular to Aristotle, is overshadowed only by his originality. That he was well acquainted with Aristotle is known, and he says, himself, "I would advise a young man . . . to read the best elementary treatises on Government, including Aristotle's, which I regard as among the best." "Letter to A. D. Wallace, December 17, 1840" in *Annual Report of The American Historical Association for the Year 1899*, ed., J. F. Jameson, Vol.II, p.468.

   The quotation is from John C. Calhoun: *Annual Report of the American Historical Association for the Year 1899*, Vol. II, ed., J. F. Jameson, pp.767-768, "To Mrs. T. C. Clemson, June 15, 1849."
2. Calhoun refers to his study, "A Discourse on the Constitution and Government of the United States" which may be found in *The Works of John C. Calhoun*, Richard K. Cralle, ed., Charleston, S. C., 1851-56, Vol.I. Most of the points treated are also to be found in the speeches reprinted here.

NOTES FOR SPEECHES:

1. The speeches have been selected to show the development of Calhoun's thought from his early nationalism to his final views and to set the theoretical tenets of his

thought in their matrix of practical politics. The contrasts of the theory of "A Disquisition on Government" with both his early nationalism and his later practical use of his views make an interesting study.

The text of the Congressional speeches reprinted here is that made of the speeches at the time they were given in Congress and printed in the various Congressional records. Grammatical constructions and the indirect form of speech have not been changed from the original source. In the interests of preserving the flavor of the practical political context, editing has been limited to a few corrections of obvious typographical errors.

The text of the speech "Remarks at the Meeting of the Citizens of Charleston," is that of *The Works of John C. Calhoun*, Richard K. Cralle, ed., Charleston, S. C., 1851-56.

2. John C. Calhoun: *Congressional Globe*, *27th Congress, 2nd Session*, p.266.